HO CHI MINH

On

Revolution

A Westview Encore Reprint

HO CHI MINH

On
Revolution

Selected Writings, 1920–66

EDITED AND WITH AN INTRODUCTION BY
Bernard B. Fall

Westview Press / Boulder and London

This is **A Westview Encore Reprint,** manufactured on our own premises using equipment and methods that allow us to reissue, by arrangement with the original publisher, and keep in stock specialized books that had been allowed to go out of print. This book is printed on acid-free paper and bound in softcovers that carry the highest rating of NASTA in consultation with the AAP and the BMI.

Copyright © 1984 by Dorothy Fall

Published in 1984 in the United States of America by Westview Press, Inc., 5500 Central Avenue, Boulder, Colorado 80301; Frederick A. Praeger, Publisher

First published in 1967 by Frederick A. Praeger, Inc., Publishers

Library of Congress Catalog Card Number: 84-40631

ISBN 0-8133-0093-2

Printed and bound in the United States of America

6   5   4   3   2   1

HO CHI MINH—A PROFILE

Bernard B. Fall

Certain great political figures in history are remembered for their talents both as writers and as leaders of men. The names of Julius Caesar, Napoleon I, Winston Churchill, and Charles de Gaulle come readily to mind. There are others whose impact on history is likely to be no less great and, for ill or for good, may be even longer lasting than that of the men in the first category. These are men who have the ability to organize, to work with a wide variety of people, and to achieve results through personal contact rather than through the persuasiveness of their writings or their thinking. Louis XIV, Marshal Tito, and, of course, Lyndon B. Johnson fall into this category of men whose deeds will endure but whose writings are unlikely material for literary anthologies.

Ho Chi Minh, as the following pages will amply show, also falls into the latter group. He has been too much the doer, the organizer, the conspirator, and, finally, the father of his own country to engage in the contemplation that serious writing generally requires. Hitler used the enforced leisure of his stay at Landsberg prison to write his *Mein Kampf*. Lenin had years of comfortable and safe exile in Switzerland to do his writing. Even Mao Tse-tung, though a guerrilla leader, had long periods of time in his Yenan redoubt, and, in later years, the protection offered by his enormous country, to produce his philosophy of revolution.

Ho Chi Minh seldom had any such leisure.* Born on May 19,

---

* For a more extensive biography of Ho, see Fall, *The Two Viet-Nams* (2d rev. ed.; New York: Frederick A. Praeger, 1967).

1890, in the village of Kim-Lien in Nghé-An province of Central Viet-Nam, he has been on the run since the age of thirteen, when he was expelled from the French *lycée* at Vinh for anti-French nationalist activities (the French side of the story says, for failing grades), and he has never stopped since. Lenin and Marx were revolutionaries, but they lived the life of the middle class of their times. Mao Tse-tung was a peasant guerrilla for two decades, but he at least benefited from the fact that he operated within a large organization; he went hungry only when everyone else went hungry and he certainly never had to worry about paying his rent. Ho Chi Minh, on the other hand, had to eke out a meager living in a completely hostile as well as alien environment. In the early days of the colonial regime, a young Vietnamese could better his status only by going abroad and either furthering his education or making money. But to go abroad in itself required funds which a poor Vietnamese could not dream of acquiring. So, in 1911, Ho Chi Minh went to sea as a mess boy on a French liner. His association with equally destitute French sailors must have been an eye-opener to him, as were his travels throughout the world—he navigated mostly on the Africa runs, but eventually landed in the major ports on the American East Coast (and perhaps also in San Francisco). The life of a mess boy aboard a ship is not one that permits much time for philosophizing, but it left some indelible impressions on Ho Chi Minh, which are clearly reflected in his early writings.

More than most other colonial revolutionaries, Ho Chi Minh understood that Viet-Nam's case as a colonial country was not exceptional but rather was typical of the whole colonial system. In his writings, Ho was to show a constant concern for other colonial struggles in Africa, the Middle East, and Latin America. His early writings also clearly reflect the personal humiliations he must have suffered at the hands of the colonial masters—not because they hated him as a person, but simply because, as a "colored" colonial, he *did not count as a human being*. This intense personalization of the whole anticolonial struggle shines clearly throughout Ho's writings. He was not interested in debating general political theories. He was far more interested in demonstrating that such-and-such French colonial official, fully named, was a sadist who enjoyed harassing his colonial charges than in patiently whittling away at the colonial structure in the hope that it would, in its own time and on its own conditions, yield a small measure of self-government to the subject nation. In fact, Ho's most important work, *French Colonization On Trial,* originally written in French, is in reality a series of highly emotional pamphlets denouncing the various abuses of the French colonial system.

Before Ho reached that stage, however, much else was to happen to him that would explain his sense of disillusionment and bitterness toward the West. At the outset of World War I, after years at sea, Ho took a job in London. It was again a menial job, as a kitchen helper, and he supplemented his meager earnings by shoveling snow in the winter for the London school system. In England, Ho made his first politically significant contact, with the Chinese Overseas Workers' Association. Yet at age twenty-four he was little more than a naïve young Asian desperately trying to make a living, like thousands of West Indians and Pakistanis in London today. At some point, the maturation process must have suddenly accelerated, but the available evidence does not throw much light on this. Toward the end of 1917, Ho moved to war-torn France, where 80,000 Vietnamese (they were still known as Annamites) were either fighting for the French Army or working in French war factories side by side with French women. Vietnamese military police units had fired into mutineering French troops in 1917, and tens of thousands of Vietnamese workers could see for themselves that the myth of the all-powerful and all-knowing white master, so assiduously fostered overseas by the colonial administration, was exactly that: a myth.

In the Europe of the last days of World War I, politics were in ferment. In Russia, Communism was moving from theory to practice —from an abstract philosophy to a system of government; Imperial Germany was cracking behind its thin layer of front-line troops, and Red banners had been flying from German warships at their base in Kiel. There was a good chance that the next German government would be Socialist, and the same was true in many areas of the collapsing Austro-Hungarian state. The latter, in fact, must have provided to a man like Ho Chi Minh an interesting case of a colonial empire losing its grip on its subjects. In French politics there was also a move to the left. The French Socialist Party had been anxiously watching events in Russia. As early as 1917, a split had occurred within its ranks between those who still believed in a slow evolutionary process and the minority who believed that the time for a Marxist revolution had come.

In all Western Socialist parties, with their equalitarian theories, the "colonials" (in the sense that the word is understood in Britain and France—i.e., the indigenous nationals of the colonies) had always loomed as politically important. This was truer in France than in Britain, since the French were propagating an assimilation theory whose goal was the eventual complete merger of all French colonies into a permanent unit. The term "Overseas France," which the French used in referring to their empire until the late 1940's, is an example of that particular delusion. All French political parties supported this policy, although only the Socialists were willing to recognize its logical implication—i.e., in effect, to give full political rights to the natives. The best way for French political parties to show their commitment to the ideal of assimilation (while at the same time acquiring a useful following in the colonies) was to grant a great deal of importance to those colonials residing in metropolitan France—as long as they were willing to play the game. (That was also the case, of course, in Britain, where such Indian nationalists as Nehru and Krishna Menon were not only the darlings of the Labour Party but, in the case of Menon, actually ran for office.) Thus a young and enthusiastic man like Ho Chi Minh was given an opportunity out of all proportion to his educational background or following at home to influence politics in the colonial mainland. By the end of World War I, he was a fully accepted member of the French Socialist hierarchy and met on a basis of equality some of the men who would hold office in France almost until Charles de Gaulle's return to power in 1958.

Yet there was one important difference between Ho Chi Minh and the many other Westernized colonials who were active in European politics, and particularly between Ho and those who eventually turned toward Communism: Ho constantly kept alive his own identification with Vietnamese national objectives. This was true even at a time when "internationalism" was the order of the day among both the Socialists and those who were eventually to become the Communists. This can be seen particularly clearly in the aliases used by Ho Chi Minh in the 1920's. The name he used the most was Nguyen Ai Quoc. "Nguyen" is the most common Vietnamese family name, like "Smith" in English, and was designed to emphasize Ho's association with the common man. It also happens to have been his real family name, since his name at birth was Nguyen That Thanh (Ho Chi Minh being merely another alias). But "Ai Quoc" reveals his clear feelings, for it means "Loves His Country," or "the Patriot." Another name Ho used in France in the 1920's, and which finally earned him a rebuke by the French Communist Party specialist on colonial affairs, Jacques Doriot,* was Nguyen O Phap ("Nguyen Who Hates the French").

For a man who was to spend twenty full years in the service of the Communist International, this ethnocentrism was remarkable. It clearly shines through all his writings, even when they deal with the creation of the Indochinese Communist Party (ICP). Throughout his whole life, Ho has never quite reconciled within himself the at times conflicting demands of over-all Communist strategy and his own love for his country. It would be quite inaccurate to say, as have some Western scholars recently, that Ho has let his Communist allegiances override his Vietnamese patriotism. The contrary, in fact, is true. Thus, recently published sources show that when international Communist tactics demanded that the anticolonial struggle in overseas areas be subordinated to a "united front" struggle against the rising fascist threat in Germany, Italy, and Japan (as at the Seventh Comintern Congress of July-August, 1935), Ho had a great deal of trouble getting this line accepted in the ICP; obviously, his heart was not in it.† This is clearly reflected in the truncated version of his 1939 report to the Comintern printed in this volume.‡ In fact, throughout the 1920's and 1930's, Ho makes anticolonialism such a central issue of all his public statements at Communist Party congresses, to the almost total exclusion of any other consideration (particularly those of Soviet diplomatic requirements), that one can well wonder where he would have stood politically had any strong nationalist Vietnamese party

---

* Jacques Doriot will eventually receive the full biographic treatment he deserves. A very able and highly regarded senior member of the Communist Party hierarchy, and its leading expert on colonial questions, Doriot broke with the party in the 1930's and formed a French fascist party, known as the Parti Populaire Français, whose admiration for the German Nazis was a matter of record even in pre-war days. After France was occupied by the Germans, the PPF built up an unsavory reputation as a military strong-arm squad for the Vichy Government. Doriot himself eventually joined the infamous Waffen-SS as a lieutenant, and for a while fought with the Germans on the Eastern Front against the Russians. Having fled France in August, 1944, he was subsequently killed by an American fighter-bomber on a road in Italy.

† See Charles B. McLane, *Soviet Strategies in Southeast Asia: An Exploration of Eastern Policy Under Lenin and Stalin* (Princeton, N.J.: Princeton University Press, 1966), pp. 214–20.

‡ See pp. 130–31.

existed in Viet-Nam, or had any French political party other than the Communist Party espoused a deliberate policy of eventual independence for the colonies.

This writer has unfortunately been unable to obtain a copy of what was probably Ho Chi Minh's earliest signed public document, his appeal on behalf of Viet-Nam to the heads of state of the victorious Allied powers assembled at Versailles in 1919. An original of this one-page flyer (with the touching misspelling of the signature as Nguyen Ai *Quac*) can be seen in the Revolutionary Museum in Hanoi.* Yet, surprisingly, the document does not appear in the four-volume *Selected Works of Ho Chi Minh,* published in Hanoi between 1960 and 1962, on which this present volume is in part based.† Perhaps it was omitted because Ho's demands in 1919 were so very modest in relation to what he eventually obtained. His eight-point program did not even include full independence, but sought equality between rulers and ruled, basic civic rights, more schools, abolishment of administrative arbitrariness and its replacement by duly enacted laws, and appointment of a Vietnamese delegation to advise the French Government on Vietnamese affairs. This hardheaded practicality—the ability to perceive what is feasible at one particular point in history and what is not—is what sets off Ho Chi Minh not only from some of his more ebullient associates in North Viet-Nam but also from most of the hopelessly unrealistic non-Communist Vietnamese politicians. Many of them, particularly former North Vietnamese nationalists who are refugees in Saigon, have reproached Ho for having accepted the division of the country at the 17th parallel in 1954, apparently forgetting that the alternative might well have been an American entry into the Indochina War right there and then in support of the French, and at the same time the commitment of a *united* Sino-Soviet bloc on the side of Ho Chi Minh. Whatever has happened in Viet-Nam between 1954 and the time of this writing, it would seem preferable to this alternative, which might have led to another world war in 1954.

---

* Unfortunately, a photograph of the text taken by the editor in 1962 failed to be completely legible.

† With the exception of the poetry and the last nine articles included in Part Five, all the selections in this volume are from the four-volume edition *The Selected Works of Ho Chi Minh* (Hanoi: Foreign Languages Publishing House, 1960, 1961, 1962) and are reprinted here with only minor stylistic changes. Some footnotes giving factual information have been reprinted from the Hanoi edition; italicized notes have been added by the editor.

One of North Viet-Nam's severest scholarly critics, Professor P. J. Honey, a lecturer at the University of London, made the point in a television interview early in 1966 that "one of the things which has impressed [him] enormously about Ho Chi Minh is how much he learned from Gandhi." There are very few Communist leaders in the world who can evoke such a comparison and even fewer to whom it would actually be applicable. Here also, it could be argued that this Gandhi-like deportment is nothing but an "act." But if so, Ho has played one and the same act successfully for audiences ranging from Western Communists to Vietnamese peasants to American OSS officers for over forty years—and without ever making a slip. In fact, Ho Chi Minh, like everyone else, no doubt play-acts part of the time, and as chief executive of his part of the country he is a captive of his mythology. But it is also true that he *means* to be exactly what he is.

There are, after all, enough writers of ability (or, for that matter, Party hacks) in North Viet-Nam who could have concocted a whole synthetic body of "collected works" of far greater importance—or at least greater volume—than those which are officially attributed to him. Yet Ho's writings, which now cover almost five decades, show little change in style, making allowance for the fact that his early writings were almost all in French (the English versions published in Hanoi represent a double translation: from original Vietnamese thoughts into French, and then into English) while his most recent ones are almost exclusively in Vietnamese. The interviews are generally conducted in French, although Ho does not object to using some English at times. His style has perhaps lost some of its erstwhile *ad hominem* virulence; for example, President Johnson is not the object of the personal invective with which French colonial governors were treated in the 1920's.

There is a quality of candor in Ho, which again is Gandhi-like—a certain deceptive simplicity not often found in Communist leaders, which has permitted him time and again to avoid paying the price in decreasing popularity for mistakes made by the regime he heads. Most bureaucracies are unwilling to admit mistakes, as becomes amply clear to anyone who looks at the Western record in Viet-Nam over the past twenty years. Yet, on August 18, 1956, three months before the farmers of his own native province rose in rebellion over the botched land reform which Hanoi had thoughtlessly rammed through, Ho Chi Minh went on the radio to admit that "the leadership of the Party Central Committee and of the Government is sometimes lacking in concreteness, and control and encouragement is disregarded. All this has caused us to commit errors and meet with shortcomings in carrying out land reform."

The same candor made him state ten years later, on July 17, 1966, that the United States would eventually destroy most of North Viet-Nam's major cities—a prospect which could hardly have heartened his fellow citizens but which, under the circumstances, he felt they must face up to. In the same speech, he also promised his people the possibility of war for perhaps another five, ten, or twenty years.

In compiling any selection of a writer's works, the editor must make the difficult choice between pieces that are most representative of the author's style and those that best reflect the times in which he lived. The process was complicated in this case by the fact that even the edition of Ho's works published in Hanoi represents a selection from a larger body of writings that has never been assembled in its entirety—including pieces that have appeared under pseudonyms to which Ho Chi Minh has thus far not admitted.* We do not know why certain pieces were omitted from the edition. In addition to the 1919 appeal to the Great Powers, already mentioned, this writer recalls a brochure on the plight of the American Negro, published by Ho Chi Minh in Moscow in the 1920's, which did not find its way into the Hanoi edition; nor did his haunting poems, written while he was imprisoned by Nationalist Chinese authorities from August 28, 1942, until September 16, 1943.† Perhaps his editors did not feel that the at times sentimental poetry fitted in too well with the image of a strong father-like leader. I have included a few of these poems because they show us another aspect of the man and another step in his historical development. Following the practice of the Hanoi editors, I have also included personal interviews granted by Ho Chi Minh in the materials I have added covering the 1960–66 period.

At the time of this writing, it was impossible to predict how long the Second Indochina War would continue and for how long Ho Chi Minh would be the leader of those Vietnamese forces which oppose the United States in Viet-Nam. Perhaps the logical ending to such a book, and perhaps the crowning achievement of two such doers as

---

* According to McLane, *op. cit.*, some of the most incisive reports on Indochinese Communism written in the 1930's were signed with the name "Orgwald"; in the view of the knowledgeable McLane, "Orgwald" may well have been still another alias for Ho Chi Minh.

† *Prison Diary* (Hanoi: Foreign Languages Publishing House, 1959).

Lyndon B. Johnson and Ho Chi Minh, would be their signatures, along with those of other interested parties, on a treaty ensuring a lasting and just peace for the Vietnamese people, both North and South. The chances are, unfortunately, that Ho's grim appeal to his people to fight on in the ruins of their country for twenty years, and President Johnson's admonition of October, 1966, to the American troops in Viet-Nam "to bring back that coon skin on the wall," are a more accurate reflection of the prevailing moods.

Saigon, South Viet-Nam
Christmas Day, 1966

CONTENTS

II. The Comintern Way (1924–30)

III. Revolution and Liberation War (1930–54)

IV. Reconstruction and Errors (1954–60)

V. At War Again (1960–66)

PART ONE

In Search of a Mission
(1920–24)

SPEECH AT THE TOURS CONGRESS*

Chairman: Comrade Indochinese Delegate, you have the floor.

Indochinese Delegate [Nguyen Ai Quoc]: Today, instead of contributing, together with you, to world revolution, I come here with deep sadness to speak as a member of the Socialist Party, against the imperialists who have committed abhorrent crimes on my native land. You all have known that French imperialism entered Indochina half a century ago. In its selfish interests, it conquered our country with bayonets. Since then we have not only been oppressed and exploited shamelessly, but also tortured and poisoned pitilessly. Plainly speaking, we have been poisoned with opium, alcohol, etc. I cannot, in some minutes, reveal all the atrocities that the predatory capitalists have inflicted on Indochina. Prisons outnumber schools and are always overcrowded with detainees. Any natives having socialist ideas are arrested and sometimes murdered without trial. Such is the so-called justice in Indochina. In that country, the Vietnamese are discriminated against, they do not enjoy safety like Europeans or those having European citizenship. We have neither freedom of press nor freedom of speech. Even freedom of assembly and freedom of association do not exist. We have no right to live in other countries or to go abroad as tourists. We are forced to live in utter ignorance and obscurity because we have no right to study. In

* The Tours Congress was the Eighteenth National Congress of the French Socialist Party held from December 25 to 30, 1920. In this Congress, Nguyen Ai Quoc sided with the left wing and, together with other comrades, approved the resolution to found the French Communist Party and join the Third International.

3

Indochina the colonialists find all ways and means to force us to smoke opium and drink alcohol to poison and beset us. Thousands of Vietnamese have been led to a slow death or massacred to protect other people's interests.

Comrades, such is the treatment inflicted upon more than 20 million Vietnamese, that is more than half the population of France. And they are said to be under French protection! The Socialist Party must act practically to support the oppressed natives.

Jean Longuet: * I have spoken in favor of the natives.

Indochinese Delegate: Right from the beginning of my speech I have already asked everyone to keep absolute silence. The Party must make propaganda for socialism in all colonial countries. We have realized that the Socialist Party's joining the Third International means that it has practically promised that from now on it will correctly assess the importance of the colonial question. We are very glad to learn that a Standing Delegation has been appointed to study the North Africa question, and, in the near future, we will be very glad if the Party sends one of its members to Indochina to study on-the-spot the questions relating to this country, and the activities which should be carried out there.

(*A right-wing delegate had a contradictory opinion.*)

Indochinese Delegate: Silence! You for the Parliament!

Chairman: Now all delegates must keep silence! Including those not standing for the Parliament!

Indochinese Delegate: On behalf of the whole of mankind, on behalf of all the Socialist Party's members, both left and right wings, we call upon you! Comrades, save us!

Chairman: Through the applause of approval, the Indochinese Delegate can realize that the whole of the Socialist Party sides with you to oppose the crimes committed by the bourgeois class.

---

* *A leader of the orthodox Socialist wing of the party, and a nephew of Karl Marx.*—Ed.

THE PATH WHICH
LED ME TO LENINISM*

After World War I, I made my living in Paris, now as a retoucher at a photographer's, now as painter of "Chinese antiquities" (made in France!). I would distribute leaflets denouncing the crimes committed by the French colonialists in Viet-Nam.

At that time, I supported the October Revolution only instinctively, not yet grasping all its historic importance. I loved and admired Lenin because he was a great patriot who liberated his compatriots; until then, I had read none of his books.

The reason for my joining the French Socialist Party was that these "ladies and gentlemen"—as I called my comrades at that moment— had shown their sympathy toward me, toward the struggle of the oppressed peoples. But I understood neither what was a party, a trade-union, nor what was Socialism or Communism.

Heated discussions were then taking place in the branches of the Socialist Party, about the question of whether the Socialist Party should remain in the Second International, should a Second-and-a-half International be founded, or should the Socialist Party join Lenin's Third International? I attended the meetings regularly, twice or thrice a week, and attentively listened to the discussions. First, I

* Article written in April, 1960, for the Soviet review *Problems of the East,* for the ninetieth anniversary of Lenin's birth. (*This is by far the most candid statement made by Ho about his reasons for joining the Communist Party, and amply demonstrates his pragmatic approach to ideological commitments.—* Ed.)

could not understand thoroughly. Why were the discussions so heated? Either with the Second, Second-and-a-half, or Third International, the revolution could be waged. What was the use of arguing then? As for the First International, what had become of it?

What I wanted most to know—and this precisely was not debated in the meetings—was: Which International sides with the peoples of colonial countries?

I raised this question—the most important in my opinion—in a meeting. Some comrades answered: It is the Third, not the Second, International. And a comrade gave me Lenin's "Thesis on the National and Colonial Questions," published by *l'Humanité,* to read.

There were political terms difficult to understand in this thesis. But by dint of reading it again and again, finally I could grasp the main part of it. What emotion, enthusiasm, clear-sightedness, and confidence it instilled into me! I was overjoyed to tears. Though sitting alone in my room, I shouted aloud as if addressing large crowds: "Dear martyrs, compatriots! This is what we need, this is the path to our liberation!"

After then, I had entire confidence in Lenin, in the Third International.

Formerly, during the meetings of the Party branch, I only listened to the discussion; I had a vague belief that all were logical, and could not differentiate as to who were right and who were wrong. But from then on, I also plunged into the debates and discussed with fervor. Though I was still lacking French words to express all my thoughts, I smashed the allegations attacking Lenin and the Third International with no less vigor. My only argument was: "If you do not condemn colonialism, if you do not side with the colonial people, what kind of revolution are you waging?"

Not only did I take part in the meetings of my own Party branch, but I also went to other Party branches to lay down "my position." Now I must tell again that Comrades Marcel Cachin, Vaillant Couturier, Monmousseau, and many others helped me to broaden my knowledge. Finally, at the Tours Congress, I voted with them for our joining the Third International.

At first, patriotism, not yet Communism, led me to have confidence in Lenin, in the Third International. Step by step, along the struggle, by studying Marxism-Leninism parallel with participation in practical activities, I gradually came upon the fact that only Socialism and

Communism can liberate the oppressed nations and the working people throughout the world from slavery.

There is a legend, in our country as well as in China, on the miraculous "Book of the Wise." When facing great difficulties, one opens it and finds a way out. Leninism is not only a miraculous "book of the wise," a compass for us Vietnamese revolutionaries and people: it is also the radiant sun illuminating our path to final victory, to Socialism and Communism.

SOME CONSIDERATIONS
ON THE COLONIAL QUESTION*

Since the French Party has accepted Moscow's "twenty-one conditions" and joined the Third International, among the problems which it has set itself is a particularly ticklish one—colonial policy. Unlike the First and Second Internationals, it cannot be satisfied with purely sentimental expressions of position leading to nothing at all, but must have a well-defined working program, an effective and practical policy.

On this point, more than on others, the Party faces many difficulties, the greatest of which are the following:

The Great Size of the Colonies

Not counting the new "trusteeships" acquired after the war, France possesses:

In Asia, 450,000 square kilometers; in Africa, 3,541,000 square kilometers; in America, 108,000 square kilometers; and in Oceania 21,600 square kilometers—a total area of 4,120,000 square kilometers (eight times its own territory), with a population of 48,000,000 souls. These people speak over twenty different languages. This diversity of tongues does not make propaganda easy, for, except in a few old colonies, a French propagandist can make himself understood only through an interpreter. However, translations are of limited

* Printed in *l'Humanité*, May 25, 1922.

value, and in these countries of administrative despotism, it is rather difficult to find an interpreter to translate revolutionary speeches.

There are other drawbacks: Though the natives of all the colonies are equally oppressed and exploited, their intellectual, economic, and political development differs greatly from one region to another. Between Annam and the Congo, Martinique and New Caledonia, there is absolutely nothing in common, except poverty.

The Indifference of the Proletariat of the Mother Country Toward the Colonies

In his theses on the colonial question, Lenin clearly stated that "the workers of colonizing countries are bound to give the most active assistance to the liberation movements in subject countries." To this end, the workers of the mother country must know what a colony really is, they must be acquainted with what is going on there, and with the suffering—a thousand times more acute than theirs—endured by their brothers, the proletarians in the colonies. In a word, they must take an interest in this question.

Unfortunately, there are many militants who still think that a colony is nothing but a country with plenty of sand underfoot and of sun overhead, a few green coconut palms and colored folk, that is all. And they take not the slightest interest in the matter.

The Ignorance of the Natives

In colonized countries—in old Indochina as well as in new Dahomey—the class struggle and proletarian strength are unknown factors for the simple reason that there are neither big commercial and industrial enterprises nor workers' organizations. In the eyes of the natives, Bolshevism—a word which is the more vivid and expressive because frequently used by the bourgeoisie—means either the destruction of everything or emancipation from the foreign yoke. The first sense given to the word drives the ignorant and timorous masses away from us; the second leads them to nationalism. Both senses are equally dangerous. Only a tiny section of the intelligentsia knows what is meant by Communism. But these gentry, belonging to the native bourgeoisie and supporting the bourgeois colonialists, have no interest in the Communist doctrine being understood and propagated. On the contrary, like the dog in the fable, they prefer to bear the mark of the collar and to have their piece of bone. Generally speaking, the masses are thoroughly rebellious, but completely ignorant. They want to free themselves, but do not know how to go about doing so.

Prejudices

The mutual ignorance of the two proletariats gives rise to prejudices. The French workers look upon the native as an inferior and negligible human being, incapable of understanding and still less of taking action. The natives regard all the French as wicked exploiters. Imperialism and capitalism do not fail to take advantage of this mutual suspicion and this artificial racial hierarchy to frustrate propaganda and divide forces which ought to unite.

Fierceness of Repression

If the French colonialists are unskillful in developing colonial resources, they are masters in the art of savage repression and the manufacture of loyalty made to measure. The Gandhis and the De Valeras would have long since entered heaven had they been born in one of the French colonies. Surrounded by all the refinements of courts martial and special courts, a native militant cannot educate his oppressed and ignorant brothers without the risk of falling into the clutches of his civilizers.

Faced with these difficulties, what must the Party do?
Intensify propaganda to overcome them.

RACIAL HATRED*

For having spoken of the class struggle and of equality among men, and on the charge of having preached racial hatred, our comrade Louzon† has been sentenced.

Let us see how the love between peoples has been understood and applied in Indochina of late. We will not speak for the time being of the poisoning and degradation of the masses by alcohol and opium of which the colonial government is guilty; our comrades in the parliamentary group will have to deal with this matter one day.

Everybody knows the deeds of derring-do of the assassin-administrator Darles. However, he is far from having the monopoly of savagery against the natives.

A certain Pourcignon furiously rushed upon an Annamese who was so curious and bold as to look at this European's house for a few seconds. He beat him and finally shot him down with a bullet in the head.

A railway official beat a Tonkinese village mayor with a cane. M. Beck broke his car driver's skull with a blow from his fist. M. Brès, building contractor, kicked an Annamese to death after binding his arms and letting him be bitten by his dog. M. Deffis, receiver, killed his Annamese servant with a powerful kick in the kidneys.

M. Henry, a mechanic at Haiphong, heard a noise in the street; the door of his house opened, an Annamese woman came in, pursued by a man. Henry, thinking that it was a native chasing after a

* Printed in *Le Paria*, July 1, 1922.
† A native of a French colony; a French Communist persecuted by the colonialists.

11

*con-gai,** snatched up his hunting rifle and shot him. The man fell, stone dead: It was a European. Questioned, Henry replied, "I thought it was a native."

A Frenchman lodged his horse in a stable in which there was a mare belonging to a native. The horse pranced, throwing the Frenchman into a furious rage. He beat the native, who began to bleed from the mouth and ears, after which he bound his hands and hung him from them under his staircase.

A missionary (oh yes, a gentle apostle!), suspecting a native seminarist of having stolen 1,000 piasters from him, suspended him from a beam and beat him. The poor fellow lost consciousness. He was taken down. When he came to, it began again. He was dying, and is perhaps dead already. . . .

Has justice punished these individuals, these civilizers? Some have been acquitted and others were not troubled by the law at all. That's that.

And now, accused Louzon, it's your turn to speak!

* *Vietnamese for "young girl"; used by the French colonialists to mean a native mistress of a Frenchman.*—ED.

ANNAMESE WOMEN
AND FRENCH DOMINATION*

Colonization is in itself an act of violence of the stronger against the weaker. This violence becomes still more odious when it is exercised upon women and children.

It is bitterly ironic to find that civilization—symbolized in its various forms, *viz.,* liberty justice, etc., by the gentle image of woman, and run by a category of men well known to be champions of gallantry—inflicts on its living emblem the most ignoble treatment and afflicts her shamefully in her manners, her modesty, and even her life.

Colonial sadism is unbelievably widespread and cruel, but we shall confine ourselves here to recalling a few instances seen and described by witnesses unsuspected of partiality. These facts will allow our Western sisters to realize both the nature of the "civilizing mission" of capitalism, and the sufferings of their sisters in the colonies.

"On the arrival of the soldiers," relates a colonial, "the population fled; there only remained two old men and two women: one maiden, and a mother suckling her baby and holding an eight-year-old girl by the hand. The soldiers asked for money, spirits, and opium.

"As they could not make themselves understood, they became furious and knocked down one of the old men with their rifle butts. Later, two of them, already drunk when they arrived, amused themselves for many hours by roasting the other old man at a wood fire. Meanwhile, the others raped the two women and the eight-year-old

* Printed in *Le Paria,* August 1, 1922.

13

girl. Then, weary, they murdered the girl. The mother was then able to escape with her infant and, from a hundred yards off, hidden in a bush, she saw her companion tortured. She did not know why the murder was perpetrated, but she saw the young girl lying on her back, bound and gagged, and one of the men, many times, slowly thrust his bayonet into her stomach and, very slowly, draw it out again. Then he cut off the dead girl's finger to take a ring, and her head to steal a necklace.

"The three corpses lay flat on the ground of a former salt-marsh: the eight-year-old girl naked, the young woman disemboweled, her stiffened left forearm raising a clenched fist to the indifferent sky, and the old man, horrible, naked like the others, disfigured by the roasting with his fat which had run, melted, and congealed with the skin of his belly, which was bloated, grilled, and golden, like the skin of a roast pig."

AN OPEN LETTER TO
M. ALBERT SARRAUT,
MINISTER OF COLONIES*

Your Excellency,

We know very well that your affection for the natives of the colonies in general, and the Annamese in particular, is great.

Under your proconsulate the Annamese people have known true prosperity and real happiness, the happiness of seeing their country dotted all over with an increasing number of spirit and opium shops which, together with firing squads, prisons, "democracy," and all the improved apparatus of modern civilization, are combining to make the Annamese the most advanced of the Asians and the happiest of mortals.

These acts of benevolence saves us the trouble of recalling all the others, such as enforced recruitment and loans, bloody repressions, the dethronement and exile of kings, profanation of sacred places, etc.

* Printed in *Le Paria*, August 1, 1922. (*Ho apparently met Sarraut at a somewhat later date, in Paris; the two men were introduced by the head of the Annam Section of the French Sûreté. It seems likely that Ho made a favorable impression on the French Minister, and vice versa. The Lycée Albert Sarraut, the last French-financed high school in North Viet-Nam, kept its name without objection by the Hanoi authorities until the threat from American air raids forced it to close in June, 1966.*—ED.)

15

As a Chinese poem says, "The wind of kindness follows the movement of your fan, and the rain of virtue precedes the tracks of your carriage." As you are now the supreme head of all the colonies, your special care for the Indochinese has but increased with your elevation. You have created in Paris itself a service having the special task—with special regard to Indochina, according to a colonial publication—of keeping watch on the natives, especially the Annamese, living in France.

But "keeping watch" alone seemed to Your Excellency's fatherly solicitude insufficient, and you wanted to do better. That is why for some time now, you have granted each Annamese—dear Annamese, as Your Excellency says—private *aides-de-camp*. Though still novices in the art of Sherlock Holmes, these good people are very devoted and particularly sympathetic. We have only praise to bestow on them and compliments to pay to their boss, Your Excellency.

We are sincerely moved by the honor that Your Excellency has the extreme kindness to grant us and we would have accepted it with all gratitude if it did not seem a little superfluous and if it did not excite envy and jealousy.

At a time when Parliament is trying to save money and cut down administrative personnel, when there is a large budget deficit, when agriculture and industry lack labor, when attempts are being made to levy taxes on workers' wages, and at a time when repopulation demands the use of all productive energies, it would seem to us antipatriotic at such a time to accept personal favors which necessarily cause loss of the powers of the citizens condemned—as *aides-de-camp*—to idleness and the spending of money that the proletariat has sweated hard for.

In consequence, while remaining obliged to you, we respectfully decline this distinction flattering to us but too expensive to the country.

If Your Excellency insists on knowing what we do every day, nothing is easier: We shall publish every morning a bulletin of our movements, and Your Excellency will have but the trouble of reading.

Besides, our timetable is quite simple and almost unchanging.

Morning: from 8 to 12 at the workshop.

Afternoon: in newspaper offices (leftist, of course) or at the library.

Evening: at home or attending educational talks.

Sundays and holidays: visiting museums or other places of interest. There you are!

Hoping that this convenient and rational method will give satisfaction to Your Excellency, we beg to remain. . . .

NGUYEN AI QUOC

AN OPEN LETTER TO
M. LÉON ARCHIMBAUD*

Deputy for Drôme
Reporter on the Budget for the Colonies
Member of the Colonial High Council

Sir,

In your speech to the Chamber of Deputies you said that if you had wished to do so, you could have denounced colonial scandals, but you prefer to pass over in silence the crimes and offenses committed by your civilizers in the colonies. This is your right and it concerns only you, your conscience, and your electors. As for us who have suffered and will continue to suffer every day from these "blessings" of colonialism, we do not need you to tell us about them.

But when, writing in *Le Rappel,* you say that the facts pointed out by citizen Bourneton† are false or exaggerated, you yourself "exaggerate"! First, the Minister of Colonies himself was obliged to recognize that a "contemptuous state of mind toward native life" exists. And that he "denied no act of brutality" denounced by Deputy Boisneuf. And then can you deny, M. Archimbaud, that during the last few years, that is to say, following the war for "the rule of law" for which 800,000 natives came to work "voluntarily" or to be killed in France, that your civilizers—with impunity—have robbed, swin-

* Printed in *Le Paria,* January 15, 1923.
† A member of Parliament, representative of the French Communist Party.

18

dled, murdered, or burnt alive Annamese, Tunisians, and Senegalese?

You write next that acts of injustice are more numerous in France than in the colonies. Then allow me to tell you, M. Archimbaud, that one should not pretend to give lessons in equality or justice to others when one is unable to apply them at home. This is the most elementary logic, isn't it?

According to you, the doings of your colonial administrators are known, commented upon, and controlled by the Governments General and the Ministry of Colonies. Hence it must be one of two things. Either you are harebrained and have forgotten the Baudoins, the Darles, the Lucases, and so many others making up the galaxy which is the honor and pride of your Colonial Administration, and who, after having committed heinous crimes, receive as punishment only promotions and decorations. Or else you are treating your readers as complete fools.

You state that if France has sinned in colonial matters it is rather from an excess of generous sentiment than anything else. Will you tell us, M. Archimbaud, whether it is out of these generous sentiments that the natives are deprived of all rights to write, speak, and travel, etc? Is it out of these same sentiments that the ignoble condition of "native" is imposed on them, that they are robbed of their land only to see it given to the conquerors, and forced thereafter to work as slaves? You yourselves have said that the Tahitian race has been decimated by alcoholism and is disappearing. Is it also from an excess of generosity that you are doing all you can to intoxicate the Annamese with your alcohol and stupefy them with your opium?

You speak finally of "duty," "humanity," and "civilization"! What is this duty? You showed what it is throughout your speech. It is markets, competition, interests, privileges. Trade and finance are things which express your "humanity." Taxes, forced labor, excessive exploitation, that is the summing up of your civilization!

While you are waiting to receive "one of the finest claims to glory that can be dreamt of," allow me to tell you, M. Archimbaud, that if Victor Hugo had known that you would write such stuff today in his newspaper, he would never have founded it.

Respectfully yours,

NGUYEN AI QUOC

THE COUNTERREVOLUTIONARY ARMY*

We are aware that colonial rivalry was one of the main causes of the 1914–18 imperialist war.

What all Frenchmen should realize is that colonial expeditions are largely responsible for aggravating the depopulation from which their country is now suffering. If one looks at the statistics of military losses in killed and wounded sustained in the colonies, one is frightened by the gap they have caused in an ever decreasing population such as that of France. From January to June, 1923, in Morocco alone, 840 soldiers were killed or wounded for the greater glory of Marshal Lyautey!

What the French working class must realize is that colonialism relies on the colonies to defeat all attempts at emancipation on the part of the working class. No longer having absolute confidence in the white soldiers, who are more or less contaminated by the idea of classes, French militarism uses African and Asian natives in their stead. Out of 159 regiments in the French Army, 10 are composed of colonial whites, i.e., seminatives, 30 of Africans, and 39 of natives from other colonies; one-half of the French Army is thus recruited in the colonies.

Now, an Annamese soldier is in service for four years and an Algerian for three years. Thus, according to the reckoning of French militarism, two native soldiers are worth almost five French.

Moreover, being ignorant of the language and politics of the coun-

* Printed in *La Vie Ouvrière* (Paris), September 7, 1923.

try, thinking that all whites belong to the race of his exploiters, and finally spurred on by his white superiors, the native soldier will march forward submissively and blindly, where the French soldier, more conscious, might refuse to go. Therein lies the danger.

One wonders for what reason thirty-one of the native regiments will be stationed on French territory. For what purpose are they intended? Are the French going to be civilized by these natives? The intention of French capitalism is thus clear. It is up to the French workers to act. They should fraternize with the native soldiers. They should make them understand that the workers of the mother country and the soldiers from the colonies are equally oppressed and exploited by the same masters, that they are all brothers of the same class, and that when the hour of struggle strikes, they will have, one and the other, to struggle against their common masters, and not between brothers.

ENGLISH "COLONIZATION"*

English capitalism, while coveting the immense wealth of China, has contented itself so far with colonizing Hong Kong and, inside China, practicing the policy of the open door, a policy which has allowed it to exploit the country without arousing the people. Today it is no longer satisfied with this policy. It wants to go further: It wants to colonize the whole of China.

Taking advantage of the Lingchen incident† and on the pretext of ensuring the security of his compatriots, the British Ambassador in Peking has just carried out the first stage of this colonization. He has begun with the railways. Here are the proposals he has made to China:

1. All lines built with British capital, or with materials bought from England and which are not yet entirely paid for, will be put under British control.

2. The land situated along the lines in question will also be put under this control.

3. Besides the railways policy, England will have the right to intervene in China's home affairs.

4. In case of armed conflicts between Chinese political factions, the

* Printed in *La Vie Ouvrière*, November 9, 1923.

† In May, 1923, a group of bandits ransacked a train at Lingchen station on the Tientsin-Poukoushi railway; an Englishman was killed and more than 100 Chinese passengers and twenty-six foreigners kidnaped. The diplomatic corps in China availed themselves of this incident to make a series of demands upon the Peking Government.

British will have the right to grant or refuse the use of these lines to whichever faction it chooses.

5. Priority of amortization of the loans advanced by the British in the use of the income derived from the railways.

Moreover, he demanded: (a) the setting up, within the Ministry of Communications in Peking, of an office of Railways Control, presided over by a foreign official (read British official), having full powers over the working of all China's railways; (b) that the management of the railways also be entrusted to foreign representatives; (c) the organization of a railway militia under the command of foreign officers; (d) that the posts of bookkeepers and railway managers be filled by foreigners.

The British have already taken in hand the salt tax and customs in China. Now they want to seize the railways. When one realizes that except for the lines in southern Manchuria, the Peking-Hankow and Lunghai lines, all others are built either with British capital or with materials bought on credit from British firms, it can be seen what this plan, if realized, will cost China.

All the Chinese, without distinction as to political trend, oppose this disguised colonization. The Peking Students' Union has launched an appeal to the working class of the world, asking it to use its influence to check this attempt against the independence of the Chinese people.

Let us hope that faced with this threat from British capitalism, the sons and daughters of China will unite in victorious resistance.

ANNAMESE PEASANT CONDITIONS*

The Annamese in general are crushed by the blessings of French protection. The Annamese peasants especially are still more odiously crushed by this protection: as Annamese they are oppressed; as peasants they are robbed, plundered, expropriated, and ruined. It is they who do all the hard labor, all the *corvées*. It is they who produce for the whole horde of parasites, loungers, civilizers, and others. And it is they who live in poverty while their executioners live in plenty and who die of starvation when their crops fail. This is due to the fact that they are robbed on all sides and in all ways by the Administration, by modern feudalism, and by the Church. In former times, under the Annamese regime, lands were classified into several categories according to their capacity for production. Taxes were based on this classification. Under the present colonial regime, all this has changed. When money is wanted, the French Administration simply has the categories modified. With a stroke of their magic pen, they have transformed poor land into fertile land, and the Annamese peasant is obliged to pay more in taxes on his fields than they can yield him.

That is not all. Areas are artificially increased by reducing the unit of measure. As a result, taxes are automatically increased by a third in some localities, by two-thirds in others. Yet this is not sufficient to appease the voracity of the protector State, which increases the taxes year by year. Thus, from 1890 to 1896, taxes doubled. They were further increased by a half from 1896 to 1898, and so on. The Anna-

* Printed in *La Vie Ouvrière,* January 4, 1924.

24

mese continued to let themselves be fleeced, and our "protectors," encouraged by the success of these operations, continued their spoliation.

Often despotism was mixed with plunder. In 1895, for example, the Administrator of a province in Tonking stripped a village of several hectares to the advantage of another village, the latter a Catholic one. The plundered peasants lodged a complaint. They were jailed. Don't think that administrative cynicism stopped there. The unfortunates who had been robbed were obliged to pay taxes until 1910 on lands which had been taken from them in1895!

On the heels of the thieving Administration came the thieving settlers. Europeans, who, for all their ideas of agriculture and farming skill, possessed only a big belly and a white skin, were given concessions whose size often surpassed 20,000 hectares.

Most of these concessions were founded on legalized theft. During the course of the conquest, the Annamese peasants, like the Alsatians in 1870, had abandoned their lands to seek refuge in the still free part of the country. When they came back, their lands had been given away. Entire villages were thus plundered, and the natives reduced to tenants of the lords of a modern feudalism, who sometimes appropriated as much as 90 per cent of the crops.

On the pretext of encouraging colonization, exemption from land taxes was made in favor of a great number of these big landholders.

After securing the land at no cost whatsoever, the landholders obtained manpower for nothing or next to nothing. The Administration supplied them with numbers of convicts who worked for nothing, or used its machinery to recruit workers for them who were paid starvation wages. If the Annamese did not come in sufficient numbers or if they showed discontent, violence was then resorted to: Landholders seized the mayors and notables of villages, cudgeled and tortured them until these unfortunates had signed a contract pledging themselves to supply the required number of workers.

Besides this temporal power, there are spiritual "saviors" who, while preaching the virtue of poverty to the Annamese, are no less zealous in seeking to enrich themselves through the sweat and blood of the natives. In Cochinchina alone, the "Sainte Mission Apostolique" on its own possesses one-fifth of the ricefields in the region. Though not taught in the Bible, the method of obtaining these lands was very simple: usury and corruption. The Mission took advantage of the years when crops failed to lend money to peasants, obliging them to pawn their lands as a guarantee. The rate of interest was usurious, and the Annamese could not pay off their debts at the due time; as a result, all pledged lands fell into the possession of the Mission. The more or less generous governors to whom the mother country entrusted the destiny of Indochina were generally dolts or blackguards. It was enough for the Mission to have in its hands certain secret, personal, and compromising papers to be able to frighten them and obtain from them whatever it wanted. In this way, one Governor General conceded to the Mission 7,000 hectares of river land belonging to natives, who were thus at one stroke reduced to beggary.

From this brief survey, one can see that behind a mask of democracy, French imperialism has transplanted in Annam the whole cursed medieval regime, including the salt tax, and that the Annamese peasant is crucified on the bayonet of capitalist civilization and on the Cross of prostituted Christianity.

LENIN AND THE COLONIAL PEOPLES*

"Lenin is dead!" This news struck the people like a bolt from the blue. It spread to every corner of the fertile plains of Africa and the green fields of Asia. It is true that the black or yellow people do not yet know clearly who Lenin is or where Russia is. The imperialists have deliberately kept them in ignorance. Ignorance is one of the chief mainstays of capitalism. But all of them, from the Vietnamese peasants to the hunters in the Dahomey forests, have secretly learned that in a faraway corner of the earth there is a nation that has succeeded in overthrowing its exploiters and is managing its own country with no need for masters and Governors General. They have also heard that that country is Russia, that there are courageous people there, and that the most courageous of them all was Lenin. This alone was enough to fill them with deep admiration and warm feelings for that country and its leader.

But this was not all. They also learned that that great leader, after having liberated his own people, wanted to liberate other peoples too. He called upon the white peoples to help the yellow and black peoples to free themselves from the foreign aggressors' yoke, from all foreign aggressors, Governors General, Residents, etc. And to reach that goal, he mapped out a definite program.

At first they could not believe that anywhere on earth could there exist such a man and such a program. But later they heard, although vaguely, of the Communist Parties, of the organization called the Com-

* Printed in *Pravda,* January 27, 1924.

27

munist International which is fighting for the exploited peoples, for all the exploited peoples including themselves. And they learned that Lenin was the leader of that organization.

And this alone was enough to make these peoples—though their cultural standard is low, they are grateful folk and of goodwill— wholeheartedly respect Lenin. They look upon Lenin as their liberator. "Lenin is dead, so what will happen to us? Will there be other courageous and generous people like Lenin who will not spare their time and efforts in concerning themselves with our liberation?" This is what the oppressed colonial peoples are wondering.

As for us, we are deeply moved by this irretrievable loss and share the common mourning of all the peoples with our brothers and sisters. But we believe that the Communist International and its branches, which include branches in colonial countries, will succeed in implementing the lessons and teachings the leader has left behind for us. To do what he advised us, is that not the best way to show our love for him?

In his lifetime he was our father, teacher, comrade, and adviser. Nowadays, he is the bright star showing us the way to the socialist revolution.

Eternal Lenin will live forever in our work.

INDOCHINA AND THE PACIFIC*

At first sight, it seems that the question of Indochina and the Pacific is of no concern to European workers. But it must be remembered that:

1. During the revolution, the Allies, not having succeeded in their attack on Russia from the West, tried to attack it from the East. And the Pacific powers, the United States and Japan, landed their troops in Vladivostock, while France sent Indochinese regiments to Siberia to support the Whites.

2. At present, international capitalism draws all its vital force from the colonial countries. It finds there raw materials for its factories, investments for its capital, markets for its products, cheap replenishments for its labor army, and above all, native soldiers for its counterrevolutionary army. One day, revolutionary Russia will have to cope with this capitalism. It is thus necessary for the Russian comrades to realize the full strength and all the immediate and long-term maneuvers of their adversary.

3. Having become the center of attraction for imperialist ambitions, the Pacific area and the neighboring colonies are likely in the future to become the seat of a new world conflagration, whose proletariat will have to bear the burden.

These statements of fact prove that the Pacific problem will concern all proletarians in general.

Therefore, to reconstruct France ruined by an imperialist war, the

* Printed in *La Correspondance Internationale*, No. 18, 1924.

French Minister of Colonies has worked out a plan for developing the colonies. The plan aims to exploit the resources of colonized countries for the benefit of the colonizing country. This plan states that Indochina must help the other colonies in the Pacific to intensify their production so that, in their turn, they too can be useful to the mother country. If the plan were carried out, it would necessarily lead to the depopulation and impoverishment of Indochina.

Lately, however, the Government Council of Indochina, despite the resistance of Annamese opinion, unanimously voted for the carrying out of the plan. To understand the importance of this unanimity, it is useful to know that this Council is composed of the Governor General of Indochina, the General Commander-in-Chief of the troops in Indochina, and about thirty high-ranking French civil servants, as well as five native mandarins, tools of the Governor. And all these gentlemen pretend to act for Indochina and in the interests of the Annamese people. Imagine Eskimos or Zulus deciding the fate of a European people.

According to an official avowal, the colonies in the Pacific are afflicted with debility, and are living—if we can call it living—at a slower and slower rate. The truth is that populous islands are being entirely depopulated, in a short time, by alcohol and forced labor. Fifty years ago, the Marquesas had more than 20,000 souls, but now have only 1,500 weak and debilitated inhabitants. Tahiti had its population reduced by 25 per cent in ten years. From these declining populations, French imperialism has further taken more than 1,500 men to serve as cannon fodder during the war. This rapid extinction of a race seems unbelievable. However, it is a fact to be observed in many colonies. (In the regions of the Congo, populations of 40,000 inhabitants fell to 30,000 in the space of twenty years. Saint-Pierre et Miquelon islands had 6,500 inhabitants in 1902; in 1922 this colony had only 3,900, etc.)

Most islands in the French Pacific have been yielded to concessionary companies which rob the natives of their land and make them work as slaves. Here is an example showing how the native workers are treated. Two hundred mother-of-pearl divers were sent by force by the French Company of Oceania to plantations 800 miles from their native districts. (It is as if tailors were sent to work in mines.) They were penned up in a small schooner fitted up for ten passengers and lacking any life-saving equipment, and embarked without being allowed to see their wives and children. For two years, these unfortunate toilers were kept prisoner in the company's jail. Many were harshly treated. Others died.

Add to this inhuman exploitation the immorality of the rascals to whom French imperialism entrusts the administration of these islands, and you will see in all its beauty the regime of exploitation and oppression which is leading the colonized countries in the Pacific to death and extinction.

Imperialism has now reached a degree of almost scientific perfection. It uses white proletarians to conquer the proletarians of the colonies. Then it hurls the proletarians of one colony against those of another. Finally, it relies on the proletarians of the colonies to rule white proletarians. Senegalese had the sad distinction of having helped French militarism to massacre their brothers of the Congo, the Sudan, Dahomey, and Madagascar. Algerians fought in Indochina. Annamese were garrisoned in Africa. And so on. During the great slaughter, more than 1 million colonial peasants and workers were brought to Europe to massacre white peasants and workers. Only recently, French soldiers in the Ruhr were surrounded by native soldiers, and native light infantry were sent against German strikers. Almost half of the French army is composed of natives, to the number of about 300,000.

Beyond this military usefulness, capitalism uses these colonies for the most skillful economic exploitation. It is often noticed that a decrease in wages in some regions in France and in some trades is always preceded by an increase in the proportion of colonial labor. The natives are employed as strikebreakers. Capitalism now uses one colony as a tool for exploiting another; this is the case of Indochina and the Pacific area. Indochina, despite the noisy untruths of the officials, is exhausted. During 1914–18, almost 100,000 Annamese (official number: 97,903 men) were dragged from their homes to be sent to Europe. Although deprived of so many hands for production, Indochina was obliged to send, for the defense of its oppressors, more than 500,000 tons of edible grains. Hundreds of millions of francs were raked off in "victory loans." Each year, the Annamese sweat blood to yield up about 450,000 francs, a sum which is almost entirely used to fatten spongers. Moreover, Indochina is responsible for big military expenses, elegantly called a "filial contribution" by the Minister of Colonies.

It is from this oppressed, weakened, and emaciated country that millions of piasters and several thousand men (40,000 to begin with) are further going to be wrung to satisfy the insatiable appetites of the concessionaries and the personal ambitions of a gang of unscrupulous politicians.

It is not enough to demoralize the whole Annamese race with alcohol and opium. It is not enough to take 40,000 "volunteers" yearly for the glory of militarism. It is not enough to have turned a people of 20 million souls into one big sponge to be squeezed by money-grubbers. We are, on top of all this, to be endowed with slavery.

It is not only the fate of the proletariat in Indochina and the Pacific area, but also that of the international proletariat, which is threatened by these imperialist actions. Japan commands the telegraphic stations on Yap Island. The United States is spending millions of dollars on improving the turret guns of its warships in the Pacific. England will turn Singapore into a naval base. France finds it necessary to build a Pacific Empire.

Since the Washington Conference,* colonial rivalries have become sharper and sharper, imperialist follies greater and greater, and political conflicts more and more unavoidable. Wars have been launched over India, Africa, and Morocco. Other wars may break out over the Pacific area if the proletariat is not watchful.

* The conference held from November 12, 1921, to February 6, 1922, and attended by the United States, the United Kingdom, Japan, France, Italy, China, Belgium, Portugal, and the Netherlands.

THE U.S.S.R. AND
THE COLONIAL PEOPLES*

Colonialism is a leech with two suckers, one of which sucks the metropolitan proletariat and the other that of the colonies. If we want to kill this monster, we must cut off both suckers at the same time. If only one is cut off, the other will continue to suck the blood of the proletariat, the animal will continue to live, and the cut-off sucker will grow again. The Russian Revolution has grasped this truth clearly. That is why it is not satisfied with making fine platonic speeches and drafting "humanitarian" resolutions in favor of oppressed peoples, but it teaches them to struggle; and helps them spiritually, as proclaimed by Lenin in his theses on the colonial question. To the Baku Congress,† twenty-one Eastern nations sent delegates. Representatives of Western workers' parties also participated in the work of this congress. For the first time, the proletariat of the conquering Western States and that of the subject Eastern countries fraternally joined hands and deliberated in common on the best means to defeat their common enemy, imperialism.

Following this historic congress, despite internal and external difficulties, revolutionary Russia has never hesitated to come to the help

* Printed in *Imprekor*, No. 46, 1924.
† The First Congress of Eastern Peoples was held in Baku in September, 1920. It was attended by nearly 2,000 representatives of Eastern countries. The Committee of Action and Propaganda of Eastern Peoples founded at the Congress was active for nearly a year.

of peoples awakened by its heroic and victorious revolution. One of its first important acts was the founding of the University of the East.

Today, this university has 1,022 students, including 151 girls and 895 Communists. Their social composition is as follows: 547 peasants, 265 workers, and 210 proletarian intellectuals.

If account is taken of the fact that Eastern countries are almost exclusively agricultural, the high percentage of students of peasant origin can readily be understood. In India, Japan, and especially in China, it is the intellectuals faithful to the working class who lead the latter in struggle; this explains the relatively large number of intellectuals among the students at the University. The relatively low number of worker students is due to the fact that industry and commerce in Eastern countries—naturally excepting Japan—are still undeveloped. Moreover, the presence of seventy-five pupils from the age of ten to sixteen years must be noted.

One hundred and fifty professors are responsible for giving courses in social science, mathematics, historical materialism, the history of the workers' movement, natural science, the history of revolutions, political economy, etc. Young people of sixty-two nationalities are fraternally united in the classrooms.

The University has ten large buildings. It also has a cinema which is put at the students' disposal free on Thursdays and Sundays; the other days of the week, it operates on behalf of other organizations. Two libraries containing about 47,000 books help the young revolutionaries to make thorough studies and to train their minds. Each nationality or "group" has its own library composed of books and publications in the mother tongue. The reading room, artistically decorated by the students, has a wealth of newspapers and periodicals. The students themselves publish a newspaper, the sole copy of which is posted on a big board by the door of the reading room. Students who are ill are admitted to the University hospital. There is a sanatorium in the Crimea for the benefit of students who need rest. The Soviets have allotted to the University two camps composed of nine buildings each for holidays. Each camp has a center where the students can learn cattle breeding. "We already have thirty cows and fifty pigs," said the "agrarian secretary" of the University with pride. The 100 hectares of land allotted to these camps are cultivated by the students themselves. During their holidays and outside working hours, they help the peasants in their labor. One of these camps was, by the way, formerly the property of a Grand Duke. It is a memorable sight to see from the top of the tower, adorned with a grand ducal crown, the red flag fluttering, and in "His Excellency's" entertainment room, the young Korean and Armenian peasants thoroughly enjoying their games.

The students of the University are fed, clothed, and lodged free. Each of them receives six gold rubles per month as pocket money.

To instill into the students a true idea of children's education, the University has a model crèche and a day nursery looking after 60 small children.

The yearly expenses of the University amount to 561,000 gold rubles.

The sixty-two nationalities represented at the University form a "Commune." Its chairman and functionaries are elected every three months by all the students.

A student delegate takes part in the economic and administrative management of the University. All must regularly and in turn work in the kitchen, the library, the club, etc. All "misdemeanors" and disputes are judged and settled by an elected tribunal in the presence of all comrades. Once a week, the "Commune" holds a meeting to discuss the international political and economic situation. From time to time, meetings and evening parties are organized where the amateur artists introduce the art and culture of their country.

The fact that the Communists not only treat the "inferior natives of the colonies" like brothers, but that they get them to participate in the political life of the country, is highly characteristic of the "barbarity" of the Bolsheviks. Treated in their native country as "submissive subjects" or "protégés," having no other right but that to pay taxes, the Eastern students, who are neither electors nor eligible for election in their own country, from whom the right even to express their political opinion is withdrawn, in the Soviet Union take part in the election of the Soviets and have the right to send their representatives to the Soviets. Let our brothers of the colonies who vainly seek a change of nationality make a comparison between bourgeois democracy and proletarian democracy.

These students have suffered themselves and have witnessed the sufferings of others. All have lived under the yoke of "high civilization," all have been victims of exploitation and oppression by foreign capitalists. Moreover, they passionately long to acquire knowledge and to study. They are serious and full of enthusiasm. They are entirely different from the frequenters of the boulevards of the Latin Quarter, the Eastern students in Paris, Oxford, and Berlin. It can be said without exaggeration that under the roof of this University is the future of the colonial peoples.

The colonial countries of the Near and Far East, stretching from Syria to Korea, cover an extent of more than 15 million square kilometers and have more than 1,200 million inhabitants. All these immense countries are now under the yoke of capitalism and imperialism. Although their considerable numbers should be their strength, these submissive peoples have never yet made any serious attempts to free themselves from this yoke. Not yet having realized the value of international solidarity, they have not known how to unite for the struggle. Relationships between their countries are not yet established as they are among the peoples of Europe and America. They possess gigantic strength and do not yet realize it. The University of the East, assembling all the young, active, and intelligent leaders of the colonized countries, has fulfilled a great task, namely:

1. It teaches to the future vanguard militants the principles of class struggle, confused in their minds by race conflicts and patriarchal customs.

2. It establishes between the proletarian vanguard of the colonies a close contact with the Western proletariat, thus preparing the way for the close and effective cooperation which will alone ensure the final victory of the international working class.

3. It teaches the colonized people, hitherto separated from one another, to know one another and to unite, by creating the bases of a future union of Eastern countries, one of the wings of the proletarian revolution.

4. It sets the proletariat of colonialist countries an example of what they can and must do in favor of their oppressed brothers.

THE FAILURE OF
FRENCH COLONIZATION*

The last reshuffling of Poincaré's ministry did not fail to have repercussions in the colonies. France always pretends that it is the first colonial power that has known how to colonize. M. Albert Sarraut, too, has always boasted that he is the first Frenchman to know how to develop the colonies. For this development, he demanded 4,000 million francs. To find this sum, he wrote a book of 656 pages. Now, this great minister has just been expelled from his Party for having voted for his boss, Poincaré. And the ungrateful Poincaré, in his turn, has just thrown the great minister out. Thus, the latter has been ousted from his post, without having his millions or his colonies developed. He has been replaced by a soldier, I beg your pardon, an "unknown colonel."† This expulsion shows us, once again, that colonization has gone bankrupt.

While waiting for something better, the French taxpayer pays, every year, more than 237 million francs (1923 budget) for his Ministry of Colonies, and more than 1,172,186,000 francs for the colonial troops and expenditure in Morocco, that is to say, 1,409,186,000 francs.

Each Frenchman—rich or poor, old man or infant, man or woman —is thus obliged to pay into the "civilizing mission" fund more than 36 francs a year. And for whose benefit? It is not for his own, that is

* Printed in *La Correspondance Internationale,* No. 26, 1924.
† From 1922 to 1924, Albert Sarrault was Minister of Colonies in the Poincaré government. When the government was reshuffled in 1924, he was replaced by Major Fabri.

to say, the taxpayer's. And still less for that of France. We shall explain this a little further on.

In 1922, for example, the general trade of the French colonies amounted to 4,358,105,000 francs (2,104,458 for imports and 2,253,-647,000 for exports). Out of this sum, the traffic between France and its colonies amounted to only 1,585 million francs, while that between the colonies and foreign countries amounted to 2,773,105,000 francs.

Concerning Indochina, the figure is still more eloquent. Of the 5,484 ships registered in Indochinese ports and which carried 7,152,-910 tons of goods, there were only 779 French ships, carrying 1,464,-852 tons, compared with 789 English vessels, carrying 1,575,079 tons.

Out of 807,729,362 francs worth of imports in 1921, France had only 247,602,029 francs.

France and its colonies had only 169,187,125 francs out of an export figure of 1,284,003,885 francs.

Is this to the natives' advantage? You will see.

In 1923, Indochina exported:

> 1,439,955 tons of rice
> 622,035 tons of coal
> 65,413 tons of cement
> 61,917 tons of maize
> 312,467 quintals of fish
> 27,690 tons of zinc
> 19,565 head of cattle
> 7,927 tons of sugar
> 6,860 tons of copra
> 46,229 tons of rubber
> 7,158 tons of dyestuffs
> 3,617 tons of cotton
> 30,760 quintals of pepper
> 21,492 quintals of beans
> 2,600 tons of hides
> 12,798 quintals of rattan
> 12,319 quintals of lac
> 8,499 quintals of coffee
> 6,084 quintals of tea
> 480,883 kilos of cinnamon
> 117,241 kilos of oil of Chinese anise
> 17,943 kilos of silk.

Well, do you know what is the native's share in this gigantic trade in the product of his land and his labor, going on under his nose? He had, all told, 542 sailing boats displacing 12,231 tons! According to this outline, we can conclude that French colonization is only practiced in favor of a gang of adventurers, dishonest and ineffectual politicians of the mother country, alcohol and opium racketeers, unscrupulous profiteers, and dubious financiers. The proof? Here it is: the Bank of Indochina had a turnover of only 24 million francs in 1876, but 145 in 1885, 222 in 1895, 906 in 1905, 2,005 in 1917, 6,718 in 1921.

And its profits have increased from 126,000 francs in 1876 to 22,854,000 francs in 1921!

Who gets them?

LENIN AND THE
PEOPLES OF THE EAST*

If in the eyes of the proletarians of the West, Lenin is a chief, a leader, a master to the peoples of the East, he is still greater and more noble, if I may venture to say so.

It is not only his genius, but his disdain of luxury, his love of labor, the purity of his private life, his simplicity, in a word, it is the grandeur and beauty of this master which exert an enormous influence upon the Asian peoples and irresistibly draw their hearts toward him.

Accustomed to being treated as backward and inferior people, they consider Lenin as the embodiment of universal brotherhood. Not only are they grateful to him, but they love him tenderly. To him, they show a veneration which is almost filial devotion. One had to see the students of the University of the East, eyes red with weeping, the young folk there who sobbed bitterly at the news of Lenin's death, to understand their love toward him.

His death was a universal mourning. The Kuomintang (the people's party in power in South China) was in session when it heard the news. All delegates stood up spontaneously and the session was closed in sign of mourning. On Sun Yat-sen's suggestion, the Canton government ordered the closure of all theaters for three days. The flags of office buildings were at half-mast. Cultural, political, and economic bodies in Peking and in the provinces, especially students' associations and workers' organizations, commemorated the great revolutionary

* Printed in *Le Paria,* July 27, 1924.

with dignity. On this occasion, they unanimously passed a resolution in favor of the immediate recognition of the Soviet government. The students decided to erect a statue of Lenin in the biggest public park in Peking.

The Chinese government sent cables of sympathy.

Lenin is also mourned by women. In China, as in all Eastern countries, the women are very little informed of world events, to which they are almost indifferent. However, they wore mourning for Lenin's death. Thus, the demonstrations by Chinese women in this sorrowful circumstance have a historic significance. On the one hand, they testify to the fact that the women of the East are awakening; on the other, they show that the great master is understood and loved by everyone, from the commonest to the most advanced people. As proof of this, here is a translation of an appeal made by a girl student, carried by the Shanghai *Women's Magazine:*

Ever since capitalism has existed, the whole social structure has been subject to its disastrous influence. Things which should belong to all, because produced by all, become the privilege of a few. Economic oppression enslaves men; it transforms women into chattels subject to the mercy of men!

For centuries, how many millions of people have been tied down in this way? How many millions of women have been sacrificed? When World War was raging, when millions of innocent people who longed for life were sent to die, Lenin stirred up the Russian proletariat and organized the Soviets in spite of the hardship and difficulties encountered.

Not only has he freed the men and women of his country, but he has shown the way to all disinherited people of the world. Notwithstanding the Whites' attacks from within and the blockade by capitalism from without, with his strong will, Lenin saved his compatriots from utter poverty and suffering, and showed the banner of the International to all oppressed people.

Does not all this merit that we should bow down to his great memory?

Must not the twenty-first of January remain forever a day of mourning for all toiling people?

Russia is advancing toward prosperity. However, there is still a long road to travel and much work to do to reach a genuine peace. Mankind is awakening, but it must struggle further to complete its emancipation. And now, our master has suddenly been taken from us without being able to see the completion of his work.

Can people of good heart refrain from weeping? Must not oppressed men and women take up the burden he has left behind and march forward? Forward!

Dear sisters, let us commemorate with dignity the memory of the man who, all his life, fought against the poverty and oppression of mankind, and who until the day of his death struggled for the people of the world!

LYNCHING*

A Little-known Aspect of American Civilization

It is well known that the black race is the most oppressed and most exploited of the human family. It is well known that the spread of capitalism and the discovery of the New World had as an immediate result the rebirth of slavery which was, for centuries, a scourge for the Negroes and a bitter disgrace for mankind. What everyone does not perhaps know, is that after sixty-five years of so-called emancipation, American Negroes still endure atrocious moral and material sufferings, of which the most cruel and horrible is the custom of lynching.

The word "lynching" comes from Lynch. Lynch was the name of a planter in Virginia, a landlord and judge. Availing himself of the troubles of the War of Independence, he took the control of the whole district into his hands. He inflicted the most savage punishment, without trial or process of law, on Loyalists and Tories. Thanks to the slavetraders, the Ku Klux Klan, and other secret societies, the illegal and barbarous practice of lynching is spreading and continuing widely in the States of the American Union. It has become more inhuman since the emancipation of the Blacks, and is especially directed at the latter.

Imagine a furious horde. Fists clenched, eyes bloodshot, mouths foaming, yells, insults, curses. . . . This horde is transported with the wild delight of a crime to be committed without risk. They are

* Printed in *La Correspondance Internationale*, No. 59, 1924.

armed with sticks, torches, revolvers, ropes, knives, scissors, vitriol, daggers; in a word, with all that can be used to kill or wound.

Imagine in this human sea a flotsam of black flesh pushed about, beaten, trampled underfoot, torn, slashed, insulted, tossed hither and thither, bloodstained, dead.

The horde are the lynchers. The human rag is the Black, the victim.

In a wave of hatred and bestiality, the lynchers drag the Black to a wood or a public place. They tie him to a tree, pour kerosene over him, cover him with inflammable material. While waiting for the fire to be kindled, they smash his teeth, one by one. Then they gouge out his eyes. Little tufts of crinkly hair are torn from his head, carrying away with them bits of skin, baring a bloody skull. Little pieces of flesh come off his body, already contused from the blows.

The Black can no longer shout: his tongue has been swollen by a red hot iron. His whole body ripples, trembling, like a half-crushed snake. A slash with a knife: one of his ears falls to the ground. . . . Oh! How black he is! How awful! And the ladies tear at his face. . . .

"Light up," shouts someone. "Just enough to cook him slowly," adds another.

The Black is roasted, browned, burned. But he deserves to die twice instead of once. He is therefore hanged, or more exactly, what is left of his corpse is hanged. And all those who were not able to help with the cooking applaud now.

Hurrah!

When everybody has had enough, the corpse is brought down. The rope is cut into small pieces which will be sold for three or five dollars each. Souvenirs and lucky charms quarreled over by ladies.

"Popular justice," as they say over there, has been done. Calmed down, the crowd congratulate the "organizers," then stream away slowly and cheerfully, as if after a feast, make appointments with one another for the next time.

While on the ground, stinking of fat and smoke, a black head, mutilated, roasted, deformed, grins horribly and seems to ask the setting sun, "Is this civilization?"

Some Statistics

From 1889 to 1919, 2,600 Blacks were lynched, including 51 women and girls and ten former Great War soldiers.

Among 78 Blacks lynched in 1919, 11 were burned alive, three burned after having been killed, 31 shot, three tortured to death, one cut into pieces, one drowned, and 11 put to death by various means.

Georgia heads the list with 22 victims, Mississippi follows with 12. Both have also three lynched soldiers to their credit. Of 11 burned alive, the first State has four and the second two. Out of 34 cases of systematic, premeditated and organized lynching, it is still Georgia that holds first place with five. Mississippi comes second with three.

Among the charges brought against the victims of 1919, we note: one of having been a member of the League of Non-Partisans (independent farmers); one of having distributed revolutionary publications; one of expressing his opinion on lynchings too freely; one of having criticized the clashes between Whites and Blacks in Chicago; one of having been known as a leader of the cause of the Blacks; one for not getting out of the way and thus frightening a white child who was in a motorcar. In 1920, there were fifty lynchings, and in 1923, twenty-eight.

These crimes were all motivated by economic jealousy. Either the Negroes in the area were more prosperous than the Whites, or the black workers would not let themselves be exploited thoroughly. In all cases, the principal culprits were never troubled, for the simple reason that they were always incited, encouraged, spurred on, then protected, by the politicians, financiers, and authorities, and above all, by the reactionary press.

When a lynching was to take place or had taken place, the press seized upon it as a good occasion to increase the number of copies printed. It related the affair with a wealth of detail. Not the slightest reproach to the criminals. Not a word of pity for the victims. Not a commentary.

The *New Orleans States* of June 26, 1919, published a headline running right across the front page in letters five inches high: "Today a Negro Will Be Burned by 3,000 Citizens." And immediately underneath, in very small print: "Under a strong escort, the Kaiser has taken flight with the Crown Prince."

The *Jackson Daily News* of the same date published across the first two columns of its front page in big letters: "Negro J. H. to Be Burned by the Crowd at Ellistown This Afternoon at 5 P.M."

The newspaper only neglected to add: "The whole population is earnestly invited to attend." But the spirit is there.

A Few Details

This evening at 7:40 P.M., J. H. was tortured with a red-hot iron bar, then burned. . . . A crowd of more than 2,000 people . . . many women and children, were present at the incineration. . . . After the Negro had been bound from behind, a fire was kindled. A little further away, another fire was kindled in which an iron bar was placed. When it was red hot, a man took it and applied it to the Black's body. The latter, terrified, seized the iron with his hands, and the air was immediately filled with the smell of burning flesh. . . . The red-hot iron having been applied to several parts of his body, his shouts and groans were heard as far away as in the town. After several minutes of torture, masked men poured petrol on him and set fire to the stake. The flames rose and enveloped the Negro who implored to be finished off with a shot. His supplications provoked shouts of derision. (*Chattanooga Times,* February 13, 1918.)

15,000 people, men, women, and children, applauded when petrol was poured over the Negro and the fire lit. They struggled, shouted, and pushed one another to get nearer the Black. . . . Two of them cut off his ears while the fire began to roast him.

Another tried to cut off his heels. . . . The crowd surged and changed places so that every one could see the Negro burn. When the flesh was entirely burned, the bones laid bare and what had been a human being was but a smoking and deformed rag curling up in the flames, everyone was still there to look. . . . (*Memphis Press,* May 22, 1917.)

. . . men of all social classes, women and children, were present at the scene. Many ladies of high society followed the crowd from outside the prison, others joined it from neighboring terraces. . . . When the Negro's corpse fell, the pieces of rope were hotly contended for. (*Vicksburg Evening Post,* May 4, 1919.)

. . . someone cut off his ears, another removed his sexual organ. . . . He tried to cling to the rope, his fingers were cut off. While he was being hoisted to a tree, a giant of a man stabbed his neck; he received at least twenty-five wounds.

. . . he was several times hoisted up, then pulled down into the brazier. Finally a man caught him in a lasso, the end of which was attached to a horse which dragged the corpse through the streets of Waco. The tree on which the hanging took place was right under a window of the mayor's house. The latter looked on while the crowd was in action. All along the way, everyone took part in the mutilation of the Negro. Some struck him with shovels, pickaxes, bricks, sticks. The body was covered with wounds from head to foot. A shout of joy escaped from thousands of throats when the fire was kindled. Some time after, the corpse was hoisted up high in the air, so that everyone could look at it, which raised a storm of applause. . . . (*Crisis*, July, 1916.)

White Victims of Lynching

It is not only the Blacks, but also the Whites who dare to defend them, such as Mrs. Harriet Beecher Stowe—author of "Uncle Tom's Cabin"—who are ill treated. Elijah Lovejoy was killed, John Brown hanged. Thomas Beach and Stephen Foster were persecuted, attacked, and imprisoned. Here is what Foster wrote from prison, "When I look at my damaged limbs, I think that, to hold me, prison will not be necessary for much longer. . . . These last 15 months, their cells have been opened to me four times, 24 times my compatriots have dragged me out of their churches, twice they have thrown me from the second floor of their houses; they have damaged my kidneys once; another time they tried to put me in irons; twice they have made me pay fines; once 10,000 people tried to lynch me, and dealt me 20 blows on my head, arms and neck. . . ."

In 30 years, 708 Whites, including 11 women, have been lynched. Some for having organized strikes, others for having espoused the cause of the Blacks.

Among the collection of the crimes of American "civilization," lynching has a place of honor.

THE KU KLUX KLAN*

The place of origin of the Ku Klux Klan is the Southern United States.

In May, 1866, after the Civil War, young people gathered together in a small locality of the State of Tennessee to set up a club. A question of whiling away the time. This organization was given the name *kuklos,* a Greek word meaning club. To Americanize the word, it was changed into Ku Klux. Hence, for more originality, Ku Klux Klan.

After big social upheavals, the public mind is naturally unsettled. It becomes avid for new stimuli and inclined to mysticism. The KKK, with its strange garb, its bizarre rituals, its mysteries, and its secrecy, irresistibly attracted the curiosity of the Whites in the Southern States and became very popular.

It consisted at first of only a group of snobs and idlers, without political or social purpose. Cunning elements discovered in it a force able to serve their political ambitions.

The victory of the Federal Government had just freed the Negroes and made them citizens. The agriculture of the South—deprived of its black labor—was short of hands. Former landlords were exposed to ruin. The Klansmen proclaimed the principle of the supremacy of the white race. Anti-Negro was their only policy. The agrarian and slave-owning bourgeoisie saw in the Klan a useful agent, almost a savior. They gave it all the help in their power. The Klan's methods ranged

* Printed in *La Correspondance Internationale,* No. 74, 1924. (*This article may well have been a part of a pamphlet on the Negro question which Ho later published in Moscow, and which was not included in the* Selected Works *as published in Hanoi.*—ED.)

from intimidation to murder. In the space of three years it committed so many crimes and misdeeds that a number of those who supported it left it in horror.

Toward 1869, under the pressure of public opinion, the Klan was given the sack by its "Emperor." It had an Emperor, who, nevertheless, had only a purely nominal authority. The local Klans carried on their own existence and crimes. Professor Mecklin—to whom we owe these details—said that every page of the thirteen big volumes containing the investigations into the acts of the Klan in 1871–72, recorded beatings-up of Blacks or Whites. These acts of violence were often done out of pure sadism. They were a favorite entertainment of the Klansmen.

A better knowledge of the Klan can be gained and a better judgment formulated by quoting the speech made by Senator Sherman of Ohio in the Senate in March, 1871. "Is there," asked Sherman, "a Senator who can name—in searching through the crimes committed through the ages—an association or gang whose acts and designs are more diabolical or criminal than those of the Ku Klux Klan? The Ku Klux Klan is a secret association, formed on oath, and whose members murder, steal, pillage, bully, insult, and threaten. They commit these crimes not against the strong and the rich but against the poor, the weak, the harmless, and the defenseless."

Yet the Klan lived and "worked" for forty-odd years without too much sensation.

The New Klan

It was in October, 1915, that William Joseph Simmons, the new "Emperor" of the Klan, together with thirty-four of his friends, brought the KKK to the American scene again. Its program was 100 per cent Americanism, that is to say, anti-Catholic, anti-Semite, anti-worker, and anti-Negro.

It is to be noted that it was following the Civil War and the emancipation of the Blacks that the old Ku Klux Klan saw the light of day, its aim being to bar the freed people's way to a social life. During the World War, America enlisted in its army and navy hundreds of thousands of Blacks who were given promises of social and political reforms and who, having made the same sacrifices as the Whites, timorously claimed the same rights. A situation equivalent to a "second emancipation." Thereupon the new Klan sprang up.

It was again in the Southern United States—region of big planters and antiabolitionists, the cradle of serfdom and lynching, the motherland of the old Klan—that "Emperor" Simmons founded the new "invisible Empire." To an interviewer, William Joseph Simmons said regarding its objectives, "We are convinced that to ensure the supremacy of the white race we must wrest from the Blacks the franchises which have been granted them. The Lord's will is that the white race shall be superior, and it was by a decree of Providence that Negroes were created slaves."

Soon after the resurrection of the Klan, more than eighty beatings-up were recorded in the state of Texas alone, in one year, and ninety-six lynchings.

The Klan flourished especially in Georgia, Mississippi, Texas, Alabama, and Arkansas. It was in those states that the victims of lynching were most numerous. In 1919, the Ku Klux Klan burned alive four Negroes in Georgia, two in Mississippi, and one in Texas. It lynched twenty-two Negroes in Georgia, twelve in Mississippi, ten in Arkansas, eight in Alabama, and three in Texas.

It attacked or pulled down jails to lynch the Negroes who were kept in custody there five times in Georgia, three in Alabama, three in Mississippi, three in Texas, and twice in Arkansas. It lynched twelve women in Mississippi, seven in Alabama, six in Texas, five in Arkansas, and five in Georgia. It burned, hanged, drowned, or shot down nine Negro former armed service personnel. The Klan carried out other lynchings in other States, but we want to quote only definite figures.

The Decline of the Ku Klux Klan

The Klan is for many reasons doomed to disappear.

1. The Negroes, having learned during the war that they are a force if united, are no longer allowing their kinsmen to be beaten or murdered with impunity. They are replying to each attempt at violence by the Klan. In July, 1919, in Washington, they stood up to the Klan and a wild mob. The battle raged in the capital for four days. In August, they fought for five days against the Klan and the mob in Chicago. Seven regiments were mobilized to restore order. In September, the government was obliged to send federal troops to Omaha to put down similar strife. In various other States the Negroes defended themselves no less energetically.

2. Like its predecessor, the new Klan has so shocked public opinion by its excesses that those who had approved of or joined it at the beginning are leaving it. Its internal quarrels, its scandals and financial frauds ended by sickening even the most indifferent and most tolerant people. The Senate has been compelled to prosecute it. Even bourgeois newspapers such as the *New York World, The Chicago Defender,* etc., are attacking it.

3. Its "100 per cent Americanism" and its antiworkerism group it against 20 million American Catholics, 3 million Jews, 20 million foreigners, 12 million Negroes, all decent Americans, and the whole working class of America.

At the last congress of Negro Associations, the following motion was carried: "We declare the Ku Klux Klan an enemy of Humanity; we declare that we are determined to fight it to the end and to make common cause with all the foreign workmen in America as well as with all those who are persecuted by it."

On the other hand, the emigration of Negroes from the agricultural South to the industrial North has forced the planters—threatened with ruin through shortage of manpower—to alleviate the lot of the black workmen, and, consequently, to condemn more and more often the methods and acts of violence of their agent: the Klan.

4. Finally, the Ku Klux Klan has all the defects of clandestine and reactionary organizations without their qualities. It has the mysticism of Freemasonry, the mummeries of Catholicism, the brutality of Fascism, the illegality of its 568 various associations, but it has neither doctrine, nor program, nor vitality, nor discipline.

PART TWO

The Comintern Way
(1924–30)

LENIN AND THE EAST*

The First International laid the foundation for the international Communist movement, but because of its short existence, it could formulate for the movement only the basic lines of action. Hence, the question of colonies was not thoroughly studied by the First International.

As for the Second International, with its representatives such as Macdonald, Vandervelde, Henderson, and Blum, etc., it paid only too much attention to this question. Its leaders did not sympathize with the struggle for self-liberation waged by the colonial peoples. Besides, after coming to office, Macdonald was no less active than Baldwin and Chamberlain in suppressing the peoples of India, the Sudan, and other colonies who courageously opposed their foreign oppressors.

On the orders of these gentlemen, native villages were bombed and colonial peoples suppressed in a ruthless and cruel manner that no words can depict. Everybody knows that the opportunists have carried out a policy of segregating the white workers from the colored workers, that the trade unions, under the influence of these wily socialists, do not want to admit workers of different color into their ranks. The colonial policy of the Second International has more than anything else laid bare the true face of this petit-bourgeois organization. Hence, until the October Revolution, socialist theories were regarded as theories particularly reserved for the Whites, a new tool for deceit and exploitation. Lenin opened a new era, which is truly revolutionary, in various colonies.

* Printed in *Le Sifflet* (Paris), January 21, 1926.

Lenin was the first man determinedly to denounce all prejudices against colonial peoples, which have been deeply implanted in the minds of many European and American workers. Lenin's theses on the question of nationalities, approved by International Communism, have brought about a momentous revolution in all oppressed countries throughout the world.

Lenin was the first to realize and emphasize the full importance of a correct solution to the colonial question as a contribution to the world revolution. The colonial question has been brought to the fore in all congresses of International Communism, the world trade-union body, and the International Communist Youth.

Lenin was the first to realize and assess the full importance of drawing the colonial peoples into the revolutionary movement. He was the first to realize that without the participation of the colonial peoples, the socialist revolution could not come about.

With his inborn clearsightedness, Lenin realized that in order to carry out work in the colonies successfully, it was necessary to know how to take full advantage of the national liberation movement which was gaining ground in these countries; he realized that with the support of the world proletariat for this movement we will have new, strong allies in the struggle for the socialist revolution.

All delegates of colonial countries who have taken part in various congresses of International Communism will never forget the concern that Lenin, their leader and comrade, displayed for them. They will forever remember with what insight he looked into the conditions of the most complex tasks peculiar to the East. Hence, every one of us will deeply understand how correct Lenin's judgments are and how valuable are his teachings.

Only Lenin's wise attitude toward the colonial question can arouse the most backward colonial peoples. Lenin's strategy on this question is applied by various Communist Parties in the world, and has won over the best and most positive elements in the colonies to take part in Communist movements.

Lenin's solution of the very complex question of nationalities in Soviet Russia, and its practical application by the Communist Party, is the sharpest propaganda weapon for the colonies.

With regard to oppressed and enslaved peoples, Lenin brought about a turn in the history of poverty of their slavelike lives and symbolized a bright future.

REPORT ON THE NATIONAL AND COLONIAL QUESTIONS AT THE FIFTH CONGRESS OF THE COMMUNIST INTERNATIONAL*

Comrades, I only wish to put forward some suggestions about Comrade Manuilsky's† criticisms of our policy on the colonial question. But before entering upon the matter, it is desirable to give some statistics in order to help us to see its importance more clearly.

COUNTRIES	MOTHER COUNTRIES		COLONIES	
	AREA (sq. km.)	POPULATION	AREA (sq. km.)	POPULATION
Great Britain	151,000	45,500,000	34,910,000	403,600,000
France	536,000	39,000,000	10,250,000	55,600,000
The United States	9,420,000	100,000,000	1,850,000	12,000,000
Spain	504,500	20,700,000	371,600	853,000
Italy	286,600	38,500,000	1,460,000	1,623,000
Japan	418,000	57,070,000	288,000	21,249,000
Belgium	29,500	7,642,000	2,400,000	8,500,000
Portugal	92,000	5,545,000	2,062,000	8,738,000
Holland	32,500	6,700,000	2,046,000	48,030,000

* Held in Moscow from June 17 to July 8, 1924.

† D. Z. Manuilsky (1883–1959), an outstanding militant of the Communist Party of the Soviet Union, who at the Fifth Congress of the Communist International delivered a report on national and colonial questions.

Therefore, nine countries, with a population of 320,657,000 and an area of 11,470,200 square kilometers, are exploiting colonies embracing dozens of nationalities, with a population of 560,193,000 and covering an area of 55,637,000 square kilometers. The whole area of the colonies is five times greater than that of the mother countries, and the whole population of the mother countries amounts to less than three-fifths of that of the colonies.

These figures are still more striking if the biggest imperialist countries are taken separately. The British colonies taken as a whole are eight-and-a-half.times more populous and about 232 times bigger than Great Britain. France occupies an area nineteen times bigger than her own. The population of the French colonies exceeds that of France by 16,600,000.

Thus, it is not an exaggeration to say that so long as the French and British Communist Parties have not brought out a really progressive policy with regard to the colonies, have not come into contact with the colonial peoples, their program as a whole is and will be ineffective because it goes counter to Leninism. I will explain myself more clearly. In his speech on Lenin and the national question, Comrade Stalin said that the reformists and leaders of the Second International dared not align the white people of the colonies with their colored counterparts. Lenin also refused to recognize this division and pushed aside the obstacle separating the civilized slaves of imperialism from the uncivilized slaves.

According to Lenin, the victory of the revolution in Western Europe depended on its close contact with the liberation movement against imperialism in enslaved colonies and with the national question, both of which form a part of the common problem of the proletarian revolution and dictatorship.

Later, Comrade Stalin spoke of the viewpoint which held that the European proletarians can achieve success without a direct alliance with the liberation movement in the colonies. And he considered this a counterrevolutionary viewpoint. But if we judge from practice to make our theoretical examination, we are entitled to say that our big Parties, excepting the Soviet Communist Party, still hold the above-mentioned viewpoint because they are inactive in this matter.

What have the bourgeois class in the colonialist countries done toward oppressing so many people enslaved by them? They have done everything. Using the means given them by the State administrative machine, they have carried out an intense propaganda. They have crammed the heads of the people of the mother countries with speeches, films, newspapers, exhibitions, and every other means so that they have a colonialist outlook; they have displayed before their eyes pictures of the easy, honorable, and rich life which seems to await them in the colonies.

As for our Communist Parties in Great Britain, Holland, Belgium, and other countries—what have they done to cope with the colonial invasions perpetrated by the bourgeois class of their countries? What have they done from the day they accepted Lenin's political program to educate the working class of their countries in the spirit of just internationalism, and that of close contact with the working masses in the colonies? What our Parties have done in this domain is almost worthless. As for me, I was born in a French colony, and am a member of the French Communist Party, and I am very sorry to say that our Communist Party has done hardly anything for the colonies.

It is the task of the Communist newspapers to introduce the colonial question to our militants to awaken the working masses in the colonies, win them over to the cause of Communism, but what have our newspapers done? Nothing at all.

If we compare the number of columns devoted to the colonial question in the bourgeois newspapers such as *The Times, Figaro, Evre* or in those of different opinions such as *Le Populaire,* or *Liberty,* with those devoted to the same question in *l'Humanité,* the central organ of our Party, we are bound to say that this comparison will not be favorable to us.

When the Ministry of Colonies worked out a plan for transforming many African regions into large private plantations and turning the people of these regions into veritable slaves attached to the new employers' land, our newspapers still remained silent. In the French West African colonies, forcible measures for enlistment unknown for centuries were carried out, and yet our newspapers maintained a close silence. The colonialist authorities in Indochina turned themselves into slave traders and sold the inhabitants of North Viet-Nam to planters in the Pacific islands; they lengthened the natives' military service from two to four years; they sold the greater part of the colonial land to financier sharks; they increased taxes by a further 30 per cent in spite of the natives' inability to pay the old ones. And all this was done while the natives were being driven to bankruptcy and dying of hunger through flood. However, our newspapers still maintained silence. Thus, it is no wonder that the natives are inclined to side with organizations for democracy and freedom, such as the Society for the Rights of Man and the Citizen, together with other, similar organizations which take care of them or pretend to take care of them.

If we go even further, we shall see incredible things, making everybody think that our Party has a disregard for all that concerns the colonies. For instance: *L'Humanité* did not publish the International Peasants' Appeal to the people of the colonies issued by the Communist International.

Prior to the Lyons conference,* the items listed for debate covered all political programs except that on the colonial question. *L'Humanité* carried many articles on the Senegal boxer Siki's success, but did not raise its voice when the dockers at Dakar port, Siki's brothers, were arrested in the middle of their work, tied hand and foot, hauled on to lorries and taken to jail. Later they were sent to the garrisons to be turned into "defenders of civilization," that is to say, into soldiers. The central organ of our Party daily informed our readers of the feats of the pilot Uadi, who flew from Paris to Indochina. But when the colonial administration pillaged the people of "Dai Nam,"† robbed them of their fields to give them to the French profiteers, sent out bombers with orders to the pilots to teach reason to the pitiful and despoiled local people, the organ of our Party did not find it necessary to bring this news to the knowledge of its readers.

Comrades, the press of the French bourgeoisie has realized that the national question cannot be separated from the colonial question. In my opinion, our Party has not thoroughly understood this. The lessons of the Ruhr, when the native troops who were sent out "to comfort" the starving German workers, encircled the suspected French regiments; the example of the Eastern troops,‡ in which the native forces were given machine guns "to mobilize the spirit" of the French

* The Third Congress of the French Communist Party was held at Lyons in January, 1924. The main problem debated at the Congress was the question of ideological struggle in the Party, its strengthening, and the elimination of alien elements.

† Name used for Viet-Nam under feudal rule.

‡ Troops press-ganged from among the various colonial peoples for the purpose of repressing revolutionary movements in the colonies and even in the metropolitan countries themselves. (*For example, when a large-scale mutiny broke out in the French Army in 1917, after the collapse of an offensive led by the inept General Nivelle, the French used battalions of Tonkinese tirailleurs to put down the rebels. As Vietnamese they could be trusted to shoot into French troops, while a French mainland unit might have hesitated to fire upon fellow Frenchmen.—*ED.)

troops worn out by the hard and protracted war; the events which occurred in 1917 at places where Russian troops were stationed in France;* the lesson of the strike of agricultural workers in the Pyrenees where native troops were forced to play the shameful part of saboteurs; and finally the presence of 207,000 colonial troops in France itself—all these have not made our Party think, have not made our Party find it necessary to lay down a clear and firm policy on colonial questions. The Party has missed many good opportunities for propaganda. The new leading organs of the Party have acknowledged that the Party is in a corner over this question. This is a good sign, because once the leaders of the Party have realized and recognized this weak point in the Party's policy, there is hope that the Party will do its utmost to rectify its errors. I firmly believe that this Congress will be the turning point and will urge the Party to correct its past shortcomings. Although Comrade Manuilsky is quite right in his remarks on the elections in Algeria, to be objective, I must say that it is true that our Party has committed errors here but has corrected them by nominating colonial representatives as candidates in the elections for the Seine department. Though this is still too little, it is fairly satisfactory as a beginning. I am very happy to see that at present our Party is again filled with the best intentions and enthusiasm, and that it needs only to be strengthened by practical deeds to be brought to a correct policy on the colonial question.

What are these practical deeds? To work out long political programs and pass high-sounding resolutions which are, after the Congress, sent to the museum, as has always been done in the past, is not enough. We must adopt concrete measures. I propose the following points:

1. To publish in *l'Humanité* a new feature of at least two columns weekly devoted to regular coverage of colonial questions.

2. To increase propaganda and choose Party members among the natives of the colonial countries in which there are already branches of the Communist International.

* During World War I, the Czarist government sent an expeditionary corps to France. In 1917, its soldiers protested against the war for the defense of the interests of the bourgeoisie. They set up Soviets and demanded their repatriation. Fearing that the Russian soldiers' revolutionary ideas might spread to the French Army, the French High Command moved the Russian corps out of their positions and sent them to the Lacourtine concentration camp, where they were surrounded by barbed wire and guarded by Senegalese and Touareg units. This led to the disarming of the Russian corps.

3. To send comrades from the colonial countries to study at the Eastern Communist University in Moscow.

4. To come to an agreement with the United General Confederation of Labor on the organization of working people from colonial countries working in France.

5. To set Party members the task of paying more attention to colonial questions.

In my opinion, these proposals are national, and if the Communist International and delegates of our Party approve them, I believe that at the Sixth Congress the French Communist Party will be able to say that the united front of the masses of the metropolitan country and colonies has become a reality.

Comrades, as Lenin's disciples, we must concentrate all our forces and energies on colonial questions as on all other questions in order to implement Lenin's teachings.

The French colonies occupy an area of 10,241,510 square kilometers, with 55,571,000 inhabitants scattered over four continents. In spite of the differences in races, climates, customs, traditions, and economic and social development, there are two common points that make them alike and can later bring about unity in the common struggle: (1) The economic situation: In all the French colonies, industry and commerce are little developed and the majority of the population are engaged in agriculture. Ninety-five per cent of the population are peasants. (2) In all the colonies, the native peoples are unremittingly exploited by French imperialist capital.

I have not enough time to make a thorough analysis of the situation of the peasants in each colony. Therefore, I shall take only a few typical examples to give an idea of the peasants' life in the colonies.

I shall begin with my country, Indochina, which naturally I know better than the other colonies.

When France occupied this colony, the war drove the peasants away from their villages. Later, on their return, they found their lands occupied by the colonists who had followed in the wake of the victorious army. They had shared among themselves the land the native peasants had cultivated for generations. In consequence the Annamese peasants were turned into serfs and forced to cultivate their own lands for foreign masters.

Numerous unfortunates who could not suffer the extremely hard conditions imposed by the occupiers left their lands and wandered about the country. They were called "pirates" by the French, who sought every means to prosecute them.

The lands thieved in this way were allotted to the planters. They needed merely to say a word in order to get tracts of land sometimes covering more than 20,000 or 25,000 hectares.

These planters not only occupied lands without any payment but also obtained all that was necessary to exploit those lands, including labor. The administration allowed them to make use of a number of prisoners without any payment, or ordered the communes to supply them with manpower.

Besides these wolves and the administration, the Catholic Mission is to be mentioned. The Catholic Mission alone occupied one-quarter of the areas under cultivation in Cochinchina. To secure for itself all those lands, it used every imaginable and unimaginable method, including bribery, fraud, and coercion. Here are a few examples. Availing itself of crop failures, it gave the peasants loans, with their rice fields on mortgage. Because the interest rates were too high, the peasants were unable to get out of debt and had to cede their mortgaged fields outright to the Mission. Using all kinds of underhand methods, the Mission did its utmost to find out secret information that could be harmful to the authorities. It used this information as a threat to force the authorities to comply with its will. Together with the big capitalists, the Mission founded companies for the exploitation of the plantations, which were occupied without any payment, and the lands stolen from the peasants. The henchmen of the Mission held high positions in the government. The Mission exploited believers no less ruthlessly than the planters. Another of its tricks was to get together poor people and force them to reclaim wasteland with promises that once the land was cultivated it would be divided among the peasants. But as soon as the land was reclaimed and the crops about to be harvested, the Mission declared that the land belonged to it and drove out those who had toiled to make it productive. Robbed by their "protectors" (Catholic or non-Catholic), the Annamese peasants were not even left in peace to work on their remaining tiny plots of land. The land registry service carried out a fraudulent cadastral survey to make the peasants pay more taxes. These increased every year. Recently, after occupying thousands of hectares of land belonging to the

Annamese highlanders to give them to the profiteers, the authorities sent airplanes to the place so that the victims dared not think of rebelling.

The despoiled peasants, ruined and driven away, again found ways and means to reclaim virgin land. But once it was under cultivation, the administration would seize it and oblige them to buy it at prices fixed by the administration. Those unable to pay would be driven out pitilessly.

Last year, the country was devastated by floods; however, land taxes increased 30 per cent.

In addition to the iniquitous taxes that ruin them, the peasants still have to go on *corvée,* pay poll tax, salt tax, buy government bonds, subscribe to various funds and many other things, and sign unequal contracts, etc.

French capitalists in Algeria, Tunisia, and Morocco have carried out the same policy of robbery and exploitation. All the good irrigated land was kept for the French. The natives were driven away to areas at the foot of the mountains or to arid spots. The financial companies, profiteers, and high functionaries divided the land in the colonies among themselves.

Through direct and indirect operations, the banks in Algeria and Tunisia in 1914 made 12,258,000 francs profit from a capital of 25 million francs. The Bank of Morocco, with a capital of 15,400,000 francs, made 1,753,000 francs profit in 1921.

The French Algerian Company has occupied 324,000 hectares of the best land. The Algerian General Company has occupied 100,000 hectares. A private company has occupied 50,000 hectares of forest without any payment, while the Capziere phosphate and railway company has occupied 50,000 hectares of land rich in ores, and in addition has secured priority rights over 20,000 hectares of land in its neighborhood. A former French deputy has occupied a plantation covering 1,125 hectares of land, with mines to the value of 10 million francs, producing a yearly income of 4 million francs. The natives, the real owners of these mines, receive annually only one-tenth of a franc per hectare.

French colonial policy has abolished the right of collective ownership and replaced it by private ownership. It has also abolished small ownership to the advantage of big ownership of the plantations. This policy has incurred for the native peasants the loss of 5 million hectares of their best land.

In 15 years, the peasants in Kabylia were robbed of 192,090 hectares.

From 1913, each year the Moroccan peasants were robbed of 12,000 hectares of land under cultivation. Since France was victorious in the war "for justice," that figure has risen to 14,540 hectares.

At present, there are in Morocco only 1,070 French people, but they occupy 500,000 hectares of land.

Like their Annamese peasant brothers and sisters, the peasants in Africa lead an unbearably hard life, going on *corvée* all the time and paying heavy taxes. Their misery and sufferings are indescribable. Due to shortage of food, they have to eat wild vegetables and grasses or rotten rice and consequently are infected with typhus and tuberculosis. Even in good harvest years, peasants are seen turning up rubbish heaps, disputing food remnants with dogs. In lean years, the corpses of peasants dead of starvation are seen everywhere in the fields and on the highways.

The peasants' life in West Africa and French Equatorial Africa is still more frightful. These colonies are in the hands of about forty companies. They occupy everything: land and fields, natural resources, and even the natives' lives; the latter lack even the right to work for themselves. They are compelled to work for the companies, all the time, and only for the companies. To force them to work for nothing, incredible means of coercion are used by the companies. All lands and fields are confiscated. Only those who agree to do the farming required by the companies are allowed to have some tiny plots of land. People are affected with all kinds of diseases through malnutrition, and the death rate, especially among the children, is very high.

Another method is to make old people, women, and children work as servants. They are lodged in small huts, ill-treated, beaten, ill-fed, and sometimes murdered. In some localities the number of permanent servants is kept about equal to the number of workers in order to discourage the latter from running away. So that work in the plantations shall not suffer, the natives are forbidden to work their own land in good time. Therefore, famine and epidemics occur very often, wreaking havoc in the colonies.

The few tribes who have fled to the forests and succeeded in escaping the planters' exploitation live like animals, feeding on roots and leaves, and die from malaria and the unwholesome climate. Meanwhile, the white masters are devastating their fields and villages. The following is an excerpt from an officer's diary describing briefly but clearly the repression of the colonial peasants:

> Raid on Colover village.
> Raid on the Fan tribe at Cuno. Villages and gardens destroyed.
> Raid on Becanit village. Village burned down; 3,000 banana trees cut down.
> Raid on Kwa village. Village destroyed. Gardens and farms razed to the ground.
> Raid on Abimaphan village. All houses burned down, all gardens and farms destroyed.
> Raid on Examphami village. Village destroyed. The whole commune along Bom river burned down.

The same system of pillage, extermination, and destruction prevails in the African regions under Italian, Spanish, British, or Portuguese rule.

In the Belgian Congo, the population in 1891 was 25 million, but it had fallen to eight-and-a-half million by 1911. The Hereros and Cama tribes in the former German colonies in Africa were completely exterminated. A total of 80,000 were killed under German rule, and 15,000 were killed during the "pacification" period in 1914. The population of the French Congo was 20,000 in 1894. It was only 9,700 in 1911. In one province there were 10,000 inhabitants in 1910. Eight years later there remained only 1,080. In another province with 40,000 black inhabitants, in only two years 20,000 people were killed, and in the following six months 6,000 more were killed or disabled.

The densely populated regions bordering the rivers were turned into deserts within a matter of fifteen years. Bleached bones were scattered throughout the ravaged oases and villages.

The life of the survivors was atrocious in the extreme. The peasants were robbed of the tiny plots of land allowed them by the companies, the artisans lost their crafts, and the breeders their cattle. The Matabélés were cattle breeders. Before the arrival of the British, they had 200,000 cattle. Two years later only 40,900 were left. The Hereros had 90,000 cattle. Within 12 years the German colonists had robbed them of half. Similar cases are numerous in all the black countries which came into contact with the Whites' civilization.

In conclusion, I quote the African writer René Maran, author of *Batuala,* who said:

> Equatorial Africa was a densely populated area, rich in rubber. There were here all kinds of gardens and farms with plenty of poultry and goats. After only seven years everything was destroyed. Villages were in ruins, gardens and farms laid waste, poultry and goats killed. The inhabitants grew weak because they had to work beyond their strength and without any payment. They were thus not sufficiently strong and lacked the time to work their fields. Diseases broke out, famine appeared, the death rate increased. We should know that they are the descendants of strong and healthy tribes imbued with an enduring and tempered fighting spirit. Here, there is nothing left that can be called civilization. . . .

To complete this tragic picture, I want to add one point: French capitalists have never hesitated to drive each region in turn to famine if it might be of advantage to them. In many colonial countries, e.g., the Reunion Islands, Algeria, Madagascar, etc., the inhabitants are no longer allowed to grow cereals but have to grow other crops required by French industry. These crops are more profitable to the planters. And this has caused the cost of living in the colonies to rise and often brings about famine.

In all the French colonies, famine is on the increase and so is the people's hatred. The native peasants are ripe for insurrection. In many colonies, they have risen many times but their uprisings have all been drowned in blood. If at present the peasants still have a passive attitude, the reason is that they still lack organization and leaders. The Communist International must help them to revolution and liberation.

FRENCH COLONIZATION ON TRIAL

BLOOD TAX

War and the "Natives"

Before 1914, they were only dirty Negroes and dirty Annamese, at the best only good for pulling rickshaws and receiving blows from our administrators. With the declaration of the joyful new war, they became the "dear children" and "brave friends" of our paternal and tender administrators and of our governors—more or less general. They (the natives) were all at once promoted to the supreme rank of "defenders of law and liberty." This sudden honor cost them rather dear, however, for in order to defend that law and that liberty of which they themselves are deprived, they had suddenly to leave their rice fields or their sheep, their children and their wives, in order to cross oceans and go and rot on the battlefields of Europe. During the crossing, many natives, after being invited to watch the wonderful spectacle of the scientific demonstration of torpedoing, sank beneath the waves to defend the fatherland of the marine monsters. Others left their skins in the poetic desert of the Balkans, wondering whether the motherland intended to enter the Harem of the Turk as first wife; otherwise, why should they have been sent to get killed in these countries? Yet others, on the banks of the Marne or in the mud of Champagne, heroically allowed themselves to be massacred to water the laurels of the chiefs with their blood and to sculpture the marshals' batons with their bones.

Finally, those who toiled at the rear, in monstrous gunpowder factories, though they didn't breathe the "Boches'" asphyxiating gases, were subject to the glowing red vapors of the French, which amounts to the same thing, because the poor devils coughed up their lungs just as if they had been gassed.

All told, 700,000 natives came to France, and of this number 80,000 will never again see the sun of their country!

Volunteering

Here is what a colleague tells us: The native proletariat of Indochina, since time immemorial squeezed in the form of taxes, forced payments, *corvées* of all kinds, and the compulsory purchase of spirits and opium, has had, since 1915–16, to put up with volunteering.

The events of the last few years have provided the pretext, throughout the length and breadth of the country, for big roundups of human material quartered under the most varied appellations: sharpshooters, skilled workmen, unskilled workmen, etc.

In the opinion of all impartial competent bodies called upon to make use in Europe of the Asian human material, this material did not produce results justifying the huge expenses that its transport and keep entailed.

And then, the chase after the said human material, called for the occasion "volunteers" (a dreadfully ironic word), gives rise to the most scandalous abuse.

Here is how this voluntary recruitment is done: the satrap, which every Indochina Resident is, informs his mandarins that within a fixed period his province must supply such and such a number of men. The means are of small importance. It is up to the mandarins to find a way. As for being in the know, they certainly are, those fellows, where coining money is concerned.

They begin by picking up hale and hearty individuals without resources, who are sacrificed without recourse. Afterwards, they call on sons of wealthy families; if they prove stubborn, it is easy enough to find an opportunity to make trouble for them or their families, and, if need be, to imprison them until they have solved the following dilemma: volunteer or finance.

It can be seen that people picked up in such circumstances are lacking in any enthusiasm for the job they are destined to perform. No sooner are they in barracks than they watch for the smallest opportunity to escape.

Others, unable to ward off their sad fate, catch the most serious diseases, the most common of which is purulent conjunctivitis, caused by rubbing the eyes with various ingredients, ranging from quicklime to gonorrheal discharge.

Notwithstanding, having promised mandarinal ranks to Indochinese volunteers who survived and posthumous titles to those who died "for the fatherland," the government general of Indochina continued its declaration thus: "You enlisted en masse, you have *unhesitatingly* left your native soil to which you are nevertheless very attached; you, *tirailleurs,* to give your blood; you, workers, to give your arms."

If the Annamese were so delighted to be soldiers, why were some taken to the chief towns in chains, and others, while awaiting embarkation, were shut in a Saigon college, under the eye of French sentinels with fixed bayonets and loaded rifles? The bloody demonstrations in Cambodia, the uprisings in Saigon, Bien Hoa, and elsewhere, were they thus a display of the eagerness to enlist "en masse" and "unhesitatingly"?

Escapes and desertions (there were 50 per cent in the reserves) provoked pitiless repression, and the latter, revolts which were stifled in blood.

The government general took good care to add that, of course, in order to deserve the "obvious benevolence" and "great kindness" of the Administration, "You [Indochinese soldiers] must behave well and not give rise to any displeasure."

The commander-in-chief of the troops in Indochina took another precaution: on each recruit's back or wrist he had an indelible number written with a solution of nitrate of silver.

As in Europe, the great poverty of some is the cause of profit for others: professional stripe wearers, for whom the windfall of recruiting and officering natives enables them to keep away from the perilous operations in Europe as long as possible; suppliers who get rich quickly by letting the unfortunate recruits die of hunger; and market keepers, who carry out shady deals in connivance with officials.

Let us add, in this connection, that there exists another kind of volunteering: volunteering to subscribe to various loans. An identical procedure. Whoever owns anything is liable to subscribe. Means of persuasion and coercion of a kind which force everyone to comply are employed against the recalcitrants.

As most of our Asian subscribers are completely unaware of our financial machinery, they consider the installments paid for the loans as new taxes and consider the bonds as of no greater value than receipts.

Let us see now how volunteering has been organized in other colonies.

Let us take, for example, West Africa, where commanding officers, accompanied by their armed forces, went from village to village to oblige local notables to supply them *immediately* with the number of men they wanted to recruit. Didn't one commanding officer think it ingenious, in order to induce young Senegalese, who were running away from him, to leave their hiding place and wear the military cap, by torturing their parents? Didn't he arrest old people, pregnant women, and young girls, making them take off their clothes which were burned before their eyes? Naked and bound, the unfortunate victims were flogged as they ran through the district at a trot, to "provide an example"! A woman carrying her baby on her back had to beg to have one hand freed to keep her child balanced. Two old people fainted on the way; young girls, terrified at such cruelty, had their periods for the first time; a pregnant woman gave premature birth to a stillborn child; another gave birth to a blind baby.

Recruiting procedure was, furthermore, carried on in various ways. The following was particularly expeditious: A rope was strung across one end of the main street in a village, and another rope at the other end. And all the Negroes who were between the two ropes at that particular time were automatically enlisted.

On March 3, 1923, at midday, wrote a witness, the quays of Rufisque and Dakar were surrounded by mounted police, and all the natives working there were picked up. As these fellows didn't seem much inclined to go at once and defend civilization, they were invited to step into trucks which took them to prison. From there, after they had had time to change their minds, they were taken to the barracks. There, after patriotic ceremonies, twenty-nine volunteers were proclaimed future heroes for the next list. All of them were now thoroughly keen to return the Ruhr to the Motherland.

"But," wrote General Mangin, who knew them well, they are troops "to be consumed before winter."

We have in our possession a letter from a native of Dahomey, an ex-soldier who did his "duty" in the just war. A few extracts from that letter will show you how the "Batouala" are protected and in what manner our colonial administrators manufacture the native loyalism which ornaments all the official speeches and feeds all the articles of the Regimansets and the Hausers of all calibers.

"In 1915," says the letter, "during the enforced recruitment ordered by Mr. Noufflard, Governor of Dahomey, my village was pillaged and burned down by police agents and guards of the Club. During this pillage and burning, all that I owned in the way of possessions was taken away from me. Nevertheless, I was enlisted by force and, notwithstanding the shocking outrage of which I was a victim, I did my duty on the French front. I was wounded on the Aisne.

"Now that the war is ended, I am going back to my country, homeless and penniless.

"This is what has been stolen from me:

1,000 francs in cash
12 pigs
15 sheep
10 goats
60 chickens
8 loincloths
5 jackets
10 pairs of trousers
7 headdresses
1 silver chain
2 trunks containing various objects.

"Here are the names of comrades living in my district who were forcibly enrolled on the same day as me, and whose houses were pillaged and burned. [Seven names follow.]

"Many are the victims of these feats of arms of Mr. Governor Noufflard, but I do not know their names to give you them today. . . ."

Wilhelm's "Boches" couldn't have done better.

The Fruit of Sacrifice

As soon as the guns had had their fill of black or yellow cannon fodder, the loving declarations of our leaders were magically silenced, and Negroes and Annamese automatically became people of a "dirty race."

As a memento of services rendered, before re-embarking at Marseilles, weren't the Annamese robbed of all they possessed: new clothes bought at their own expense, watches, souvenirs of all kinds, etc.? Weren't they submitted to the control of brutes who struck them without reason? Weren't they fed like pigs and made to sleep as such in damp holds, without bunks, without air, without light? Back in their country, weren't they warmly welcomed by this patriotic speech by a grateful administrator: "You have defended the motherland, that is good. Now we don't need you any more, go away!"

And the former "poilus"—or what remained of them—after valiantly defending right and justice, returned empty-handed to their indigenous state where right and justice are unknown.

According to Indochinese newspapers, opium-house licenses are granted to widows of French soldiers killed in the war and to French war-wounded.

In this way, the colonial government has in one stroke committed two outrages against humanity. On the one hand, it doesn't want to do its own dirty work as a poisoner but it wants to associate with it its poor victims of fratricidal butchery. On the other, it values so low the lives and blood of its dupes that it considers it is paying sufficiently for the loss of a limb or mourning for a husband by throwing them this rotten bone.

We do not doubt that the war-wounded and war widows will spurn this repugnant offer, spitting their indignation in the face of its author; and we are sure that the civilized world and the good Frenchmen are on our side in condemning the sharks of the colonies who do not hesitate to poison a whole race to line their pockets.

Festival at Bien Hoa

According to an Annamese custom, if in a village someone dies, the rice huskers must show that they respect the rest of the deceased's soul and the family's sorrow by abstaining from singing during work as they usually do. Modern civilization, implanted by force in our country, doesn't make so much ado. Read the following anecdote published in a paper in Cochinchina:

> The Commission in charge of organizing the festivities for the benefit of the memorial to the fallen Annamese of the province of Bien Hoa is actively working to draw up a wonderful program.

A garden party, a village fair, an open air ball, etc. are mentioned. . . . In short, the attractions will be numerous and varied, to enable everyone to participate in a good work in the pleasantest way in the world.

Messrs. the airmen of the Bien Hoa club will give their assistance and the organizers can already count on the presence of the highest authorities from Saigon to enhance the sparkle of the festival with their presence.

Let us add that then ladies and gentlemen of Saigon will not need to return to the capital for dinner, which would only result in cutting short their share of pleasure; a wonderful, carefully prepared and well-furnished buffet will give satisfaction to the most delicate gourmets.

Let us go to Bien Hoa on January 21st, we will be present at a fine festival and we will have shown the families of the Annamese who died during the war that we know how to remember their sacrifice.

The following letter has been communicated to us from Saigon:

. . . If there exists an anomaly which is both painful and grotesque, it is to have the victory of "right" and "justice" celebrated by a people which is suffering every injustice and has no rights whatever. That is, however, what we have done here. No need to describe to you the festivities and "public rejoicing" which took place in this town on November 11. It's the same everywhere and at all times. Torchlight tattoos, fireworks, troop reviews, a ball at the Governor's palace, flower processions, patriotic collections, advertising speeches, banquets, etc. Out of all these masquerades, I have retained only one psychologically interesting fact. Like the crowd in all countries, the crowd in Saigon are very keen on the cinema. Therefore a compact mass was standing in front of the Palace Hotel, where films succeeded each other and Charlie Chaplin, cowboys, and wonderful people filed past one after another. People crowded into the boulevard and streets. Then the proprietor of the Saigon Palace, wanting to clear the pavement in front of his hotel, began hitting the crowd with a stick. Madame helped him, and she too struck the crowd. A few ragamuffins managed to "pinch" Madame's stick, and people clapped. Furious, Monsieur came to the rescue, with a bigger stick this time, and heroically struck about with all his might. The *nha que* ("peasants") drew back to the boulevard, but drunk with his "victory," this good Frenchman bravely crossed the road and continued to rain his big stick on the head, shoulders, and backs of these poor natives. He caught a child and gave him a sound beating. . . .

The Militarism Continues

Immediately on arriving in Casablanca, Marshal Lyautey addressed to the occupation troops in Morocco, the following order of the day:

It is to you I owe the highest military dignity with which the government of the Republic has honored me, because for nine years, you have unstintingly given your devotion and your blood.

We are going to undertake a campaign which will ensure the definite pacification of Morocco for the common benefit of its loyal population and of the protector nation, etc.

Now on that day (April 14) the following communiqué arrived: "During an engagement with the Beni Bon Zert, at Babel-Harba, there were twenty-nine killed and 'wounded.' "

When it is remembered that it needed the blood of 1,500 workers to make six marshal's batons, the death of twenty-nine poor devils does not sufficiently applaud the Marshal Higher Resident's eloquent speech. So where is the right of peoples to dispose of themselves, for which people cut each other's throats for four years? And what a strange way to civilize: To teach people to live well, a start is made by killing them!

Here (in Haiphong) there are also sailors' strikes. Thus, on Thursday (August 15) two steamers were due to leave carrying a large number of Annamese *tirailleurs* bound for Syria.

The sailors refused to leave, under the pretext that their pay was not given them in piasters. In effect, the piaster being worth 10 francs at the rate of exchange instead of 2.50 francs, the Companies, with unbelievable abuse, drew up the sailors' accounts in francs, while the officials were paid in piasters. Everyone was then disembarked and the crew were immediately arrested. As can be seen, the sailors of the Yellow sea have nothing to envy the sailors of the Black sea.

We protest with all our might against the dispatch to Syria of Annamese contingents. Is it considered, in higher circles, that not enough of our unfortunate yellow brothers were killed on the battlefields between 1914 and 1918, during the "war of civilization and right"?

It is usual for our illustrious ones to "educate" the natives with kicks and sticks. The unfortunate Nahon—doubly assassinated, first by Captain Vidart, then by the sawbones officer in charge of the autopsy, who to save his pals' skins, did not hesitate to steal and hide the dead man's brain—is not, alas! the only victim of colonial militarism. One of our colonial colleagues notified us of another:

This time, it was at Maison-Carrée, Algeria, at the 5th *Tirailleurs*. The victim was a young soldier of the 21 class, Terrier, from Ténès.

The circumstances of his death are especially painful. On August 5th, the young soldier Terrier went to the regimental infirmary to ask for a laxative. It was given to him, or to be more precise, what he thought was a laxative; he took it, and a few hours later he was writhing with terrible pains and died.

Mr. Terrier senior then received a telegram announcing, without consideration or explanations that his son—his only son—had died and would be buried the next day, Sunday.

Mad with grief, the poor father dashed to Algiers, to the 5th *Tirailleurs* at Maison-Carrée. There he learned that his son's body was at the Maillot hospital. (How was he taken there? Is it true that to avoid the regulation inquiry prescribed for all deaths occurring at the infirmary, he had been taken *dead* to the hospital, with the pretense that he had died on the way?)

At the hospital, the unfortunate father asked to see the body; he was told to wait.

A long time after, a Major came and told him that the autopsy which had just been carried out had revealed nothing and left him there without giving him permission to see his son's body.

According to the latest news, it appears that Mr. Terrier senior, who had asked the Colonel of the 5th *Tirailleurs* for an explanation, received this answer from him: his son had died from poisoning!

POISONING OF THE NATIVES

The worthy Mr. Sarraut, former radical Minister of Colonies, little father of the natives (so he says), adored the Annamese and was adored by them.

In order to instill French civilization into them, of which he was the principal agent, he did not stop at anything, not even infamy and crime. Here is proof of this: it is a letter which, in his capacity of Governor General of Indochina and to swell the pockets of the colonial bandits and his own, he addressed to his subordinates:

Mr. Resident,
In accordance with instructions from Mr. Director General of the Excise, I have the honor to beg you to be so kind as to second the efforts of my department in the establishment of new alcohol and opium houses.

To this effect, I am taking the liberty of sending you a list of the homes which should be installed in the various villages mentioned, most of which are entirely without spirits and opium.

Through the channels of Cambodian governors and village heads, your preponderant influence could be fortunately used to draw the attention of certain native small traders to the advantages of going in for some additional business.

On our side, the agents of the active service, on their rounds, will endeavor to install premises, unless you would prefer, Mr. Resident, that they should wait until you have first acted with the authorities in order that they may second your action, in which case, I beg you to be so kind as to inform me.

It is only through complete and constant understanding between your administration and ours that we shall obtain the best results, in the best interests of the Treasury.

There were at the time 1,500 alcohol and opium houses for a thousand villages, while there were only ten schools for the same number of localities. Already, before this famous letter, the 12 million natives—women and children included—had been made to swallow 23 or 24 million liters of spirits yearly.

"For the monopolies, Indochina will be represented by a magnificent stag pitilessly bound, dying under the curved beaks of insatiable vultures."

The society for the monopoly of alcohol had among its subscribing members the most eminent personalities in Indochina, and all branches of the Administration were brilliantly represented. Most of them had the advantage of being undeniably useful:

Justice, to settle differences with those on whom they wished to impose:

2 Attorneys General

1 Public Attorney

1 Clerk notary

The Army, to suppress a revolt considered as a possibility by mere fact of the application of the coveted monopoly:

1 Brigadier General

1 Lieutenant Colonel

2 High-ranking military doctors

1 Major

2 Captains

The Administration, whose disinterested complaisance was to be the best guarantee for the success of the operation:

1 Resident of France

1 District Tax Collector

1 Paymaster General

1 Inspector of Posts

1 Registrar

1 Civil Service administrator

2 Professors, etc.

Finally: the honorable Mr. Clémentel, deputy for Puy-de-Dôme.

"Let France look and be proud!" cried Mr. Sarraut at the Colonial Exhibition in Marseilles. In effect, here beside the majestic caymans of West Africa, the camels of Tunisia yawn philosophically; friendly Malagasy crocodiles chat familiarly with august Indochinese cows. Never was understanding so perfect and, opposite the peaceful invasion of colonial fauna, the legendary sardine from the Vieux-Port, as a good hostess, smiles graciously.

The visitors examine with lively interest the historic settle of a certain Governor General, the administrator's sword with which Resident Darles pricked the thighs of Tonkinese detainees, and the torch which administrator Bruère used to smoke out alive more than 200 natives of Houassas.

The pavilion of the Cameroons attracts particular attention. A signboard bearing these patriotic words can be seen there: "The Germans imported large quantities of spirits into the Cameroons. The French prohibited its use."

However, under this signboard a waggish hand had stuck a copy of the letter from Mr. Sarraut advising his subordinates to increase the number of alcohol and opium houses in Annamese villages with the following inscription: "While the Annamese have already: 10 schools, and 1,500 alcohol and opium houses for 1,000 villages."

A significant fact concerns an official who was at the head of a province in Tonkin, Son Tay. In this province there was a population estimated at 200,000 inhabitants. For the needs of the cause, when it was a question of pushing consumption, this population rose with sudden rapidity: It was brought up to 230,000 inhabitants. But as these 230,000 inhabitants consumed too little, the Resident of Son Tay managed, at the end of a year, to obtain a consumption of 560,000 liters of spirits. Thereupon, his promotion assured, he was congratulated.

Mr. de C. affirmed that another Resident showed him a letter from hierarchical superiors in which was stated: "Spirits consumed in the prefecture of X have dropped to less than Z per head of those registered. Do you not think it necessary to make an example?" The Resident thus called upon convened the notables and explained that if they consumed so little it was because they were engaged in smuggling; and the villagers, in order to be left in peace, forthwith bought the quantity of official alcohol, proportionate to the number of inhabitants, that estimates by the offices wished to impose on them.

Factually, if not legally, the annual consumption of each native was determined. And when we say each native, it should not be forgotten that this does not mean only adult natives; it means the whole population, it means old people, women, and children, even at the breast; the parents are in a way forced to substitute for them to consume not one, but two or three liters of spirits.

The inhabitants of a village in Tonkin, finding they were forced to consume in view of the threat hanging over them, approached their European official: "We haven't even anything to eat."

The official replied: "You are accustomed to taking three meals of rice a day; you can cut out one meal, or, if need be, one-and-a-half meals, so as to be able to consume the government spirits."

Until then, the native consumers had been accustomed to obtaining spirits in small quantities and could collect them in whatever receptacle they wished. But a system of stamped bottles was established. Spirits could only be delivered in official half-liter or one-liter bottles. The Annamese were accustomed to 20- or 22-proof spirits; 40- to 45-proof spirits were imposed on them. They were used to drinking spirits with a kind of pleasant empyreumatic flavor, due to the amount of raw materials that they used, and among which was a most delicate kind of rice. The drug the Annamese are forced to swallow is made with cheap rice and chemical ingredients, and has a bad taste.

The monopolizers put out a circular prescribing that their employees should water the spirits on sale: To one hectoliter of spirits were to be added eight liters of water. It was worked out that as 500 hectoliters of these spirits are sold daily in Indochina, that makes 4,000 liters of water, and that 4,000 liters at 30 centimes a day make 1,200 piasters a day, 36,000 piasters a month; say a small benefit from the fountain alone of 432,000 piasters or 4 million francs yearly!

Thus the spirits as they are made and sold in Indochina do not correspond, either as to the proof or the taste, to what the natives wish for, and they have to be imposed on them by force.

The Administration, pressed by a constant need for money because of having to meet the growing expenditure by the Government General on big loans and military constructions and because of the need to find—if not genuine employment—at least salaries for a host of officials imposed on it by Paris, used every means to urge the officials and agents, from the Resident to the most humble State employee, to increase the consumption of spirits.

THE CIVILIZERS

A question: Is it true in the Sûreté of the Government General of Indochina a Frenchman named C—— is employed? That C——, sent on a "mission" to Phu Xuyen, obliged the Annamese in the area to call him *quan lon* ("great mandarin"), and violently struck those who didn't do so quickly enough? Is it true that the same C—— violated a *linh le* ("Annamese militiaman")? Everything is allowed, everything is possible in this Indochinese paradise.

In the middle of December, 1922, a European sergeant in the Saigon urban police—completely tipsy—went into a native house and seriously injured two of the occupants, one of them a woman.

Questioned by the examining magistrate, the policeman declared that he remembered nothing, while denying that he had been drunk. The witnesses, one of them a European, affirmed on the contrary that this guardian of law and order was not in a normal state at the time of the tragic incident. Whether this civilizer was mad or drunk matters little, we wish with all our heart that he may be decorated for the act of courage he has accomplished.

In the colonies, if one has a white skin, one belongs to the aristocracy: One is of a superior race. In order to maintain his social status, the least of European customs officers has at least one servant, a "boy" who, quite often, is a maid of all work.

As native domestic labor is very malleable and cheap, it is not rare to see colonial officials returning to France on leave or retirement, taking their domestics with them.

This was the case of Mr. Jean le M...rigny, living in Rue Carnot at Cherbourg. This gentleman, home from Indochina, brought with him a boy, at a wage of 35 francs a month. Needless to say, the native had to drudge from morning till night. Weekly rest times and days off were unknown in this house. In addition, bad board and lodging.

One day, Mr. Jean le M...rigny wanted to send his "protégé" to work in the country. The son of Annam, having previously tasted of the happy country existence his kind boss had in store for him, declined the offer. Thereupon, the ex-civilizer, in a temper, threw the Annamese out after thoroughly hauling him over the coals. Despite repeated requests by the native, Mr. le M...rigny would not return his belongings to him: money, trunk, clothes, etc. Thrown suddenly out into the streets, not knowing the language of the country, without resources, friendless, removed from his usual surroundings, this unfortunate individual was in dire straits.

Colonial officials are the main cause of the high cost of living in the colonies. In order better to understand to what heavy extent this parasitic factor weighs on the budget, that is to say, on the backs of the working people:

British India has 4,898 European officials for 325 million inhabitants. French Indochina has 4,300 European officials for 15 million inhabitants.

That is to say, in the British colony there is one European official for 66,150 inhabitants, and in the French colony there is one European official for 3,490 inhabitants.

In India, the Customs and Excise administration has 240 European officials. In Indochina, the same administration has 1,100 European officials.

In India, there are 26,000 post and telegraph offices with 268 European officials. Indochina has 330 offices and 340 European officials.

Why this disproportionate number of budgetivorous people in Indochina? Because the colony is an earthly paradise where, apart from a few very rare exceptions, all the refuse of politics, finance, journalism, etc., thrown out by the metropolitan country, find a very favorable field for their development. . . . Let us begin with the biggest bigwig of all, the Governor General. On this subject, an impartial colonial settler writes as follows: "On arriving in Tonkin, the governors have but one aim: to place people, friends, sons, relatives, electoral brokers, of all those it is of interest to them to gain the support; often, it is a man weighed down with debts, harried by his creditors, so that one needs money. . . ."

For the noble writer who writes the glorious history of civilizing colonialism, the so-called war of right and justice will be an inexhaustible source of documentation. Mr. Albert Sarraut, in a surge of eloquence and enthusiasm, said: "It was in the conquest of the colonial Empire that most of the big military leaders, who have led us to victory and whose glory and exploits French opinion was already celebrating when they carried our flag under the skies of Africa and Asia, became versed in combat."

As frank in idea, but less of a juggler with verbs, the *Journal de Genève* says outright that "the Republic has seen in the building of its colonial empire, a derivative of the defeat of 1870. The French race has found therein a revenge for its European rebuffs and the military, a fresh opportunity to distinguish themselves in successful combats."

And be hanged to you, if after such authoritative evidence, you persist in not believing that colonization is neither more nor less than a civilizing and humanitarian mission.

A theft of 5,000 francs was committed to the detriment of Mr. Guinaudeau. In order to obtain confessions from the natives employed by him, this good employer and great civilizer submitted them to electric current. The author of the theft was later discovered; it was not a native, but another civilizer: Mr. Guinaudeau's son! Mr. Guinaudeau was acquitted. And the eight unfortunate natives are still in the hospital.

Mr. Vollard, a civilizer and businessman, does not regularly pay his native employees. One of them asked the overseer to demand the wages due to him. Mr. Vollard handed the following note to the overseer: "Tell that pig to eat shit, it's the only food fit for him." This happened in Tunisia in 1923, at the actual time when Mr. Millerand was making a presidential tour of that country.

If one has a white skin, one is automatically a civilizer. And when one is a civilizer, one can commit the acts of a savage while remaining the most civilized.

An overseer in charge of public works in Cochinchina obliged the Annamese he met on his way to give him the correct form of greeting due to the superior race by the conquered race.

One day, a native clerk left work reading a novel. Coming to an amusing passage, the reader began to laugh. Just then, he passed Mister overseer of public works and the latter flew into a rage, first of all because the native, absorbed in his reading, hadn't noticed him and greeted; secondly, because the native had taken the liberty of laughing as he passed a white man. Our civilizer therefore stopped the Annamese and, after asking his name, asked if he wanted a slap in the face. Naturally, the clerk declined the far too generous offer and expressed surprise at such a storm of abuse. Without more ado, the official grabbed the native by the jacket and dragged him before the head of the province.

The same overseer of public works, under the pretext of bringing houses and gardens into line, ordered the inhabitants living along the sides of provincial roads, under the threat of fines, to move out, uproot their trees and do away with their gardens in a time limit set by him.

And people are surprised at the discontent on the part of the natives in the colonies!

Not only can Governors and Residents do as they think fit, but also customs officers, policemen, and all those who hold a scrap of authority, make use of and abuse it, in the certainty of remaining unpunished.

A commissioner of police in Tuyen Quang (Tonkin) struck a native and broke his arm. Another commissioner, the one in Dalat (Cochinchina), has just inaugurated a tremendously interesting trading system which we take pleasure in relating here for the benefit of Mr. Dior and Mr. Sarraut. One day this official needed some planks. He sent his militiamen to buy some in town. To buy in a manner of speaking, for Mr. Commissioner hadn't given his men any money. The latter went to town, however, chose the wood and wanted to take it with them, without paying, of course. The salesman wouldn't let his goods be taken away without being paid. The militiamen gave their white chief an account of the tradesman's extraordinary demands.

Furious, Mister Commissioner delegated three armed men to go and seize the assuming tradesman. The latter, suffering from influenza, refused to let himself be taken away. The militiamen came back to inform their superior. Exasperated, Mister Commissioner doubled the team, ordering them to bring the recalcitrant alive or dead. The armed guards surrounded the salesman's house and carried out the orders.

A European trader intervened on behalf of the native trader and wrote to Mister Commissioner. But the energetic collaborator of Mr. Maurice Long stuck to his "summons" and let it be known that if the native persisted in refusing to come, he would lay himself open to considerable trouble. The native trader was obliged to leave his business and his country to escape the "civilizing" anger of the white official.

They were seven poor Annamese in a long, narrow boat which, driven by the current and the effort of their seven oars each pulled by two arms, slid along the river as fast as a steam launch. The customs officer's sampan emerged from an arroyo hidden by mangroves, with the French flag flying aft. A sailor called to them to halt. They went on rowing; they hadn't understood. And the customs sampan wasn't going fast. The customs officer took a Winchester and fired. The boat carried on. Bang! Bang! A rower gave a cry and fell. Bang! Another. Meanwhile, a European, a brick-maker, wandering about there by boat too, surprised the "pirates" at a bend. Bang! Bang! Bang! He was a good marksman. Three bullets, three victims. The boat with two survivors disappeared in the arroyos. . . .

Another day, the same customs officer, followed by six armed sailors, had discovered a poor devil hidden in a pond, buried in the mud, breathing through a straw, one end of which was held in his mouth, the other emerging; lotus leaves were artistically arranged on the surface. The customs officer brought to the Residence the head of this "pirate," an ordinary villager who had been afraid on seeing frightening-looking strangers armed with revolvers and cartridge belts and carrying Winchesters coming toward his village. In the huts were found three cartridge cases, some Chinese cakes, and a wood-cutter's knife. How could there be any doubt that this was a pirate village and which supplied the pirates!

A young officer newly arrived from France came to a village, saw the huts empty and the population assembled in the square. He imagined he had fallen into a trap and fired on this inoffensive crowd who were celebrating a religious festival and who dispersed in a panic. He pursued them and exterminated them.

"When I arrived in Tonkin," relates an old Tonkinese, "do you know what the life of an Annamese was worth on the boats of a big exploiter? Not a cent!" It is true.

Look here! I remember when we were going up the Red River on our steamers we played for a drink of absinthe to be stood to whoever could, from the boat, "bowl over" the greatest number of Annamese on the banks with ten carbine shots. A few of them, Winchester in hand, held the villagers and the boats to ransom.

A marine infantry company left for Vinh Thuong. The local mandarin, out of courtesy, set out with great ceremony with his *linhs* ("militiamen") to meet the arrivals. The head of the company's scouts gave order to his section to fire on the mandarinal escort and collected several bodies.

When an insurgent cannot be got rid of, his village is burned down. Thus the region around Hung Hoa was razed.

Along a lonely path, we passed a yellow-skinned man who was staggering because he was carrying two big baskets of peanuts slung from a shoulder pole. He didn't get out of our way as we neared him. He was taken and shot.

People spend all day hitting the Annamese with sticks or the flat of a sword to make them work.

The Annamese are very gentle and very submissive; but they are spoken to only through kicks on the backside.

We consider Annamese patriots as brigands. That is how Doi Van,* a patriot who had struggled against domination for several years, was beheaded in Hanoi, his head exhibited in Bac Ninh and his body thrown in the Red River.

Tong Duy Tan,† captured after ten desperate years of struggle, was beheaded.

Phan Dinh Phung,† a high mandarin, resisted for ten years; he died finally in the forest. This death does not mollify us; his body is exhumed and the remains dispersed. He is pursued beyond the tomb.

* Doi Van, or Tuan Van: one of the military leaders of the Bai Say maquis (1885–89). On August 17, 1889, at the head of 500 men equipped with 100 rifles, he crossed the Canal of Rapids and the Cau River to entrench himself in the north of Yen The during the height of the battle between the French Army and De Tham partisans, who were thus reinforced. The French launched against him two columns commanded by Major Dumont and Captain Piquet. Doi Van, then ill, fell into the hands of reactionaries and was given up by a missionary to the French, who beheaded him in Hanoi on November 7, 1899.

† After the capitulation of the Court of Hue, a broad resistance movement, the "Royalist Movement," spread throughout Viet-Nam from 1885 to 1896. The struggle headed by Phan Dinh Phung and Tong Duy Tan was a part of this movement led by scholars and former court mandarins. Phan Dinh Phung, a former official, set up his headquarters at Huong Khe, Ha Tinh province (Central Viet-Nam), but operated throughout the mountain area north of Central Viet-Nam, where he had many forts built. Well organized, experienced in guerrilla warfare, armed with self-made rifles, his partisans inflicted serious losses on the enemy. It was not until his death that the resistance ended after twelve years of struggle.

Tong Duy Tan, a Doctor of Literature, entrenched himself in the mountain area of Thanh Hoa, north Central Viet-Nam; he was seconded by an excellent military chief, Cao Dien. The resistance lasted six years. After ordering his partisans to stop fighting to prevent useless sacrifice, he withdrew into the mountains where he was surprised and caught by the French in 1892.

In the province of Quang Tri, a drunken overseer of public works, with a shot from his rifle, brought down a native guilty of not having heard or understood his orders.

A customs officer, drunk too, with a cudgel stroke in the midriff, knocked down an Annamese sailor assigned to his service in Baria (Cochinchina).

A French contractor killed a militiaman at Dalat where, furthermore, following violence by another civilizer, a native carpenter also succumbed.

A contractor compelled his workmen to work in the water night and day to dig a tunnel. Many of them died, the rest went on strike. The contractor himself burned down the strikers' houses to oblige them to go back to work. A whole village was in flames during the night.

A senior artillery-company sergeant major set fire to a house, under the pretext that the owner, whose husband was away, would not receive him at midnight. The poor woman was naturally terrified.

A polygamous lieutenant threw a young woman to the ground and knocked her senseless with a cane under the pretext that she wouldn't live with him.

An official in the naval arsenal murdered an Annamese railway employee by pushing him into a furnace after violently striking him.

Nowhere in the world, writes Vigné d'Octon, is there a vanquished people who are the object of more ill treatment than the native.

Another traveler writes: "Colonial life only develops an individual's defects: lack of morals, debauchery and dishonesty, cruelty among those who have seen war; among profiteers and other adventurers, a taste for plundering and theft. Opportunities for this sort of thing were lacking in France, and fear of the police was stronger! Here, this kind is sometimes alone with a few natives, in their junk or in some village; they are more thieving than Europeans in the market and more brutal towards peasants who protest."

All the Frenchmen, writes a third, arrive here with the idea that the Annamese are their inferiors and must serve them as slaves. They treat them like brutes good only for leading with a stick. All of them have got into the habit of considering themselves as members of a new and privileged aristocracy. Whether they are military men or colonial settlers, they normally visualize no other kind of relations with the natives than those they have with their servants. It seems that their "boy" is for them the representative of the entire yellow race. You should hear with what idiotic disdain a Frenchman of Indochina speaks of the "yellow-skinned man." You should see how boorishly a European treats a native.

The conqueror attaches a great price to signs of submission or respect on the part of the conquered. The Annamese in the towns, like those in the countryside, are obliged to take off their hats before a European.

An agent of the security service brutally struck any Annamese who forgot to call him "Great Mandarin." A customs clerk obliged natives passing by his house to doff their hats or get off their mounts. One day, this civilizer brutalized an Annamese woman who, though she had greeted him, had forgotten to call him Great Mandarin. This woman was pregnant. A violent kick right in the stomach aimed by the agent caused a miscarriage; the unfortunate woman died shortly after.

If our protectors demand that the Annamese be humble, submissive, docile, and polite, on the other hand, "it seems that nothing is done but to make our presence odiously unbearable," says a writer who has visited Indochina. And he continues: "In Europe, the yellow race is considered as being full of every trickery and deceit. Yet we care very little for making our frankness appreciated."

There are officers who pull bonzès' beards during services. A daddy's boy gave an Annamese official a third-degreeing because the latter, the occupier of a seat in a bus, would not give it up to him.

On the arrival of a governor general in Marseilles, at the lunch given for him, it was suggested that the mandarins living in that town should be brought. "If the mandarins are brought," replied the Governor General of Indochina, "I shall bring my house boy."

We have extracted from a colonial soldier's travel diary the following fact:

> While the Tonkinese are amusing themselves, to starboard a few junks are selling fruit and shellfish. To reach us, the Annamese hold up big poles holding baskets in which they display their goods. One has only the trouble of choosing. By way of money, those who allow themselves the luxury of paying deposit the most varied objects in the bottom of these baskets: pipe stems, trouser buttons and cigarette ends. (That is perhaps how one teaches commercial honesty to the natives!) Sometimes, just for a laugh, a stoker throws a bucket of boiling water onto the unfortunates' backs. Then there are cries of pain and a frantic

flight of oars which bumps the canoes together.

Just below me an Annamese is burning from head to toe; completely maddened, he wants to throw himself into the sea. His father, forgetting the danger, lets go the oars, grabs hold of him, and forcibly stretches him out on the bottom of the sampan. The struggle hasn't lasted two seconds, is barely over, when another bucket of water, thrown with unerring aim, scalds the rescuer. I see him twisting in the boat, his flesh raw, with cries that have nothing human about them! And it makes us laugh, it seems exceedingly funny. We already have a colonial soul!

At the time I was there (in Tonkin) not a week passed without our seeing a few heads fall.

From these spectacles, I have noted but one thing, it is that we are crueler and more barbarous than the pirates themselves. Why these physical tortures, these processions of prisoners through the villages?

Mr. Doumer, a former Governor General of Indochina, pronounced the following solemn words at a session of the Chamber of Deputies: "I have known the police in the colonies and have even increased the number of their brigades, after noting that it was the police force which gave the natives the guarantee of being defended against the possibility of abusive measures taken by some settlers. The police were popular among the natives."

We shall see how the gentlemen of the police interpret working up their "popularity." Let us say straight away that they are generally very gentle and paternal with wrongdoers, this is an established fact. But as far as peaceful natives are concerned, it's another story. Without mentioning for the moment the tragic affair of the Saigon central prison in 1916, when, driven by a highly patriotic zeal, the police gentlemen made haphazard arrests, and innocent people thus arrested were condemned and executed. If the Annamese blood reddening the Plain of Tombs disappears with time, the bruised hearts of the widows, orphans, and mothers will never heal. The guilty ones, of whom the police were the vile instruments, will not be punished, and justice is not yet done. Today, let us quote only a few particular cases.

A commissioner in Tonkin, under the pretext of keeping the gutters clean, walked along by the outlets all day long and, as soon as he noticed the smallest scrap of grass in the water, distributed countless punishments and fines to the unfortunate inhabitants of the area.

To avoid accidents on the waterways used by craft in the west of Cochinchina, a police post has been installed along each canal with the task of preventing the junks from sailing too fast or hampering circulation. With the presence of the police, a veritable dam of fines and transgressions has been opened. Nearly all the junks passing through this locality find fines ranging from one to two piasters inflicted on them. To the crushing taxes levied by the State is added the toil instituted by the "popular" police, and the Annamese are happy, very happy!

Besides the promotion awaiting the most zealous, it appears that the gentlemen of the police are entitled to a commission of 20 per cent on the proceeds of the fines! What a wonderful system!

A native paper said that "the native population no longer wants French policemen, who are too often a calamity for honest people."

One Pourcignon, furious, threw himself on an Annamese who had the curiosity and audacity to look for a few seconds at the European's house. He struck him and finally brought him down with a revolver shot in the head. . . .

Seeing three natives taking their sheep to pasture in his olive woods, a French settler sent his wife to fetch a rifle and cartridges. He hid in a bush, fired three times, and seriously injured the three natives.

Another French settler had two native workmen, Amdouni and Ben Belkhir, working for him. These had, it appears, stolen a few bunches of grapes. The settler summoned the natives and beat them black and blue with bull pizzle until they fainted. When they regained consciousness, our protector had them bound with their arms behind their backs and hung up by the hands. This odious torture lasted four hours and ended only on the protests of a neighbor.

Taken to the hospital, they each had to have a hand amputated. It is not certain that the other hand can be saved.

An Annamese, aged fifty, who had been employed in the railway services of Cochinchina for twenty-five years was murdered by a white official. Here are the facts:

Le Van Tai had under him four cther Annamese. Their duties consisted in lowering a bridge when trains passed, and opening it for craft. Instructions prescribed the lowering of the bridge ten minutes before trains were due to pass.

On April 2, at 4:30 P.M., one of the Annamese had just closed the bridge and lowered the signal. Just then arrived an administrative launch carrying an official of the naval arsenal returning from a hunt. The launch began to whistle. The native employee ran to the middle of the bridge, waving his red flag to make the agents of the small steamer realize that the train was going to pass. But then the launch came alongside a pillar of the bridge. The official jumped down and, looking furious, went toward the Annamese. The latter, being prudent, ran toward the house of his chief, Tai. The official ran after him pelting him with stones. Hearing the noise, Tai came out of his house and went up to the representative of civilization, who exclaimed, "You brute! Why don't you open up?" For answer, Tai, who couldn't speak French, pointed to the red signal. This simple gesture exasperated Mr. Long's collaborator who, without more ado, fell on Tai and, after giving him a good "third-degreeing," pushed him onto a nearby brazier.

Terribly burned, the Annamese crossing keeper was taken to the hospital, where he died after six days of atrocious suffering.

The official was not worried. In Marseilles, the official prosperity of Indochina is exhibited; in Annam, people are dying of starvation. Here loyalism is sung, over there, murder is done!

While the life of an Annamese dog isn't worth a cent, for a scratch on the arm Mr. Inspector General Reinhart receives 120,000 francs indemnity.

The civilizing of the Moroccans by gunshots is continuing.

A Zouave major garrisoned at Settat, speaking to his men, told them: "We must put an end to these savages. Morocco is rich in agricultural and mineral products. We civilized Frenchmen are here with two aims: to civilize it and enrich ourselves."

He is right, this major. He is frank enough, especially, to admit that if one goes to the colonies, it is to steal from the natives. For, after only ten years of protectorate, 379,000 hectares of arable land in Morocco are occupied by Europeans, 368,000 of which by civilizing Frenchmen. The surface of the colony being 815,000 square kilometers, if civilization continues to march on in this way, in a few years the unfortunate Moroccan will no longer have an inch of land free to live and work on in his own fatherland without putting up with the yoke of exploiting and enslaving colonialism.

Administrative Fraud

The budget for Cochinchina, for example, amounted to 5,561,680 piasters (12,791,000 francs) for 1911; it was 7,321,817 piasters (16,840,000 francs) for 1912. In 1922, it rose to 12,821,325 piasters

(96,169,000 francs). A simple reckoning shows us that in 1911 and 1922 there was a difference of 83,369,000 francs in the budget for this colony. Where does this money go? Quite simply, to expenditure on staff, which swallows up more or less 100 per cent of the total receipts.

Other follies are piled one on top of the other to waste the money the poor Annamese have sweated for. We do not yet know the exact number of piasters spent for the King of Annam's trip to France, but we do know that, to await the propitious day, the only one on which the Bamboo Dragon could embark, the steamship *Porthos* had to be compensated for four days' delay at the rate of 100,000 francs a day (400,000 francs). Traveling expenses, 400,000 francs. Expenses for the reception, 240,000 francs (not counting the salaries of the police entrusted with watching the Annamese in France). To provide board in Marseilles for Annamese militiamen for "presenting arms" to His Excellency and His Majesty, 77,600 francs.

Since we are in Marseilles, let us take advantage of this to see what the Colonial Exhibition has cost us. First of all, besides the favored ones from the metropolitan country, thirty high officals have been brought from the colonies who, while they sip cocktails along the Cannebière, are collecting bonuses both at the Exhibition and in the colonies. Indochina alone has to spend 12 million for this Exhibition. And do you know how this money was spent? Here is an example: the famous reconstruction of the palaces of Angkor took 3,000 cubic meters of timber at 400 or 500 francs a meter. Total: 1,200,000 to 1,500,000 francs!

Other examples of waste:

To transport Mr. Governor General, luxury cars and coaches are not enough; he needs a special carriage, the fitting up of which cost the Treasury 125,250 francs.

In eleven months of functioning, the Economic Agency has burdened the economy of Indochina with a sum of 464,000 francs.

In the Colonial School, where future civilizers are made, forty-four professors of all kinds are subsidized for thirty to thirty-five students. Several thousand francs more.

The permanent inspection of defense works in the colony costs the budget 785,168 francs yearly. Now these gentlemen the inspectors have never left Paris and don't know the colonies any better than they know the moon.

If we go to other colonies, we find the same fraud everywhere. To receive an unofficial "economic" mission, the Treasury of Martinique is "relieved" of 40,000 francs. Within the space of ten years, the budget of Morocco has risen from 17 to 290 million francs, although local expenditure has been reduced by 30 per cent, that is to say, expenditure which would have been of advantage to the natives!

On his return from a visit to the colonies, a former deputy exclaimed: "Highway robbers are honest people compared with the officials in our colonies!" Although favored with huge salaries (a European agent, even illiterate, starts at 200 piasters [2,000 francs]), these gentlemen are never satisfied. They want to earn more, by any means. Scholarships have been awarded to daddy's boys who, as residents or administrators on duty, earn meager salaries (40,000 to 100,000 francs).

Certain sessions of the Colonial Council are, so to speak, solely devoted to a methodical plunder of the budget. A certain president has, for himself alone, nearly 2 million francs for supplying contracts. Yet another, a director of the Interior representing the government within the Council, asks for his salary to be doubled and obtains this. The building of a road, prolonged from year to year and carried out without control, provides regular benefits for a third. The functions of a doctor for the officials in the colony procure considerable emoluments for a fourth. The fifth is a doctor for the municipal services; the sixth is a stationery supplier and printer to the Administration. And so on.

If the cashbox seems a bit empty, there are some who do not take long to have it filled up. On their own authority, they notify the natives that they need a certain sum. The charges are distributed among villages, which hasten to comply so as not to incur immediate reprisals.

When a resident general has some expense or other to meet, he issues mandarin's certificates. A certain province is quoted where an operation of this kind took place to the tune of 10,620 francs. And these facts are not rare.

One of our residents superior, whose credits for a steamer had run out a few months too early, had the charges reimbursed from some festival or other during which the king was invited onto the steamer.

The commercial travelers of civilization and democracy know all the angles.

A former governor general of Indochina one day confessed that

that colony is covered with officials who are too numerous for its budget and often useless. A good half of these officials—province chiefs and others—writes a settler, fulfill only very imperfectly the qualities demanded from men on whom such wide and formidable powers are conferred. All of them are good at wasting public funds, and the poor Annamese wretches pay, and pay again. They pay not only officials whose functions are useless, but they also pay employees whose employment doesn't exist: In 19–, 250,000 francs were volatilized in this way.

For the journey of an Excellency, a warship was detailed. The fitting-out amounted to 250,000 francs, not counting the "petty expenditure" which cost Indochina more than 80,000 francs for each journey.

Mr. Governor was not content with the sumptuous palaces he occupies in Saigon and Hanoi, he also needed a villa by the sea. It was again Indochina which forked out.

In 19–, a noted foreign Thingumbob came to Saigon, and the governor received him in a princely manner. For four days it was a debauchery of festivities, blowouts and champagnes; poor Cochinchina paid the bill: 75,000 francs.

The administrators are petty potentates who like to surround themselves with luxury and sumptuousness to enhance, so they say, their prestige with the natives. One resident formed a company of lancers to serve him as guard, and he doesn't go out without an escort. In all the residences there are from six to eleven horses, five or six coaches: victorias, mylords, tilburies, malabars, etc. To these already superfluous means of transport are added luxurious cars costing the budget tens of thousands of piasters. One administrator even keeps a string of racehorses. These gentlemen are housed and provided with furniture and lighting at the expense of the state; in addition, their coachmen, chauffeurs, stablemen, and gardeners, in a word, their domestic staff, are paid by the administration.

Even literary entertainment is supplied free to these fortunates. One administrator puts down to the budget 900 piasters for his heating and 1,700 piasters subscription costs for papers! Another, by juggling with the accounts, managed to transform the purchase of dresses, pianos, and toilet articles into the purchase of materials needed for the maintenance of the residence or other similar qualification, in order to make the State budget bear the cost!

Whether they have been restaurant keepers or college ushers, once they arrive in the colonies our civilizers lead a princely life. One administrator employs five or six militiamen to mind his goats. Another has had made for him, by sculptor militiamen, pretty statues of Buddha or elegant chests in camphor wood.

The case is cited of a brigade inspector who, according to the regulations, was entitled to only one militiaman as an orderly and who employed: 1 sergeant steward, 1 butler, 3 waiters, 2 cooks, 3 gardeners, 1 manservant, 1 coachman, and 1 groom. And Madame had in her service: 1 tailor, 2 laundrymen, 1 embroiderer, and 1 basketmaker. The child had a special boy who never left his side.

A witness cites a meal at an administrator's—an ordinary meal and not a banquet—where each guest had a militiaman behind him to change the plates and pass him the dishes. And all the militiamen in the room were under the orders of a sergeant major.

EXPLOITATION OF THE NATIVES

After stealing fertile land, the French sharks levy tithes on
poor land a hundred times more scandalous than feudal
tithes.

Vigné d'Octon

Before we were occupied, the roll of land taxes listed according to category of crops all village lands, common property, and private property. The tax rate varied from 1 piaster to 50 cents for rice fields. For other lands from 1 piaster 40 cents to 12 cents. The surface unit was a *mow,* each side 150 *thuoc.* The length of the *thuoc* varied. It was, according to provinces, 42, 47, or 64 centimeters, and the corresponding surfaces of the *mow* were 3,970, 4,900, and 6,200 square meters.

To increase State revenue, as a basis for all measurements, a length of 40 centimeters was adopted, which was less than all the measurements in use. The surface of the *mow* was thus fixed at 3,600 square meters. Land taxes were thereby augmented in the proportions varying in the different provinces: a dozen in some localities, one-third in others, two-thirds in the less favored.

From 1890 to 1896, direct taxes had doubled; from 1896 to 1898, they increased by half again. When an increase was imposed on a village, the latter resigned itself and paid. To whom would it have taken its complaints? The success of these operations encouraged the Residents to repeat them. In the eyes of many Frenchmen, the docility of the communes was manifest proof that the limits had not been overstepped!

Personal tax went up from 14 cents, to 2 piasters 50 cents. Those not registered, i.e., young people under eighteen, who had until then had nothing to pay, were hit by a tax of 30 cents, say more than double that which those registered formerly paid. According to a decree by the Resident superior in Tonkin dated December 11th, 1919, all natives aged from eighteen to sixty were subject to a uniform personal tax of 2 piasters 50 cents.

Every Annamese was required constantly to carry his card and to present it on demand. Anyone who forgot or lost this card was arrested and imprisoned.

To remedy the fall in the piaster, Governor General Doumer simply increased the number of taxable people registered!

Every year, each village is assigned a certain number of registrations and a certain area of land of various categories; are additional resources wanted? The figures are modified during the carrying out, the villages are obliged to pay a number of registrations and a surface of land higher than that distributed at the beginning. That is how in the province of Nam Dinh (Tonkin), the total area of which does not reach 120,000 hectares, the statistics mention 122,000 hectares of rice fields and the Annamese is forced to pay taxes for nonexistent land! If he shouts, no one hears him.

Not only are taxes crushing, they vary every day. The same applies for certain rights of circulation. It is, moreover, impossible to collect taxes of this kind equitably: A permit for 150 kilos of tobacco is delivered, and things are so contrived that the same product is hit many times in succession, when these 150 kilos have been distributed among three or four different buyers. There exist no rules other than the whims of the customs officials. They inspire such fear that the Annamese, at the sight of them, abandon along the road the basket of salt, tobacco, or areca nuts they are carrying; they prefer to give up their property rather than pay eternal dues on it. In some regions, people are obliged to pull up tobacco plants and cut down areca palms so as not to have to put up with the bother the new tax would entail.

In Luang Prabang, poor, pitiful women loaded down with iron are employed at cleaning the roads. They are guilty only of having been unable to pay.

Devastated by floods, the province of Bac Ninh (Tonkin) was compelled to pay 500,000 piasters in contributions.

You have heard M. Maurice Long, Governor General of Indochina, M. Albert Sarraut, Minister for the Colonies, and their press—a disinterested press—loudly proclaiming the success of the Indochinese Loan. However, they carefully refrain from telling you by what means they obtained this success. They are probably right in not divulging their professional secret, and the secret is this. First, they begin by luring gullible folk with a bait of benefits. As this does not bring in enough, the villages are stripped of their communal property. This is still not enough. Then well-off natives are called, they are given a receipt in advance, and it is up to them to manage to pay in the sums entered. As the government cashbox is big and the native industrialists and businessmen are not numerous, compulsory loans from the latter do not fill the fathomless bottom of this cashbox. Then the hitting-state hits the pack of the most hit: Two, three, four, or several wretches are obliged to subscribe in common to a shareholding!

Here, for example, is a trick our administrators use to get money out of the pockets of the native *cai ao*.* It was in a western province, a few weeks before the opening of the Indochinese Loan. The head of this province gathered together all the heads of cantons within his competence, and after having explained to them, through an interpreter, the terms of the loan, said to them in conclusion: "There, it is my duty to give you these explanations. Now subscribe!" Then, catching sight of a canton head standing next to him, the distinguished *"quan lon"* asked: "And you, what can you get from your canton?"

The poor man, taken unawares by the question, stammered a few words to indicate that he couldn't supply figures, not yet having seen his subordinates in order to realize their possibilities.

"Shut your mouth. You're not worthy of our office. I dismiss you!"

The loan was opened. The Governor of Cochinchina, during his tour, stopped in the chief town and inquired what the subscription figure for the week was. "73,000 piasters," he was told. The governor didn't seem satisfied with the figure, seeing that the province is reputed to be the richest in west Cochinchina, and that it made more than this at the last loan.

After the departure of the colony's head, the province head decided to make a propaganda tour in his fief. He saw all the wealthy natives possessing a firearm. He fixed a figure for every one, and, to make the person concerned realize that it was not a joke, he con-

* Jacket or dress worn by the Vietnamese.

fiscated a rifle. "You know, if you don't go along, your rifle won't be returned to you!"

And people went along.

Let us note in passing that the same administrator spent 30,000 piasters to build a 9-kilometer-long road, which is crumbling into a neighboring canal. Let us hope that the Trans-Indochinese will meet a better fate.

A pagoda was being built. The labor was supplied by prisoners led by a notable. The duty roster and workmen's days were regularly marked and regularly paid by the contractors. But it was Mr. Resident who pocketed the money.

Mr. Resident had just been decorated. To celebrate his decoration, a public subscription was opened. The total of the subscription was peremptorily determined for the officials, agents, and notables; the minimum was six piasters. The sum collected: 10,000 piasters. A fine rosette, wasn't it?

Supplies for the building of wooden bridges and communal schools left our upright administrator a little pocket money of about 2,000 piasters. The registration of animals being free, Mr. Resident allowed his employees to collect from 0.50 to 5 piasters per head of animals registered. In return, he receives a monthly income of 200 piasters. A faked classification of rice fields brought in for this official—now decorated—4,000 piasters. An illegal concession of a few hectares of land added 2,000 piasters to the residential funds.

Civilizer, patriot, and right-to-the-ender, Mr. Resident has been able to benefit greatly from Victory loans. Some villages subscribed to the 1920 loan—note that we have a loan for every victory and a victory for every year—55,900 francs, at the rate of 10.25 francs to the piaster, say 5,466 piasters. In 1921, the piaster having fallen to 6 francs, Mr. Resident generously took all these stocks himself and had 5,466 piasters reimbursed. He later collected 9,325 piasters following a rise.

We call attention to the following fact from the *Journal Officiel*, first session of December 22, 1922: "During the war, African *tirailleurs* sent money orders to their families which often amounted to considerable sums. These money orders never reached the addressees."

A colleague quite recently notified us of a similar "phenomenon."

This time, in Réunion Island. For months, the inhabitants of the island haven't received a single parcel addressed to them.

The *Journal Officiel* wrote:

Such a phenomenon surprised both those who sent and those who didn't receive.

There were complaints. There was an inquiry, and hardly had it opened when, together with an explanation of the mystery, it brought about the discovery of a series of thefts committed with remarkable diligence and persistence.

One employee was arrested, then another, then a departmental head, and finally, when all the employees were under lock and key, the director joined his staff in prison.

Every day the inquiry revealed some new fact. More than 125,000 francs worth of parcels had been stolen; the books had been juggled and were in such a mess that it took six months to put the accounts in order.

Though a dishonest employee is sometimes encountered in an administration, it is rare for a whole department, from top to bottom, to be affected, but what is even stranger is that this whole gang of thieves has been able to operate undisturbed for several years.

On the occasion of this discussion of the draft bill relating to air forces expenditure, expenditure for which the colonies, i.e., the natives will have to cough up (Indochina, 375,000 francs; West Africa, 100,000 francs), Mr. Morinaud, deputy for Algeria, said this:

On this occasion, permit me, dear colleagues, after all the congratulations which have been addressed them, including one in the *Times,* which described this feat as miraculous, in turn to pay the homage of our admiration to the valiant Frenchmen who recently accomplished such a fine exploit, a homage which deserves to be shared by Mr. Citroen, the disinterested industrialist, who did not hesitate to supply them with the financial and technical means.

What happened the day after this great event? Just that the military posts we have in southern Algeria immediately ordered those means of transport unparalleled for the Sahara, called caterpillar trucks.

The posts at Touggourt and Ouargla—this information was given to me recently by the Governor of Algeria—have just ordered two.

All our other forts will evidently soon be supplied with them.

It is necessary, within a short space of time, to install four or five more, so that they succeed each other every 200 kilometers.

New posts will thus be created. They will immediately order caterpillar trucks. In this way all the Sahara forts will easily be able to intercommunicate. They will be able to ensure their supplies from post to post with surprising facility. They will receive their mail regularly.

(From the *Journal Officiel,* November 1, 1923.)

JUSTICE

Is it true that through an excess of humanitarian feelings so many times proclaimed by Mr. Sarraut, the prisoners in the prison of Nha Trang (Annam) were put on a dry diet, that is to say, they were deprived of water with their meals? Is it true that the prisoners' noses were daubed with iodine to make them more easily recognizable in case of escape?

Concerning the precautions taken to combat the plague, the *Independent* of Madagascar dated July 13th, 1921, published a report of which the following is an extract: "A number of dwellings have been burned, notably a rather attractive one last Monday, that of Rakotomanga in Rue Gallieni. Mr. Desraux's dwelling did not undergo the same fate; it is estimated to be too valuable with all it contains (50,000 francs); consequently it was decided simply to disinfect it, and that it would be forbidden to inhabit it for a fairly long time—six months, we think."

We may add that Mr. Desraux is a French citizen, while Rakotomanga is subject because he is a native. We remind our readers that the law of 1841 was voted for all French peasants.

In Madagascar, six natives were arrested on a settler's concession for not having paid their taxes. In court, the accused declared that the settler who employed them, M. de la Roche, had promised (1) to pay their taxes; (2) to have them exempted from prestations due to the public services; and (3) to give them 10 francs salary for 30 days' work. It should be noted that this settler only employs them for one day a week. To meet their needs, these natives are obliged to go and work for Malagasies in the neighborhood of the concession. Furthermore, not only has M. de la Roche not paid their taxes, as he had promised, but has, moreover, it seems, kept the money these natives had handed to him for payment of these taxes.

The Administration for once opened an inquiry. But you will see. . . . Notified of the matter, the Agricultural Syndicate of Mahanoro, of which M. de la Roche is probably a member, telegraphed to the Governor General to protest against the inopportune raid by the police on M. de la Roche's property and to demand a sanction against the chief of the police station, whose crime was to have uncovered the abuses committed by a Frenchman to the detriment of the natives.

The Governor General, so as to avoid a fuss, purely and simply hushed up the scandal.

The Council of War in Lille condemned to twenty years hard labor Von Scheven, a German officer who during the occupation horse-whipped the natives of Roncq.

But why, in Indochina, the French gentleman who shoots down an Annamese with a revolver shot in the head; the French official who shuts up a Tonkinese in a dog's cage after savagely beating him; the French contractor who kills a Cochinchinese after binding his arms and making his dog bite him; the French mechanic who "brings down" an Annamese with a hunting rifle; the French naval employee who kills a native crossing-keeper by pushing him into a furnace, etc. Why are they not punished?

And why are only eight days' prison, with reprieve, "inflicted" on these young gentlemen in Algeria who, after having punched and kicked a little native boy of thirteen, impaled him on one of the spikes surrounding the "Tree of Victory"?

And why does the NCO who horsewhipped Nahon and the officer who murdered him remain unpunished?

It is true that Annam and Algeria are conquered countries, as was Roncq, but the Frenchmen in these countries are not "Boches," and what is criminal for the latter is an act of civilization when committed by the former; and that the Annamese and the Algerians are not men, they are dirty *"nha que"* and "goats." There is no justice for them.

The ironic Vigné d'Octon was not mistaken when he wrote: "Law and justice for the natives? Get along! The stick, the revolver, and the rifle, that is all they deserve, these vermin!"

In the terribly well-stocked arsenal of hardships to be weighed on the heads of the natives are encountered fines ranging from 200 to 3,000 piasters.

Mr. Doumer is not unaware that the Annamese will never be able to pay such sums; yet he wants to make money at all costs, and this clever man foresaw that the villages could be made responsible. (Article 4.)*

To have a whole village condemned, it is necessary, you will say, to establish its complicity.

Not at all; with Article 4, this is not necessary. Any village is responsible for an individual offense if it has not been able to prevent this offense.

* *The reference is to a new Income Tax Code passed by the French Government after World War I.*—ED.

This Article 4 is infernally clever, as it suffices for the farmers' agents, paid to bring the greatest number possible of infractions to notice, to declare that the village has done nothing to prevent such and such an offense.

Heading III rules the method of ascertaining offenses which the farmers' agents are empowered to carry out.

But there is a stumbling block. More often than not, these agents, who are illiterate, draw up irregular reports. This inconvenience is obviated by having reports drawn up by customs officers in the chief towns, on the strength of the reports prepared by the farmers' agents.

Indochina is a darling daughter. She is worthy of mother France. She has all that the latter has: her government, her means, her justice, and also her little conspiracies. We will speak only of the two latter.

Justice is represented by a good lady holding scales in one hand and a sword in the other. As the distance between Indochina and France is so great, so great that, on arrival there, the scales lose their balance and the pans melt and turn into opium pipes and official bottles of spirits, the poor lady has only the sword left with which to strike. She even strikes innocent people, and innocent people especially.

As for the conspiracies, that is another story. We will not recall the famous conspiracies of 1908 and 1916,* thanks to which a good number of French protégés were able to appreciate the blessings of civil-

---

* Conspiracy of 1908: The conspirators planned to poison the French garrison and attack Hanoi by surprise. The plan of attack was disclosed before it could be carried out, and the conspiracy failed.

Conspiracy of 1916: On the night of December 15, 1916, the people of Saigon, in arms, attempted to take the Saigon Central Prison. The French rushed in reinforcements and put down the poorly organized and led insurgents. The conspiracy failed.

(*It should be added that the 1916 conspiracy was led by the young Vietnamese emperor Duy Tan, whose tragic life deserves full biographic treatment. Duy Tan was imprisoned, deposed, and deported to Réunion Island, where he became an electrical engineer. Twenty-five years later, realizing that his country would never gain independence from the Vichy regime, he became a leader in the island's Free French movement. Raised by de Gaulle to the rank of major in the French Army, Duy Tan persuaded the French to let him return to Viet-Nam in 1946. But on his way to Réunion to pick up his family prior to returning to Viet-Nam, he was killed in a plane crash near Ganui (Central African Republic). He is buried there, under a simple tombstone bearing his personal name—Vinh San—and the inscription: "Major, French Army. Mort pour la France." Neither of the two Viet-Nams has thus far seen fit to return his body to his native country, which he had served so well.—*ED.)

ization on the scaffold, in prison, or in exile; these conspiracies are already old and leave traces only in the memory of the natives.

Let us speak only of the most recent conspiracy. While the metropolitan country had the resounding Bolshevik conspiracy, the colonialist gentlemen of Indochina—like the frog in the fable—also wanting a conspiracy, puffed themselves up and ended by having one.

This is how they went about it. A French mandarin (Resident of France, if you please), an Annamese subprefect, and a native mayor took it upon themselves to manufacture a conspiracy. The administrative trinity put out the rumor that the conspirators had received 250 bombs intended to blow up the entire Tonkinese territory.

Now on February 16, the Criminal Court of Hanoi recognized that not only was the existence of a revolutionary organization disposing of destructive engines not established, but that the conspiracy was simply a provoking maneuver by government agents desirous of winning administrative favors.

Do you think that after this decision the incarcerated Annamese were going to be released? No! The prestige of the conquerors must at all costs be maintained. For this, instead of simply decorating the clever inventors of the affair, twelve Annamese, most of them scholars, were condemned to two to five years in prison. On the door of this prison can be read—in French, of course—Liberty, Equality, Fraternity.

And the so-called nativophile newspapers hasten to extol the impartiality of this caricature of justice.

Listen rather to the *Dépêche Coloniale,* which holds the championship for Annamesophobia: "French justice has just given its verdict. It is an acquittal for half of the accused and light sentences for the other half. . . . Scholars who had, through bad rhymes of circumstance, celebrated the blessings of liberty."

You see, it is a real crime for Annamese to praise the blessings of liberty, and they are given five years in prison, merely for that!

"We must," continues the same newspaper, "rejoice over the highly impartial verdict of our magistrates and our juries," etc.

Furthermore, the *Dépêche Coloniale* noted with joy the highly impartial verdict of French justice in the affair of the famous conspiracy of Vinh Yen: The Annamese in Paris, like their far-off compatriots, have displayed their confidence in our magistrates and have declared that they were right and that the affair in question has been concluded to their entire satisfaction.

No, M. Pouvourville, you are too much of a humbug.

The newspaper *France-Indo-Chine* has noted the following fact:

> A few days ago, the firm of Sauvage notified the security services of the disappearance from their workshops of a very large quantity of iron, about a ton. As soon as the complaint was received, our policemen immediately got down to the job of discovering the authors of the crime, and we learn with pleasure that a European detective-inspector assisted by a few native police recently laid hands on the thieves as well as their accomplice.
>
> Mr. S . . . , the manager of the firm of Sauvage, as well as a certain Tran Van Loc, an apprentice mechanic, and a certain Tran Van Xa, have been apprehended and handed over to the Public Prosecutor for theft and complicity. . . .

Have you noticed our colleague's great tactfulness? When it is a question of Mr. the French thief, manager of the firm of Sauvage, his name is hushed up, it is replaced by dots. The prestige of the superior race must be saved above all. But for common Annamese thieves, their surname and first name are quoted, and it is no longer Mr., it is "a certain."

By a decree dated October 10, 1922, the government has just brought about an important change in the colonial magistrature. We quote, among other names, those of Messrs. Lucas and Wabrand. It is well to recall in a few words the history of these two magistrates.

M. Lucas, who was then Deputy Public Prosecutor in French West Africa, is the same who was in question on the occasion of the recent scandals in Togoland. In a communiqué to the press, the Minister of Colonies was obliged to declare that "the inquiry also brings to light that M. Lucas' part in the affair brings the heaviest responsibilities to bear on this magistrate."

It is probably to compensate him for these heavy responsibilities that he is today being pushed up as President of the court of appeal in French Equatorial Africa.

As for Wabrand, his story is simpler and less known. In 1920, a Frenchman called Durgrie, an agent of the trading firm of Peyrissac in Kankan (Guinea), was out hunting. He shot down a bird, which fell into a river. A little native boy passed by. Durgrie caught him and threw him into the river, telling him to go and fetch the game. The water was deep and the current strong. The child, who couldn't swim, drowned. His parents complained, and Durgrie, summoned by the district commissioner, agreed to give 100 francs to the bereaved family.

The unfortunate parents refused this disgraceful bargain. M. Commissioner, angered, sided with his compatriot, the murderer, and threatened to put the parents in prison if they persisted in prosecuting the assassin. Then he "filed" the matter. However, an anonymous letter denounced the fact to the Public Prosecutor in Dakar. This high magistrate sent Public Prosecutor Wabrand to investigate. M. Wabrand went to Kankan, spent the evening with the stationmaster and the next day with M. Cousin de Lavallière, the Assistant District Commissioner. He left the next day, without even having begun his investigation. This did not prevent M. Wabrand from concluding that the denunciation was slanderous. The Intercolonial Union brought the fact to the notice of the League for the Rights of Man (December 22, 1921), but the latter, probably thinking that the matter was not sensational enough, didn't deal with it.

Since his visit to Kankan, M. Wabrand has stayed quietly at his port, receiving chickens and sacks of potatoes sent by his friend M. Cousin de Lavallière, Assistant District Commissioner, while awaiting promotion. As you see, M. Wabrand well deserves the . . . just reward the government has recently granted him by naming him Public Prosecutor at Dakar.

With the Darleses and the Beaudoins, the Wabrands and the Lucases, higher civilization is in good hands and so is the fate of the natives in the colonies.

The court of summary jurisdiction has just awarded thirteen months' imprisonment to Fernand Esselin and the widow Gère, and ten months to Georges Cordier, for having owned, transported, and sold one kilo of cocaine or opium.

Very well. And that makes—by a simple reckoning—thirty-six months of prison for one kilo of drug! It would therefore be necessary—if justice were equal for all, as it is said—for the life of M. Sarraut, Governor General of Indochina, to be enormously long in order to pay the whole of his penalty; for he would have to do at least *one million three-hundred-and-fifty thousand* months' prison *every year,* because every year he sells to the Annamese more than *one-hundred-and-fifty thousand* kilograms of opium.

Unable to rid themselves of the famous De Tham,* not having succeeded in killing him or in making him disappear by poisoning or dynamite, they had the remains of his parents exhumed and thrown into a river.

After the demonstrations in South Annam, many scholars were condemned to death or exiled. Among others, Dr. Tran Qui Cap,† a distinguished scholar revered by everyone, was arrested at his post as a professor and, without being questioned, was beheaded twenty-four hours later. The Administration refused to return his body to his family.

At Haiduong, following a riot which had not caused a single victim, sixty-four heads fell without judgment.

At the time of the execution of the *tirailleurs* in Hanoi, the Administration had their fathers, mothers, and children brought by force to make them witness this ceremonial killing of those dear to them. To prolong the impression and to "give the population a lesson," there was a repetition of what was done in the eighteenth century in England, when in the streets of the City or on London Bridge, the heads of the defeated Jacobites were planted on stakes. For weeks along the main streets of Hanoi could be seen grinning on bamboo stakes the heads of victims of French repression.

Weighed down by ruinous charges and exposed to countless vexations, the Annamese of the Center demonstrated in 1908. Despite the altogether peaceful nature of these demonstrations, they were pitilessly repressed. There were hundreds of heads cut off and mass deportations.

Everything is done to arm the Annamese against their own and to provoke betrayals. Villages are declared responsible for disorders which occur on their territory. Any village which gives shelter to a

---

* A leader of the resistance movement against the French colonialists in Yen The, a central region of Tonkin. The main stages of the resistance were as follows: From 1887 to 1894, the French, being unable to get the better of the partisans, ceded the administration of four cantons and twenty-two villages to De Tham. From 1894 to 1897, the French, with fresh troops, launched an offensive which again failed. This was followed by a new truce of eleven years. From 1909 to 1913, the French vigorously pursued the partisans. They only overcame them in 1913, after having De Tham murdered.

† A scholar, one of the leaders of the renovation campaign in Central Viet-Nam during the first years of the twentieth century, following the Royalist Movement.

patriot is condemned. To obtain information, the procedure—always the same—is simple: The mayor and notables are questioned, whoever remains silent is executed on the spot. In two weeks, a militia inspector had seventy-five notables executed!

Not for an instant is there any thought of distinguishing patriots who struggle desperately from the riffraff of the towns. To destroy the resistance, no other means are conceived than to entrust "pacification" to traitors to our cause, and in the Delta, in Binh Thuan, and in Nghe Tinh, to these terrible columns of police, the awful memory of which will remain forever.

THE MARTYRDOM OF NATIVE WOMEN

From what we have related in the preceding pages, it can be seen in what manner the Annamese woman is "protected" by our civilizers. Nowhere is she secure from brutality. In town, in her home, at the market or in the countryside, everywhere she is exposed to ill-treatment from the administrator, the officer, the policeman, the customs officer, the station employee. It isn't rare to hear a European call an Annamese woman *con di* ("prostitute") or *bouzou* ("monkey"). Even in the Central Market in Saigon, a French town so they say, European guards do not hesitate to strike native women with bull pizzles or truncheons—to make them circulate!

We could multiply these sad examples infinitely, but the facts quoted are sufficient, we hope, to enlighten our sisters in the metropolitan country on the misery and oppression of which the unfortunate Annamese woman suffers. Let us see now whether the native woman in other colonies—also under the protection of the mother country—is better respected.

At Fedj-M'Zala (Algeria), a native was condemned to one year's imprisonment for theft. The prisoner escaped. A detachment commanded by a lieutenant was sent to surround the dower. After a thorough search, the escaped man was not found. Then thirty-five women belonging to his family and people connected with him were assembled. Among them were twelve-year-old girls, seventy-year-old grandmothers, expectant women, and mothers breast-feeding their babies. Under the kindly eye of the lieutenant and the administrator who had come, every soldier got hold of a woman. Notables and heads of confraternities were forced to witness this spectacle. To impress them, so it was said. After which, houses were demolished, cattle were taken away, and the raped women were pushed into the premises where they were watched by their tormentors and where the same sadistic acts were renewed for more than a month.

It was said: "Colonization is theft." We add: rape and assassination.

Under the title "Colonial Bandits," Victor Méric told us of the incredible cruelty of the administrator who poured liquid rubber into a Negress's private parts, then he made her carry a huge stone on her head in the blazing sun until death overtook her. This sadistic official is today carrying on his exploits in another district.

Facts as odious as this are unfortunately not rare in what the worthy press calls "overseas France."

In March, 1922, a customs and excise officer in Baria (Cochinchina) almost killed an Annamese woman salt carrier, under the pretext that she had disturbed his siesta by making a noise under the veranda of his house. The best of the affair is that this woman was threatened with dismissal from the site on which she worked if she complained.

In April, another customs and excise officer, who succeeded the first, was worthy of his predecessor by his brutalities. An old Annamese woman, also a salt carrier, had had a discussion with her forewoman concerning money held back from her wages. The former complained to the customs officer. The officer, without more ado, gave the salt carrier two hard slaps in the face. As she bent down to pick up her hat, the civilizer gave her a violent kick in the stomach, causing an immediate and severe hemorrhage.

She fell down in a faint. But M. Sarraut's collaborator, instead of picking her up, sent for the village chief and ordered him to take the injured woman away. The notable refused. Then the official sent for the victim's husband, *who was blind,* and instructed him to take his wife away.

Would you like to bet that, like their colleague the administrator in Africa, the two customs and excise officers in Cochinchina weren't in the least bit worried. They were probably even promoted.

The little natives in Algeria are hungry. To have something to eat, children of six or seven become shoeshine boys or basket carriers in the market. The colonial and civilizing government thinks these little pariahs earn too much. It compels each of them to be registered and pay a license fee of from 1.50 francs to 2 francs a month.

Workers in the metropolitan country who protest against the iniquitous tax on salaries, what do you think of this odious tax?

Before the war, in Martinique sugar was sold at 280 francs a ton; rum at 35 francs a hectoliter. Today, the former sells at 3,000 francs and the latter at 400 francs. *The boss makes a profit of 1,000 per cent.*

Before the war, a workman earned 3 francs a day. Today, he earns 3.75 francs to 4 francs a day. *The increase in wages is thus barely 30 per cent.* The cost of living has increased by at least 300 per cent.

To this scandalous disproportion add the decrease in purchasing power of the franc and you will gain some idea of the native workman's poverty.

In February, 1924, following the bosses' refusal to increase wages, the workers went on strike. Like everywhere, and in the colonies more than elsewhere, the employers do not hesitate to spill the blood of the workers. That is how, in this strike, two young workers of Martinique, one aged eighteen and the other nineteen, were assassinated in a cowardly manner.

The savagery of the employers spared neither children nor women. This is what *Le Paria* told us in its issue of May, 1923:

> The prejudice of the authorities against the workers is obvious. All those who refused to work for the wages offered by the bosses were denounced, arrested, and searched by the police who everywhere displayed the greatest ill-will toward the unfortunates.
>
> Thus, the day before yesterday, two policemen went to fetch a woman, Louise Lubin, from the Trinité almshouse; she had both her thighs struck by bullets on February 9 during the fusillade at Bassignac. She was thrown into prison under the pretext that "by assault or threats, she had endangered the freedom of work."
>
> But, what is certain is that the poor woman couldn't walk, and the policemen intended to take her on foot, *32 kilometers away,* to appear before the magistrate.
>
> At the time she was arrested, it was five or six days since she had seen the doctor, who lives at Fort-de-France, 32 kilometers from there.
>
> Who said she could leave the hospital, since this mother of three children, imprisoned, declares that she is not cured, that she is still an invalid and cannot walk?
>
> I have quoted this fact out of so many others, just as revolting, which are repeated more or less everywhere in the colony.
>
> During the strike, on some properties, the "engaged" workers were compelled to work under the supervision of police and marines, just like in times of slavery.

We read in a paper:

> In Constantine, groups of prostitutes go around begging. One of these unfortunates died near the El-Kantara bridge, holding her child in her arms.
>
> From Bogharic to Djelfa, the trains are assailed by old people, women and children, carrying babies in their arms and begging for alms.
>
> They are like skeletons covered in rags. They are prevented from approaching the stations.

It is a painful irony that civilization—symbolized in its various forms: liberty, justice, etc., by the gentle image of woman and managed by a type of men who pride themselves on their manners—should cause its living image to undergo the most ignoble treatment and shamefully strike at her in her morals, her modesty, and her life.

Colonial sadism is unbelievably frequent and cruel, but we will merely recall here a few facts seen and related by witnesses not to be suspected of taking sides, and which will enable our sisters in the West to understand the value of the "civilizing mission" and the sufferings of their sisters in the colonies. . . .

After the taking of Cho Moi (Tonkin), one evening an officer of the Africa battalion saw a prisoner alive and unwounded. In the morning he saw him dead, burnt, his fat running, the skin of his stomach swollen and golden. Some soldiers had spent the night roasting this unarmed individual, while others had tormented a woman.

A soldier obliged an Annamese woman to give herself up to his dog. She refused. He killed her with a bayonet thrust in the stomach. The same witness says that "one festival day a tipsy soldier threw himself on an old Annamese woman and ran her through with his bayonet without the slightest reason."

A soldier gardener, seeing a group of men and women entering his garden one morning at ten o'clock, a peaceful group of market gardeners drawn by curiosity, immediately shot at them with a sporting gun and killed two young girls.

A customs officer, refused entry into a native's house, set it on fire and broke the wife's leg just as, blinded by smoke, the unfortunate woman was coming out to escape with her children.

The unrestrained sadism of the conquerors knows no limits. They carry their cold cruelty as far as the refinements of a bloodthirsty civilization allows them to imagine.

Crushing taxes hit not only lands, animals, and men, but their blessings (!) also extend to the female population: Poor native women, loaded with irons, are employed to clean the roads. They are guilty only of having been unable to pay.

Among all the efforts the civilizers have made to improve the Annamese race and lead it toward progress (?), the enforced sale of official spirits must be noted. It would take too long to enumerate here all the abuses born of the sale of a poison, intended to give proportionate doses of democracy and get it swallowed.

We have described how, in order to enrich the sharks in the metropolitan country, the criminal government of Indochina allows its lackeys to oblige women and children to pay for spirits they do not drink. To please the monopolizers, laws destined to punish contraband are invented, a terribly well-stocked arsenal of punishments weighs on the head of the natives. The customs men are armed. They have the right to enter private property.

We are somewhat surprised—and there is good reason to be—when we see arriving in Hanoi or Haiphong long files of old folk, expectant women, and children tied together in twos, led by policemen to render account of their defaults in the matter of customs. But this is nothing beside what happens in the provinces, especially in Annam, where the Resident judges and locks up all together young and old, men and women.

A witness recounts the procession of relatives at the prison doors: "Old folk, women, kiddies, all these people were dirty, ragged, hollow-cheeked, their eyes burning with fever; the children were dragged along, unable to follow on their little legs. And all these worn-out people were carrying the most varied objects: hats, rags, balls of cooked rice, food of all kinds, meant to be secretly passed to the accused father, husband, breadwinner, in nearly every case the head of the household."

Everything that can be said is less than the truth. Never at any time and in any country has the violation of all human rights been practiced with such cruel cynicism. It is not only incessant visits into the home, but corporal visits which can be operated everywhere on natives of both sexes! Customs officers go into native dwellings, oblige women and young girls to undress completely in front of them and, when they are in the garb of Eve, carry their lewd whims as far as affixing the customs stamp on the body.

French mothers, women, daughters, what do you think of this, sisters? And you, French sons, husbands, and brothers? It is certainly "colonialized" French gallantry, isn't it?

The enthusiasm of the Annamese for modern education frightens the Administration of the Protectorate. That is why it is closing down communal schools and turning them into stables for the officer gentlemen, driving out the pupils, and locking up the teachers. A native woman teacher was arrested and taken bareheaded in the burning sun to the chief town, a cangue around her neck.

A senior company sergeant major of artillery set fire to a house, under the excuse that the owner, a woman, would not receive him at midnight.

A polygamous lieutenant threw a young Annamese woman to the ground and lashed her with a cane because she didn't want to be his concubine.

Another officer had violated a little girl in odiously sadistic conditions. Summoned before the Criminal Court, he was acquitted because the victim was an Annamese.

In all the speeches, in all the reports, in every place where they have the opportunity to open their mouths, and where there are idlers to listen to them, our statesmen ceaselessly affirm that only barbarous Germany is imperialist and militarist, while France, this peaceful, humanitarian, republican, and democratic France, this France represented by them, is neither imperialist nor militarist. Oh, not at all! If these same statesmen send soldiers—children of workers and the workers themselves—to massacre the workers of other countries, it is simply to teach the latter to live properly.

AWAKENING OF SLAVES

In Indochina

In November, 1922, following a cut in wages, 600 dyers in Cholon (Cochinchina) decided to stop work.

The bosses' offensive is being launched everywhere, and everywhere the working class is beginning to be aware of its strength and its value.

If these unfortunate native workers, normally very docile and very manageable, uneducated, and unorganized, were driven—through an

instinct of preservation, if we can express it thus—to group themselves together and struggle against the savage demands of the bosses,
it is because their situation is much more unfortunate than people
imagine in Europe. It is the first time that such a movement has
appeared in the colony. Let us note this sign of the times and let us
not forget that our duty—workers of the metropolitan country—is not
only to show verbal solidarity with our class brothers over there,
but to educate them and teach them the spirit and methods of organization.

In Dahomey

French capitalism, anxious at the awakening of the working class
in the metropolitan country, is trying to transfer its domination to
the colonies. It draws from there both raw materials for its factories
and human material for its counterrevolution. Bourgeois newspapers
in Paris and the provinces regularly devote whole pages to colonial
items. Generals and members of Parliament hold conferences on
colonies. These virtuous pen-pushers and braggarts cannot find
enough words to extol our loyalism and the blessings of "their"
civilization.

Sometimes these gentlemen carry their impudence so far as to
oppose their generosity to British colonial banditry: They describe
British policy as a "cruel method," or "heavy handed," and uphold
that the French practice is full of justice and charity.

It suffices to glance at our colonies to judge how "fine and gentle"
this civilization is.

In Dahomey, the already crushing native taxes are being increased.
Young men are dragged from their homes and their lands to be turned
into "defenders of civilization." The natives are forbidden to possess
arms to defend themselves against wild animals which devastate whole
communes. Education and hygiene are lacking. On the other hand,
no means are neglected to submit the "protected" of Dahomey to
the abominable native status, an institution which places men on a
level with animals and which dishonors the so-called civilized world.
The natives, their patience at an end, revolt. Then comes bloody
repression. Energetic measures are taken. Troops, machine guns,
mortars, and warships are sent; a state of siege is proclaimed. Mass
arrests and imprisonments are carried out. That is the gentleness of
civilization!

In Syria

The population of Syria is pleased, very pleased with General Gouraud's administration, say the official gazettes. But the following facts prove the opposite:

In March, 1922, Mustapha Kemal went to Messina. To welcome him, the Moslems in Syria had erected a triumphal arch decorated with black flags bearing the inscriptions: "Turko-Arab Fraternity," "Do Not Forget Your Syrian Brothers!," "Deliver Us!," etc.

Mustapha Kemal's visit to Adana provoked enthusiastic demonstrations. The irredentists of Antioch and Alexandretta carried black flags about the streets for two days, uttering hostile shouts against the Administration of the French representative.

Replying to the manifesto of the irredentist delegation, Mustapha Kemal is said to have answered: "A center dating back so many centuries cannot remain in foreign hands."

French colonialism hasn't altered its motto: "Divide and rule." That is why the empire of Annam—that country inhabited by a people descended from the same race, having the same customs, the same history, the same traditions, and speaking the same language— was divided into five parts. Through this hypocritically exploited division, it is hoped to cool off the feeling of solidarity and fraternity in the hearts of the Annamese and to replace it by an antagonism of brother against brother. After throwing them one against the other, the same elements were artificially regrouped in a "union," the Indochinese Union.

The same tactics can be seen in the new colonies. After dividing Syria into a series of "States," the French High Commissariat in Beirut claimed the constitution of a Syrian "Federation" formed by the "States" of Aleppo, Damascus, and the Alaouites. A flag was devised to this end. As with the flag of Annam, it was not forgotten to add to this federal flag—on top, near the flagpole—the "protector color." December 11, 1922, was the "solemn" day on which this flag was hoisted for the first time on the federal palace in Aleppo.

On this occasion, official speeches were made. Soubhi Barakat Bey, the federal President, spoke of the "generous protector," the "sincere guide," of "victorious leaders," and hosts of things. M. Robert de Caix, High Commissioner ad interim, discoursed at length, too. Among other things, this high official recalled that "independent Syria is not the first people over whose cradle France has watched," etc. All this high-sounding palaver deceives no one, however. And the Syrio-Palestinian delegation, responsible for defending Syria's genuine independence and unity at the Lausanne Conference, sent a letter of protest, which was published by our colleague *La Tribune d'Orient* and which we are happy to reproduce here.

Your Excellency,

At a time when an endeavor is being made to repair the breaches that the Sèvres Treaty has opened in the question of the Near East and when the Arab people are, in proportion to the sacrifice they have made, the most directly harmed by the evils resulting from this treaty, the voices of the representatives of its various districts unfortunately continue to find no echo at this conference which has, however, met to establish a firm and lasting peace.

And this is the moment which the French authorities find opportune solemnly to crown the task of colonization which they undertook four years ago, by hoisting the emblem of eternal slavery, the tricolor, on the flag which the so-called Syrian Confederation has recently been made to adopt. Once again, the declaration of the Allies, the engagements undertaken in their name by England concerning the Arabs, and even the promises made by French statesmen guaranteeing independence to this unfortunate country are repudiated. Syria, which has indisputable claims to speedy and total independence and which is no less worthy of it than any other country in the East or the West, is deprived of her own national flag. As a sign of mandate, which camouflages annexation, the three colors are imposed on her in her national flag.

Mr. President, we have always protested against the mandate, we have never recognized it, and we now protest energetically against the adoption of its symbol in our national flag.

Hardly any of the powers, even those which are no less great than France, have adopted this humiliating method, even in their most backward colonies.

The pact of the League of Nations specifies the provisional nature of mandates (Art. 22, para. 4). On what do the French authorities therefore base themselves to have their colors adopted by a country they claim to be leading toward the independence already recognized by the aforementioned pact?

Your Excellency, we beg you to consider our protest on this subject and reiterate our keen desire to have our just claims put forward at the conference.

We beg you to accept, etc.

> For the Head of the
> Syrio-Palestinian Delegation:
> The Secretary General
> EMIR SHEKIB ARSLAN

Furthermore, the inhabitants of Hama, many of whom are government employees, lawyers, teachers, journalists, and businessmen, addressed a letter to the President of the French Council of Ministers, of which the following are the main passages:

We have the honor, Mr. President of the Council, to put forward our claims, and to protest against the reactions of this Council, which we deem are contrary to our interests and those of the country in general.

1) The said Council was not elected by universal suffrage of the nation. Its members cannot in any way be the representatives of the nation, nor reflect its thoughts.

2) The said Council is devoid of powers; it cannot even deal with questions vitally concerning the country, compelled as it is to be acquainted only with matters submitted to it. Finally, its decisions are at the discretion of the High Commissariat, which can carry them out or reject them.

3) The actual basis of the said Council is falsified by the fact that each State possesses only a single voice in it despite the numerical inequality of the States. Added to this inexplicable peculiarity is that no majority exists in this Council and that each divergence cancels the debate, which is then taken before the High Commissioner.

4) The said Council, which is put forward as a progress of the path of unity, is in truth a negation of the unity and actual personality of the country, in the sense that this Council, being officially appointed, in no way reflects national ideas; it might even perhaps go counter to these ideas, while in the eyes of the whole world it would be considered as the interpreter of national aspirations and would supply an argument against the nation itself.

As for our wishes, we can formulate them in the following way:

a) The recognition of the effective independence and the unity of Syria;

b) The census at present being undertaken, once finished, an election will be carried out by universal suffrage of a National Assembly which will enact the constitution and will determine the form of government of the country. This Assembly could be convoked towards the end of 1922, the date on which the federal Council will be convoked;

c) The formation of a government responsible before the Assembly having full legislative powers within its functions.

These are the true aspirations of the population of Hama, they are also those of the majority of the Syrian people.

Since this booklet was written, serious events have taken place in many colonies. Let us quote the bomb thrown by an Annamese in Canton, the bombs in the Antilles, and the strikes with bloodshed in

Guadeloupe, the no less bloody demonstrations in Damascus, Bizerte, and Hammanlif, and the unrest in Tunisia.

The Russian Revolution and the Colonial Peoples

Capitalism is a leech with one sucker on the proletariat in the metropolitan country and another on the proletariat in the colonies. If the animal is to be killed, both suckers must be cut off at once. If only one is cut off, the other will continue to suck the blood of the proletariat; the animal will go on living and the cut off sucker will grow again.

The Russian Revolution clearly understood this. That is why it was not content to make fine platonic speeches and to vote for humanitarian motions in favor of the oppressed peoples, but it is teaching them to struggle. It is helping them morally and materially, as Lenin wrote in his colonial thesis. It summoned them to the Baku Congress, to which twenty-one nationalities of the East sent delegates. Representatives of workers' parties in the West took part in the Congress. It was the first time in history that the proletariat of conquering countries and that of conquered countries fraternally shook hands and together sought for a means effectively to combat capitalism, their common enemy.

After this historic Congress, and despite difficulties from within and without which assailed it, revolutionary Russia never hesitated to come to the aid of these peoples which it had already—through the example of its heroic and victorious Revolution—drawn out of lethargy. Its first gesture was the creation of the University of the East. . . .

The Near and Far East, which stretches from Syria to Korea—we speak only of colonial and semicolonial countries—covers an area of more than 15 million square kilometers and has a population of more than 1,200 million inhabitants. All these huge countries are today under the yoke of capitalist imperialism. And despite their numbers, which should be their strength, these oppressed peoples have never seriously attempted to emancipate themselves, in the sense that they have not understood the value of national and international solidarity. They have not—like the peoples of Europe and America—any intercontinental relations. They have in themselves a gigantic force and are unaware of it! The foundation of the University of the East marks a new era and the University, by gathering together youthful, active, and intelligent elements from the colonial countries, is undertaking an imposing task:

a) Teaching these future combatants the principle of class struggle, a principle which the struggles among races on the one hand and patriarchal customs on the other have confused in their minds;

b) Putting the vanguard of the workers in the colonies in close contact with the proletariat in the West, in order to pave the way for an impending and effective collaboration, which alone will be able to guarantee the international working class final victory;

c) Teaching the colonial peoples—up till now isolated from one another—to get to know each other better and to unite, thus laying the foundations for a Federation of the East, which will be one of the pinions of the proletarian revolution;

d) Setting the proletariat of the countries whose bourgeoisie own colonies, the example of what they can and must do for their subject brothers.

Proletarians and Peasants of the Colonies!

The worldwide carnage has opened the eyes of millions of proletarians and peasants in the colonies concerning their intolerable living conditions. A series of powerful but so far unorganized revolutionary outbreaks marked the end of the world war. This spontaneous and irresistible force, which aspires to combat for a better future, has been led and organized by the national and native bourgeoisie. Grown up and strengthened during the war, this bourgeoisie has no longer wished to remain in the claws of imperialism and surrender to the latter the greater part of the exploitation of "its workers and peasants." The struggle for national liberation, watchword of the young colonial bourgeoisie, has been enthusiastically welcomed and powerfully supported by the laboring masses in India, Egypt, Turkey, etc.

The Communist International is struggling unremittingly against the rapacious capitalists in all the countries in the world.

Could it hypocritically turn away from the struggle for national liberation of the colonial and semicolonial countries?

The Communist International has openly proclaimed its support and assistance for this struggle and, loyal to its aims, is continuing to furnish this support.*

* This was followed by an extract from the Manifesto of the Executive Committee of the Third International.

An Appeal from the Peasant International
to the Working Peasants in the Colonies

The Peasant International, gathered in its first Congress, which was held recently in Moscow, wished to show its interest in the working peasants in the colonies by addressing the following appeal to them:

To the working peasants in the colonies!
Peasants in the colonies, modern slaves who, in millions, in the fields, savannas, and forests in the two continents, are suffering under the double yoke of foreign capitalism and your local masters.
The International Peasant Conference, meeting for the first time in Moscow to work out the organization of the struggle in which the workers of the world are so far lacking, appeals to your class consciousness and calls on you to come and swell its ranks.
Even more than your peasant brothers in the metropolitan countries, you put up with long working hours, poverty, and insecurity.
You are compelled to do forced labor, backbreaking porterage, and endless *corvées.*
You pay crushing taxes.
Exploiting capitalism is keeping you in obscurantism, oppressing you ideologically, and decimating your race by the use of spirits and opium.
The odious system of denizenship, imposed by capitalist imperialism, is depriving you of all individual liberty, and all political and social rights, thus placing you on the lower level of beasts of burden.
Not content with thus reducing you to poverty and ruin, capitalism is dragging you from your homes and your fields, to turn you into cannon fodder and throw you, in fratricidal wars, against other natives or against the peasants and workers of the metropolitan country.
Pariahs of the colonies! Unite! Organize yourselves!
Join your action to ours; let us struggle together for our common emancipation!
Long live the deliverance of the natives in the colonies!
Long live the Workers' International!
Long live the International Peasants' Council!

*Trade Union Organization in the Colonies**

Present-day imperialism is based on the exploitation of several million workers in the colonial and semicolonial countries. Moreover, the dislocation of imperialism will be complete and definite only when we will have succeeded in tearing out these foundations of the imperialist edifice. From this point of view, the organization of trade unions in the

* Extract from a report of the session held on June 27, 1923, by the Central Council of the Red International of Labor Unions.

colonial countries acquires an especially great importance. The partisans of the RILU have done hardly anything in this direction, either in Egypt, in Tunisia, or in any of the countries under the heel of French imperialism. The liaison which exists among the various workers' groups in the French colonies and the French trade unions is merely a chance effect. No systematic work is being carried out. Now it is quite evident that without winning over the masses in the colonies, we shall be powerless to undermine the imperialist system. What is needed is to undertake in the colonies a major propaganda effort to form trade-union organizations (in the colonies) and develop those already existing in an embryonic form. It is also necessary for us to overcome the suspicion of the workers in the colonies regarding the representatives of the dominating races, by demonstrating to them the effective class brotherliness between workers of all nations and all races. A coordinated liaison between the colonial trade unions and those of the metropolitan country can only be the result of very lengthy work in the colonies.

Not to forget the workers in the colonies, to help their organizations and struggle constantly against the governments of the metropolitan countries who are oppressing the colonies, that is one of the most pressing duties of the revolutionary trade unions, especially in countries whose bourgeoisie is enslaving and exploiting the colonial and semi-colonial countries.

Manifesto of the "Intercolonial Union," an Association of the Natives in All the Colonies

Brothers of the colonies! In 1914, the powers, at grips with a frightful cataclysm, turned to you and asked you then to agree to contribute your share of sacrifice to safeguard a country said to be yours and of which you had until then known only the spirit of domination.

To induce you to do so, the advantages your cooperation would bring you were unfailingly dangled before your eyes. But once the storm was over, as before, you remain subjected to the system of denizenship, exceptional jurisdiction, and deprived of the rights which make the dignity of a human being: freedom of association and to hold meetings; freedom of the press; the right to circulate freely, even in your own country. So much for the political side.

From the economic point of view, you remain subjected to the heavy and unpopular head tax and porterage tax; to the salt tax; to poisoning by and enforced consumption of spirits and opium, as in Indochina; to night watching as in Algeria to guard the property of the colonial sharks.

For equal work, your efforts remain less remunerative than those of your European comrades.

In a word, you were promised wonders.

You have now realized that they were only lies.

What is to be done to achieve your emancipation?

Applying the formula of Karl Marx, we say to you that your deliverance can only come through your own efforts.

It is to help you in this task that the Intercolonial Union has been founded.

It includes, with the cooperation of metropolitan comrades sympathetic to our cause, all those originating from the colonies now residing in France.

Means of action: In order to accomplish this work of justice, the IU intends to set the problem before public opinion with the help of the press and the spoken word (conferences, meetings, use of the tribunes of deliberating assemblies by those of our friends who hold elective mandates), and finally, by every means in our power.

Oppressed brothers of the metropolitan country! The dupes of your bourgeoisie, you have been the instruments of our conquest: carrying out this same Machiavellian policy, *your bourgeoisie today intends to use us to repress any desire on your part for independence.*

In the face of Capitalism and Imperialism our interests are the same: Remember the words of Karl Marx:

"Workers of all lands, unite!"

To the Annamese Youth

Mr. Paul Doumer, ex-Governor General of Indochina, writes: "When France arrived in Indochina, the Annamese people were ripe for slavery." More than half a century has gone by since. Tremendous events have shaken the world. Japan has been classed in the front rank of world powers. China has brought about its revolution. Russia has driven out its tyrants and has become a proletarian republic. A great breath of emancipation is rousing the oppressed peoples. The Irish, the Egyptians, the Koreans, the Hindus, all these defeated of yesterday and slaves of today, are struggling heroically for their independence of tomorrow. Only the Annamese remain as they were: ripe for slavery.

Listen to these words spoken by a guest at a banquet for 200 served in honor of the honorable Outrey, Valude and Co., where, to sniff the smell of these so-called nationalist blocs' socks, the Annamese did not hesitate to pay 85 francs for a blowout!

I am proud (said the speechifier), I am proud to express to you, in the name of everyone, our feelings of profound respect, of joy and gratitude toward you, who, in our dazzled eyes, synthetize the government of the glorious French nation.

No fine enough word comes to my mind to state precisely the meaning of our innermost thoughts, but, gentlemen, you can be quite sure of our faithful attachment, our sincere loyalty and veneration for Tutelary and Protector France, which considers us all as her children, without distinction as to race and color.

We have all seen for ourselves how many advantages we owe to the High Administration and the representatives of France in this country through the just and clearsighted application of liberal and benevolent laws.

At the funeral of Governor General Long, Mr. N. K. V., Doctor of Laws, Doctor of Political Science and Economics, attached to the public prosecutor's office in Saigon, said that if the whole of Indochina could express itself through his voice, he was sure that that voice would be raised in sorrow to thank the Governor for all he had done for the Annamese people. And then Mr. V.'s turn to exclaim:

> Those who, thanks to your liberal measures, are today taking part, together with the representatives of the protector nation, in the growing prosperity of Indochina, thank you from the bottom of their hearts and revere your memory. The economic question was your major preoccupation. You wanted to endow Indochina with all the economic apparatus to make of it a second France, the France of the Far East, strong and powerful, and which will be a subsidiary of republican France.
>
> You put your heart and soul in your mission of civilizing a people halted on the path of progress by a conjunction of historic and climatic circumstances. You were the champion of progress and the apostle of civilization. . . .

For his part, Mr. Cao Van Sen, engineer, President of the Association of Indochinese, said that Indochina is in mourning because of the premature death of Mr. Long. And he ended his speech with these words: "We sincerely mourn for you, Mr. Governor General, for you were for all of us a benevolent and paternal head."

From all this, I have concluded that if all the Annamese were really such grovelers as these tools of the Administration, it would have to be admitted that they have only the fate they deserve.

It is not without its use for our youth to know that there are at present more than 2,000 young Chinese in France, and about 50,000 in Europe and America. Nearly all of them hold diplomas in Chinese characters and they are all student workers. We here have seen scholarship students and just plain students, who, thanks to the generosity of the State or their family's fortune (one or the other are unfortunately inexhaustible pumps), spend half their time in the academy of billiards, half of the other half in other pleasure spots, and the rest, and there rarely remain any, at college or the Faculty.

But the Chinese student-workers, they have nothing less in view than the effective recovery of their country's economic condition, and whose motto is: "To live by the fruits of their own labor, and to learn while working."

This is how they proceed: As soon as they arrive at their destination, all those who have the same aptitude and wish to learn the same trade form themselves into groups to approach the employers. Once they have been admitted to a workshop or a factory, they naturally begin as apprentices, then as ordinary workmen. It is very trying for many of them who have been brought up surrounded by luxury and family comforts to do hard and tiring work. If they weren't endowed with a firm will and impelled by prodigious moral strength, most of them would have given up. But up till now, all of them have continued their work. Another obstacle they have been able to overcome, thanks to a sense of observation which is almost a privilege for us Far Easterners, and which our young neighbors are able to use to their advantage, is the language. If they cannot understand their employers or understand them only with difficulty, they attentively observe what the latter show them.

They do not earn much. With the little they earn, they have first of all to support themselves. They then make it a point of honor not to allow themselves to ask for any financial assistance from the government or their families. Finally, according to their earnings, they pay in a percentage to the mutual aid fund they have founded. This fund has been set up with a double aim: (1) to help students who are sick or unemployed, the former producing a doctor's certificate and the latter, one from the employer; (2) to give an allowance for one year to all those who have completed their apprenticeship, to enable them to undergo a period of improvement.

In all the countries in which they work, they have founded a magazine (with contributions from the student-workers). The magazine, in Chinese characters, acquaints them with what is happening in their native country, the important events of the day in the two worlds, etc. In the publication, a tribune is reserved for readers in which the latter impart information useful to their apprenticeship, let each other know of everyone's progress, and give each other advice and encouragement. They work during the day; they study at night.

Proceeding from such tenacity, such will power and such a spirit of solidarity, our "young uncles" will certainly reach their goal. Assisted by a working army of 50,000 men endowed with admirable courage and trained through discipline and in modern technique, China will soon win its place among the industrial and commercial powers.

We have in Indochina all that a people can wish for: ports, mines, huge fields, and vast forests; we have a capable and hard-working labor force.

But we lack organization and organizers! That is why our industry and trade are worth nothing. And what are our Youth doing? It is sad, very sad to say so: They are doing nothing. Those who are without means dare not leave their villages; those who have any, wallow in their laziness; and even those who are abroad think only of satisfying the curiosity of their age!

Poor Indochina! You will die, unless your old-fashioned Youth comes to life.

PART THREE

Revolution and Liberation War
(1930–54)

APPEAL MADE ON THE
OCCASION OF THE FOUNDING OF
THE COMMUNIST PARTY OF INDOCHINA*
(February 18, 1930)

Workers, peasants, soldiers, youth, and pupils!
Oppressed and exploited compatriots!
Sisters and brothers! Comrades!
Imperialist contradictions were the cause of the 1914–18 World
War. After this horrible slaughter, the world was divided into two
camps: One is the revolutionary camp including the oppressed
colonies and the exploited working class throughout the world. The
vanguard force of this camp is the Soviet Union. The other is the
counterrevolutionary camp of international capitalism and imperialism whose general staff is the League of Nations.

* The Communist Party of Indochina, founded on February 3, 1930, was the
outcome of the conference convened in Hong Kong by the Communist International. This historic conference merged the three Communist groups in the
three parts of Viet-Nam (North, Center, and South) into a single Communist
Party. Comrade Nguyen Ai Quoc was charged by the Communist International
to attend the conference. Basing itself on Nguyen Ai Quoc's proposals, the
conference approved of the general political thesis on the revolutionary line in
Viet-Nam at that stage and decided to unify the Party under the name of the
Communist Party of Indochina, to draft the Party's political program, its constitution, and the statutes of various mass organizations, and to appoint the
Party's Provisional Central Committee.

During this World War, various nations suffered untold losses in property and human lives. The French imperialists were the hardest hit. Therefore, in order to restore the capitalist forces in France, the French imperialists have resorted to every underhand scheme to intensify their capitalist exploitation in Indochina. They set up new factories to exploit the workers with low wages. They plundered the peasants' land to establish plantations and drive them to utter poverty. They levied many heavy taxes. They imposed public loans upon our people. In short, they reduced us to wretchedness. They increased their military forces, firstly to strangle the Vietnamese revolution, secondly to prepare for a new imperialist war in the Pacific aimed at capturing new colonies, thirdly to suppress the Chinese revolution, fourthly to attack the Soviet Union because the latter helps the revolution of the oppressed nations and the exploited working class. World War II will break out. When it breaks, the French imperialists will certainly drive our people to a more horrible slaughter. If we give them a free hand to prepare for this war, suppress the Chinese revolution, and attack the Soviet Union, if we give them a free hand to stifle the Vietnamese revolution, it is tantamount to giving them a free hand to wipe our race off the earth and drown our nation in the Pacific.

However the French imperialists' barbarous oppression and ruthless exploitation have awakened our compatriots, who have all realized that revolution is the only road to life, without it they will die out piecemeal. This is the reason why the Vietnamese revolutionary movement has grown even stronger with each passing day. The workers refuse to work, the peasants demand land, the pupils strike, the traders boycott. Everywhere the masses have risen to oppose the French imperialists.

The Vietnamese revolution has made the French imperialists tremble with fear. On the one hand, they utilize the feudalists and comprador bourgeois in our country to oppress and exploit our people. On the other, they terrorize, arrest, jail, deport, and kill a great number of Vietnamese revolutionaries. If the French imperialists think that they can suppress the Vietnamese revolution by means of terrorist acts, they are utterly mistaken. Firstly, it is because the Vietnamese revolution is not isolated but enjoys the assistance of the world proletarian class in general and of the French working class in particular. Secondly, while the French imperialists are frenziedly carrying out terrorist acts, the Vietnamese Communists, formerly working separately, have now united into a single party, the Communist Party of Indochina, to lead our entire people in their revolution.

Workers, peasants, soldiers, youth, pupils!

Oppressed and exploited compatriots!

The Communist Party of Indochina is founded. It is the party of the working class. It will help the proletarian class to lead the revolution in order to struggle for all the oppressed and exploited people. From now on we must join the Party, help it and follow it in order to implement the following slogans:

1. To overthrow French imperialism, feudalism, and the reactionary Vietnamese capitalist class.

2. To make Indochina completely independent.

3. To establish a worker-peasant and soldier government.

4. To confiscate the banks and other enterprises belonging to the imperialists and put them under the control of the worker-peasant and soldier government.

5. To confiscate the whole of the plantations and property belonging to the imperialists and the Vietnamese reactionary capitalist class and distribute them to poor peasants.

6. To implement the eight-hour working day.

7. To abolish public loans and poll tax. To waive unjust taxes hitting the poor people.

8. To bring back all freedoms to the masses.

9. To carry out universal education.

10. To implement equality between man and woman.

THE PARTY'S LINE IN THE PERIOD OF
THE DEMOCRATIC FRONT (1936–39)*

1. For the time being, the Party cannot put forth too high a demand (national independence, parliament, etc.). To do so is to enter the Japanese fascists' scheme. It should only claim for democratic rights, freedom of organization, freedom of assembly, freedom of press and freedom of speech, general amnesty for all political detainees, and struggle for the legalization of the Party.

2. To reach this goal, the Party must strive to organize a broad Democratic National Front. This Front does not embrace only Indo-chinese people but also progressive French residing in Indochina, not only toiling people but also the national bourgeoisie.

3. The Party must assume a wise, flexible attitude with the bourgeoisie, strive to draw it into the Front, win over the elements that can be won over and neutralize those which can be neutralized. We must by all means avoid leaving them outside the Front, lest they should fall into the hands of the enemy of the revolution and increase the strength of the reactionaries.

4. There cannot be any alliance with or any concession to the Trotskyite group. We must do everything possible to lay bare their faces as henchmen of the fascists and annihilate them politically.

5. To increase and consolidate its forces, to widen its influence, and to work effectively, the Indochinese Democratic Front must keep close

* This is an excerpt from the report made by Nguyen Ai Quoc to the Communist International in July, 1939.

contact with the French Popular Front because the latter also struggles for freedom, democracy, and can give us great help.

6. The Party cannot demand that the Front recognizes its leadership. It must instead show itself as the organ which makes the greatest sacrifices, the most active and loyal organ. It is only through daily struggle and work that the masses of the people acknowledge the correct policies and leading capacity of the Party and that it can win the leading position.

7. To be able to carry out this task, the Party must uncompromisingly fight sectarianism and narrow-mindedness and organize systematic study of Marxism-Leninism in order to raise the cultural and political level of the Party members and help the non-Party cadres raise their level. We must maintain close contact with the French Communist Party.

8. The Central Executive Committee must supervise the Party press to avoid technical and political mistakes. (E.g., in publishing comrade R's biography, the Lao-Dong revealed his address and his origin, etc. It also published without comment his letter saying that Trotskyism is a product of boastfulness, etc.)

LETTER FROM ABROAD*

(1941)

Elders!

Prominent personalities!

Intellectuals, peasants, workers, traders, and soldiers!

Dear compatriots!

Since the French were defeated by the Germans, their forces have been completely disintegrated. However, with regard to our people, they continue to plunder us pitilessly, suck all our blood, and carry out a barbarous policy of all-out terrorism and massacre. Concerning their foreign policy, they bow their heads and kneel down, shamelessly cutting our land for Siam; without a single word of protest, they heartlessly offer our interests to Japan. As a result, our people suffer under a double yoke: they serve not only as buffaloes and horses to the French invaders but also as slaves to the Japanese plunderers. Alas! What sin have our people committed to be doomed to such a wretched plight!

Living in such painful and lamentable conditions, can our people

* The Eighth Plenum of the Central Committee of the Communist Party of Indochina, held at Pac Bo (Cao Bang province) May 10–19, 1941, decided on a new line highlighting the slogan "national liberation," establishing the Viet Minh Front, changing the names of various mass organizations into Associations for National Salvation, and speeding up the preparations for an abortive armed uprising against the French on June 6, 1941. This letter calls on revolutionary fighters at home, together with all other Vietnamese, to rise up and overthrow the Japanese and the French.—ED.

132

bind their own hands to doom themselves to death? No! Certainly not! More than 20 million sons and daughters of Lac Hong are resolute to do away with slavery. For nearly eighty years under the French invaders' iron heels we have unceasingly sacrificed ourselves and struggled for national independence and freedom. The loyal and heroic spirit of our predecessors such as Phan Dinh Phung, Hoang Hoa Tham, and Luong Ngoc Quyen is still alive; the heroic feats of our revolutionaries in Thai Nguyen, Yen Bai, Nghe An, and Ha Tinh provinces remain forever in our memory. The recent uprising in the South and at Do Luong and Bac Son have testified to the determination of our compatriots to shed their blood as their glorious predecessors did, heroically to annihilate the enemy. If we did not succeed, it was not because the French invaders were strong, but only because the situation was not yet ripe and our compatriots throughout the country did not yet have the same heart and mind.

Now, the opportunity has come for our liberation. France itself is unable to dominate our country. As to the Japanese, on the one hand they are bogged in China, on the other they are hamstrung by the British and American forces and certainly cannot use all their forces to contend with us. If our entire people are united and single-minded, we are certainly able to smash the picked French and Japanese armies.

Compatriots throughout the country! Rise up quickly! Let us follow the heroic example of the Chinese people! Rise up quickly to organize the Association for National Salvation to fight the French and the Japanese.

Elders!

Prominent personalities!

Some hundreds of years ago, when our country was endangered by the Mongolian invasion, our elders under the Tran dynasty rose up indignantly and called on their sons and daughters throughout the country to rise as one in order to kill the enemy. Finally they saved their people from danger, and their good name will be carried into posterity for all time. The elders and prominent personalities of our country should follow the example set by our forefathers in the glorious task of national salvation.

Rich people, soldiers, workers, peasants, intellectuals, employees, traders, youth, and women who warmly love your country! At the present time national liberation is the most important problem. Let us unite together! As one in mind and strength we shall overthrow the Japanese and French and their jackals in order to save people from the situation between boiling water and burning heat.

Dear compatriots!

National salvation is the common cause to the whole of our people. Every Vietnamese must take part in it. He who has money will contribute his money, he who has strength will contribute his strength, he who has talent will contribute his talent. I pledge to use all my modest abilities to follow you, and am ready for the last sacrifice.

Revolutionary fighters!

The hour has struck! Raise aloft the insurrectionary banner and guide the people throughout the country to overthrow the Japanese and French! The sacred call of the Fatherland is resounding in your ears; the blood of our heroic predecessors who sacrificed their lives is stirring in your hearts! The fighting spirit of the people is displayed everywhere before you! Let us rise up quickly! Unite with each other, unify your action to overthrow the Japanese and the French.

Victory to Viet-Nam's Revolution!

Victory to the World's Revolution!

Command gave us an order to destroy everything in order to transform this region into a desert. This order was observed to the letter. Houses were burned down. Animals and poultry were killed. Havoc was wrought to gardens and plants and trees hewn down. Rice fields and crops were set afire. Many days on end, black smoke covered the sky and there was not a single soul alive, except the French soldiers. The conflagration lasted until November 25, when the Viet-Nam People's Army unexpectedly attacked and annihilated our unit."

The examples quoted above can be counted by the thousands and are sufficient proof to substantiate the essence of the French colonialists' and U.S. interventionists' "civilization."

Achievements Recorded by the Democratic Republic of Viet-Nam

In 1951, the Vietnamese people made a big stride forward. In the political field, the founding of the Viet-Nam Workers' Party, the amalgamation of the Viet Minh and Lien Viet, and the setting up of the Committee of Action for Viet-Nam, Cambodia, and Laos greatly consolidated the unity and enhanced the confidence of the Vietnamese people. They strengthened the alliance between the three brother countries in their struggle against the common enemies—the French colonialists and the U.S. interventionists—in order to realize their common goal, i.e., national independence.

So we were able to frustrate the enemy's policy of divide and rule.

In the economic field, the National Bank of Viet-Nam has been established, our finance is placed under centralized and unified supervision, and communications have been reorganized.

Formerly, we demolished roads to check the enemy's advance; at present, we repair them to drive the enemy to an early defeat. Formerly, we did our utmost to sabotage roads; now we encounter great difficulties in mending them, but have managed to complete our work quite rapidly. This is a hard job, especially when we lack machines. However, thanks to the enthusiasm and sacrificing spirit of our people, this work was carried through. To avoid enemy air raids, it was done at night by workers often knee-deep in water. In the bright torchlight, hundreds of men, women, and young people dug the earth to fill the gaps in the roads, broke stones, felled trees, and built bridges. As in any other work, the workers' enthusiasm was roused by emulation drives. I am sure that you would be astonished to see teams of old volunteers of from sixty to eighty years competing with teams of young workers.

Here it must be pointed out that in the free zone, most of the work is done at night—children go to school, housewives go to market, and guerrillas go to attack the enemy.

Great successes have been achieved in the elaboration of the agricultural tax. Formerly, the peasants were compelled to pay taxes of various kinds and make many other contributions; nowadays, they have only to pay a uniform tax in kind. Households whose production does not exceed 60 kilograms of paddy per year are exempt from the tax. Households who harvest greater quantities have to pay a graduated tax. Generally speaking, the taxes to be paid do not exceed 20 per cent of the total value of the annual production. To collect taxes in time, the Party, the National United Front, and the Government have mobilized a great number of cadres to examine the new tax from the political and technical points of view. After their study, these cadres go to the countryside and hold talks and meetings to exchange views with the peasants and explain to them the new taxation policy.

After this preparatory period, the peasants of both sexes appoint a committee composed of representatives of the administration and various people's organizations, whose duty it is to estimate the production of each household and fix the rate to be paid after approval by a Congress in which all the peasants take part.

This reform was welcomed by the population, which enthusiastically took part in this tax collection.

The agricultural tax has been established simultaneously with the movement for increased production. At present, the Government possesses adequate stocks of foodstuffs to cater for the soldiers and workers. So we have thwarted the enemy's cunning plot of blockading us to reduce us to starvation.

As far as mass education is concerned, in 1951 we scored worthwhile results. Though great difficulties were created by the war, such as frequent changes of school site, schooling at night time, lack of school requisites, the number of schools rose from 2,712 in 1950 to 3,591 in 1951, with an attendance of 293,256 and 411,038 pupils, respectively.

In South Viet-Nam, the situation is all the more ticklish. There,

ON THE ANNOUNCEMENT OF WILLKIE'S
RECEPTION IN THE NEWSPAPERS

Both of us are friends of China,
Both are going to Chungking,
But you are given the seat of an honored guest,
While I am a prisoner, thrown under the steps.
Why are we both so differently treated?
Coldness to one, and warmth toward the other:
That is the way of the world, as from time immemorial
The waters flow down to the sea.

WORD PLAY

Take away the sign 人 (*man*) from the sign 囚 for *prison*,
Add to it 或 (*probability*), that makes the word 國 (*nation*).
Take the head-particle from the sign 患 for misfortune:
That gives the word 忠 (*fidelity*).
Add the sign 亻 for *man* (standing) to the sign 憂 for *worry*
That gives the word 優 (*quality*).
Take away the *bamboo* top 竹 from the sign 籠 for *prison*,
That gives you 龍 (*dragon*).

People who come out of prison can build up the country.
Misfortune is a test of people's fidelity.
Those who protest at injustice are people of true merit.
When the prison doors are opened, the real dragon will fly out.

AUTUMN NIGHT

In front of the gate, the guard stands with his rifle.
Above, untidy clouds are carrying away the moon.
The bedbugs are swarming round like army tanks on maneuvers,
While the mosquitoes form squadrons, attacking like fighter planes.
My heart travels a thousand li toward my native land.
My dream intertwines with sadness like a skein of a thousand threads.
Innocent, I have now endured a whole year in prison.
Using my tears for ink, I turn my thoughts into verses.

AFTER PRISON, A
WALK IN THE MOUNTAINS

The clouds embrace the peaks, the peaks embrace the clouds,
The river below shines like a mirror, spotless and clean.
On the crest of the Western Mountains, my heart stirs as I wander
Looking toward the Southern sky and dreaming of old friends.

INSTRUCTION TO ESTABLISH
THE VIET-NAM PROPAGANDA
UNIT FOR NATIONAL LIBERATION*

(December, 1944)

1. The Viet-Nam Propaganda Unit for National Liberation shows by its name that greater importance should be attached to the political side than to the military side. It is a propaganda unit. To act successfully, in the military field, the main principle is concentration of forces. Therefore, in accordance with the new instruction of the Organization,† most resolute and energetic officers and men will be picked out of the ranks of the guerrilla units in the provinces of Cao Bang, Bac Can, and Lang Son and a great amount of weapons will be concentrated to establish our main force.

Because ours is a national resistance by the whole people, we must mobilize and arm the whole people. Therefore, when concentrating

---

* *The Viet-Nam Propaganda Unit for National Liberation was set up on December 22, 1944, from small guerrilla units that had formerly operated in the provinces of Cao Bang and Lang Son. At the beginning, it comprised thirty-four men and officers under the command of Vo Nguyen Giap, a history professor who in 1945 became the commanding general of the Viet-Nam People's Army, which grew out of that first guerrilla unit. To this day, December 22 is celebrated as the official "birthday" of the North Vietnamese Armed Forces. For a biography of Giap, see Vo Nguyen Giap,* People's War, People's Army *(New York: Frederick A. Praeger, 1962).*—ED.

† The Communist Party of Indochina, now the Viet-Nam Workers' Party.

our forces to set up the first unit, we must maintain the local armed forces, coordinate their operations and assist each other in all aspects. On its part, the main unit has the duty to guide the cadres of the local armed units, assist them in drilling, and supply them with weapons if possible, thus helping these units to grow unceasingly.

2. With regard to local armed units, we will gather their cadres for training, send trained cadres to various localities to exchange experience, maintain liaison, and coordinate military operations.

3. Concerning tactics, we will apply guerrilla warfare, which consists in being secret, rapid, active, now in the East, now in the West, arriving unexpectedly and leaving unnoticed.

The Viet-Nam Propaganda Unit for National Liberation is the first-born unit. It is hoped that other units will soon come into being.

At first its size is small, however, its prospect is brilliant. It is the embryo of the Liberation Army and can move from North to South, throughout Viet-Nam.

APPEAL FOR
GENERAL INSURRECTION*

Dear compatriots,

Four years ago, in one of my letters, I called on you to unite to-gether. Because unity is strength, only strength enables us to win back independence and freedom.

At present, the Japanese army is crushed. The National Salvation movement has spread to the whole country. The Revolutionary Front for the Independence of Viet-Nam (Viet Minh) has millions of members from all social strata: intellectuals, peasants, workers, business-men, soldiers, and from all nationalities in the country: Kinh, Tho, Nung, Muong, Man, etc. In the Front our compatriots march side by side without discrimination as to age, sex, religion, or fortune.

Recently, the Viet Minh Front convened the Viet-Nam People's Congress and appointed the National Liberation Committee to lead the entire people in the resolute struggle until national independence is won.

* The National Congress held on August 16, 1945, at Tan Trao (Tuyen Quang province) was called by the Viet Minh Central Committee. The con-ference was convened so hastily that few non-Viet Minh organizations had an opportunity to express their views. The Congress approved the ten policies and the order of general insurrection issued by the Viet Minh Front and appointed the Viet-Nam National Liberation Committee, which was in fact the Provi-sional Government of the Democratic Republic of Viet-Nam, presided over by Ho Chi Minh. After the closing of the Congress, Ho wrote this letter calling on the Vietnamese people to rise up and regain their independence.— ED.

This is a great advance in the history of the struggle waged for nearly a century by our people for their liberation.

This is a fact that enraptures our compatriots and fills me with great joy.

However, we cannot consider this as good enough. Our struggle will be a long and hard one. Because the Japanese are defeated, we shall not be liberated overnight. We still have to make further efforts and carry on the struggle. Only a united struggle will bring us independence.

The Viet Minh Front is at present the basis of the struggle and solidarity of our people. Join the Viet Minh Front, support it, make it greater and stronger!

At present, the National Liberation Committee is, so to speak, in itself our provisional government. Unite around it and see to it that its policies and orders are carried out throughout the country!

In this way, our Fatherland will certainly win independence and our people will certainly win freedom soon.

The decisive hour in the destiny of our people has struck. Let us stand up with all our strength to free ourselves!

Many oppressed peoples the world over are vying with each other in the march to win back their independence. We cannot allow ourselves to lag behind.

Forward! Forward! Under the banner of the Viet Minh Front, move forward courageously!

DECLARATION OF INDEPENDENCE
OF THE DEMOCRATIC REPUBLIC
OF VIET-NAM*
(September 2, 1945)

All men are created equal; they are endowed by their Creator with certain unalienable Rights; among these are Life, Liberty, and the pursuit of Happiness.

This immortal statement was made in the Declaration of Independence of the United States of America in 1776. In a broader sense, this means: All the peoples on the earth are equal from birth, all the peoples have a right to live, to be happy and free.

The Declaration of the French Revolution made in 1791 on the Rights of Man and the Citizen also states: "All men are born free and with equal rights, and must always remain free and have equal rights."

Those are undeniable truths.

Nevertheless, for more than eighty years, the French imperialists, abusing the standard of Liberty, Equality, and Fraternity, have violated our Fatherland and oppressed our fellow citizens. They have acted contrary to the ideals of humanity and justice.

In the field of politics, they have deprived our people of every democratic liberty.

* *The borrowing from the United States Declaration of Independence was open and intended. American members of the OSS mission parachuted to Ho in the summer of 1945 recall several of Ho's attempts to obtain a copy of the Declaration, or, failing this, a close approximation of its essential passages.* —ED.

They have enforced inhuman laws; they have set up three distinct political regimes in the North, the Center, and the South of Viet-Nam in order to wreck our national unity and prevent our people from being united.

They have built more prisons than schools. They have mercilessly slain our patriots; they have drowned our uprisings in rivers of blood.

They have fettered public opinion; they have practiced obscurantism against our people.

To weaken our race they have forced us to use opium and alcohol.

In the field of economics, they have fleeced us to the backbone, impoverished our people and devastated our land.

They have robbed us of our rice fields, our mines, our forests, and our raw materials. They have monopolized the issuing of bank notes and the export trade.

They have invented numerous unjustifiable taxes and reduced our people, especially our peasantry, to a state of extreme poverty.

They have hampered the prospering of our national bourgeoisie; they have mercilessly exploited our workers.

In the autumn of 1940, when the Japanese fascists violated Indochina's territory to establish new bases in their fight against the Allies, the French imperialists went down on their bended knees and handed over our country to them.

Thus, from that date, our people were subjected to the double yoke of the French and the Japanese. Their sufferings and miseries increased. The result was that, from the end of last year to the beginning of this year, from Quang Tri Province to the North of Viet-Nam, more than two million of our fellow citizens died from starvation. On March 9 [1945], the French troops were disarmed by the Japanese. The French colonialists either fled or surrendered, showing that not only were they incapable of "protecting" us, but that, in the span of five years, they had twice sold our country to the Japanese.

On several occasions before March 9, the Viet Minh League urged the French to ally themselves with it against the Japanese. Instead of agreeing to this proposal, the French colonialists so intensified their terrorist activities against the Viet Minh members that before fleeing they massacred a great number of our political prisoners detained at Yen Bay and Cao Bang.

Notwithstanding all this, our fellow citizens have always manifested toward the French a tolerant and humane attitude. Even after the Japanese *Putsch* of March, 1945, the Viet Minh League helped many

Frenchmen to cross the frontier, rescued some of them from Japanese jails, and protected French lives and property.

From the autumn of 1940, our country had in fact ceased to be a French colony and had become a Japanese possession.

After the Japanese had surrendered to the Allies, our whole people rose to regain our national sovereignty and to found the Democratic Republic of Viet-Nam.

The truth is that we have wrested our independence from the Japanese and not from the French.

The French have fled, the Japanese have capitulated, Emperor Bao Dai has abdicated. Our people have broken the chains which for nearly a century have fettered them and have won independence for the Fatherland. Our people at the same time have overthrown the monarchic regime that has reigned supreme for dozens of centuries. In its place has been established the present Democratic Republic.

For these reasons, we, members of the Provisional Government, representing the whole Vietnamese people, declare that from now on we break off all relations of a colonial character with France; we repeal all the international obligation that France has so far subscribed to on behalf of Viet-Nam, and we abolish all the special rights the French have unlawfully acquired in our Fatherland.

The whole Vietnamese people, animated by a common purpose, are determined to fight to the bitter end against any attempt by the French colonialists to reconquer their country.

We are convinced that the Allied nations, which at Teheran and San Francisco have acknowledged the principles of self-determination and equality of nations, will not refuse to acknowledge the independence of Viet-Nam.

A people who have courageously opposed French domination for more than eighty years, a people who have fought side by side with the Allies against the fascists during these last years, such a people must be free and independent.

For these reasons, we, members of the Provisional Government of the Democratic Republic of Viet-Nam, solemnly declare to the world that Viet-Nam has the right to be a free and independent country— and in fact it is so already. The entire Vietnamese people are determined to mobilize all their physical and mental strength, to sacrifice their lives and property in order to safeguard their independence and liberty.

ON THE OCCASION
OF THE "GOLD WEEK"*
(September 17, 1945)

To compatriots all over the country!

The "Gold Week" organization committee in Hanoi has invited me to attend the opening ceremony of the "Gold Week." Being busy and unable to come, I send this message to compatriots all over the country.

Thanks to the sacrifice in struggle of our compatriots all over the country for nearly eighty years, especially during these last five years, we have succeeded in building up our freedom and independence.

Today we need to consolidate this freedom and independence to resist the aggressive intentions of the French imperialists.

The consolidation of such freedom and independence requires the sacrifice in struggle of our compatriots all over the country, but we are also badly in need of donations from the people, mainly from well-to-do families.

This is the meaning of "Gold Week."

"Gold Week" will collect the gold given by the people, and mainly

* The "Gold Week" was held for the specific purpose of obtaining means to pay for the American weapons given the Chinese Nationalist troops under wartime Lend-Lease agreements and which the latter were selling freely in North Viet-Nam. In that way, the D.R.V.N. also acquired the Japanese stocks the Chinese had supposedly come to impound—a total of close to 40,000 weapons, including mortars, artillery, and eighteen tanks.—ED.

146

by the well-off families, to devote it to our most pressing and important task at present, which is national defense.

"Gold Week" will show all our compatriots and the whole world that, while the Vietnamese fighters on all battle fronts are determined to sacrifice the last drop of their blood to safeguard the homeland, freedom, and independence, our compatriots in the rear, especially well-to-do people, can sacrifice a small quantity of their gold to serve their Fatherland.

By so doing, "Gold Week" does not only mean a contribution to the finance of national defense but it also conveys an important political meaning.

Therefore I expect you, compatriots throughout the country, especially well-to-do people, to do your utmost to sacrifice for our country.

I am confident that all our compatriots, the rich chiefly, will show in this collection, that they merit the sacrificing spirit of our patriotic fighters on all fronts. I trust that our compatriots throughout the country will carry through their task.

Long live independent Viet-Nam!

MESSAGE TO
SOUTHERN COMPATRIOTS
(September 26, 1945)

Dear southern compatriots!

Our newly won national independence is threatened by foreign invasion. When fighting the Japanese, the French colonialists either surrendered or fled; now, the war having just ended, they are coming back either secretly or openly. Within a period of four years, they sold out our country twice, now they still want to dominate our people once more.

I believe, and our compatriots throughout the country believe, in the firm patriotism of the southern compatriots. We should remember the heroic words of a great French revolutionary, "I'd rather die as a free man than live as a slave."

I am sure, and the southern compatriots are also sure, that the Government and our compatriots throughout the country will do their utmost to support the fighters and people who are making sacrifices in their struggle to maintain national independence.

I am sure, and all our compatriots are sure, that individuals and peoples the world over who love equality and freedom all sympathize with us.

Victory will definitely be ours because we have the united force of our entire people. We are sure to win the battle because our struggle is a just one.

I want to recommend to our southern compatriots just one thing: as far as the Frenchmen captured in the war are concerned, we must watch them carefully, but we must also treat them generously. We must show to the world, and to the French people in particular, that we want only independence and freedom, that we are not struggling for the sake of individual enmity and rancor.

We must show to the world that we are an intelligent people, more civilized than the homicidal invaders.

Long live independent Viet-Nam!

Long live our southern compatriots!

TO THE PEOPLE'S EXECUTIVE COMMITTEES AT ALL LEVELS (BOS,* PROVINCES, DISTRICTS, AND VILLAGES)

(October, 1945)

Our country was oppressed by the French for more than eighty years and by the Japanese for four or five years. The poverty suffered by our people was indescribable. It is a heartbreaking thing to remember it now. Thanks to our people's monolithic unity and the Government's wise guidance, we have been able to break the bonds of slavery and win back our independence and freedom.

If there are insufficient people, we will not have enough strength; if there is no Government, no one will guide the people. Hence, the Government and the people must unite into a bloc. We have now built our Democratic Republic of Viet-Nam. But if our country is independent without our people enjoying happiness and freedom, then this independence is meaningless.

Our Government has promised the people that it will do its best so that every citizen may enjoy his share of happiness. In the building of our country, the things to be restored will have to be restored slowly. They cannot be accomplished in a month or a year. But from the very beginning, we must correctly follow our guiding principles. We must realize that all Government organs, from the Central to the communal

* Bo: one of the three parts of Viet-Nam (North, Center, South).

150

level, are the people's servants, that is to say they are appointed to work for the sake of the whole people's interests and not to oppress the people as under the French and Japanese.

We must exert ourselves to do what is of benefit to the people.

We must exert ourselves to avoid what is harmful to them.

We must love them so that they may love and respect us.

I know that many of you have correctly carried out the Government's policies and won the people's confidence. But there are also many of you who have committed very serious mistakes. The main ones are:

1. Breaches of the law. Traitors whose guilt is clearly established must be punished, and they have no grounds for complaint. But sometimes, because of personal enmity and rancor, you arrest honest people and confiscate their property, causing them distress.

2. Arrogance. Abusing your position as members of such and such committees, you become unruly and do things in your own way. You hold public opinion in contempt, disregard the people's interests. You forget that you are elected by the people to serve them, and should not be arrogant toward them.

3. Debauchery. If you make good cheer, dress yourselves in fine clothes, becoming more and more wasteful, more and more romantic, you must ask yourselves where the money comes from. You have gone so far as to appropriate public wealth for yourselves, forgetting integrity and virtue. You, members of committees, use official cars, your wives use them, and even your children use them. Ask yourselves who is paying for these expenses.

4. Sectarianism and connivance. You group your friends and relatives around you and give them positions for which they have no ability. Those who are competent and satisfactory but do not please you, are discarded. You forget that this is a public affair and not a private concern of anyone.

5. Division. You oppose one section of the people against another. You do not make various sections of the people become reconciled one with another and so live on good terms. In some places, you have gone so far as to let fields lie fallow and made the peasants dissatisfied with you. You forget that at this moment we must unite the whole people, that no distinction can be made between the old and the young, the rich and the poor; this in order to safeguard our independence and fight the common enemy.

6. Conceit. Thinking that an official is someone, you look upon the people with contempt. You always want to show off that you are "mandarin revolutionaries." You do not realize that through your conceit you will lose the people's confidence and harm the Government's prestige.

Mistakes are not to be feared, but they are to be corrected when discovered. Hence, he who has not fallen into the above-mentioned mistakes should try to avoid them to make further progress. He who has committed them must endeavor to correct them. If he does not correct himself, the Government will not forgive him.

It is for the sake of the people's happiness and national interests that I have mentioned the above mistakes. We must always bear the words "justice" and "integrity" in mind.

I hope you will make progress.

ADDRESS TO THE
FRENCHMEN IN INDOCHINA
(October, 1945)

I want to address a few words to you not as President of the Democratic Republic of Viet-Nam, but as a sincere friend of the honest Frenchmen.

You love France and want it to be independent. You love your compatriots and want them to be free. Your patriotism is a glory to you because it is mankind's highest ideal.

But we also have a right to love our fatherland and want it to be independent, have we not? We also have a right to love our compatriots and want them to be free, have we not? What you consider as your ideal must be ours too.

We neither dislike nor hate the French people. On the contrary, we respect them as a great people who were the first to propagate the lofty ideals of liberty, equality, and fraternity and have greatly contributed to culture, science, and civilization.

Our struggle is not directed against France, nor is it directed against honest Frenchmen, but we are fighting the cruel domination of French colonialism in Indochina. You will understand to what extent this colonialism has misused the reputation of France and imposed upon us disastrous calamities: forced labor, *corvées,* salt tax, compulsory consumption of opium and alcohol, heavy taxes, complete absence of freedom, incessant terrorism, moral and material sufferings, and ruthless exploitation. Ask yourselves who has benefited by making us suffer in such a way. Is it France and the French people? No, France does not become richer from colonialist exploitation, and it is not due to the absence of this exploitation that it will become poorer. On the contrary, expenditure for the colonies is another burden loaded upon the French people's shoulders.

Do the French planters and industrialists in Indochina profit? Before you give an answer, I want you to put yourselves in our situation for a moment. What would you do if foreigners came and imposed on you an endless string of plagues and sufferings? I strongly believe that you would struggle to the last against this domination. Then why do you want us shamefully to accept French domination?

You have also known that this domination profits neither France nor the French people. It only enriches the few colonialist sharks and blemishes France's reputation.

Some people say that it is to save face that France is trying to cling to Indochina.

The recognition of Viet-Nam's independence will not lower France's prestige, but will heighten it before the world and history. This gesture will show to the world at large, and particularly to the Vietnamese, that today's France is completely different from the old imperialist France. It will win the respect of all peoples and the love of the Vietnamese who now, as always, want nothing else than to see their Fatherland independent.

Frenchmen in Indochina! Don't you think that mankind's blood has been shed too much? Don't you think that peace, a genuine peace built on justice and democratic ideals must be a substitute for war, that freedom, equality, and fraternity must be realized in all countries with no discrimination between nationalities and races?

We do not fear death, because we want to live. Like you, we want to live free, not to be trampled underfoot and strangled. Hence, we have made a distinction between good Frenchmen and bad ones.

I repeat that we are struggling for our independence, we are struggling against domination and not against honest Frenchmen.

At present the French colonialists have started their offensive against us in the South. They have begun to kill so many of our compatriots, committed arson and sacking. We are obliged to fight these invaders in order to safeguard our families and Fatherland.

However, everywhere in Viet-Nam the lives and property of the

Frenchmen are being protected and will continue to be protected, provided they are content to live quietly and do not cause trouble.

I solemnly guarantee that the Frenchmen who earn their living honestly and live quietly will always be treated by us as friends and brothers. We are a people advocating peace and respecting others' interests and freedom.

Frenchmen in Indochina! It is now up to you to show that you are worthy children of the glorious heroes who formerly struggled for freedom, equality, and fraternity.

APPEAL TO VIETNAMESE
RESIDENTS IN FRANCE
(November 5, 1945)

Dear compatriots,

The Vietnamese people wholeheartedly acclaim the protest you have sent to the British government demanding the withdrawal of British and Indian troops from South Viet-Nam; they also whole-heartedly acclaim the meeting you organized, and which enabled the French people to get a clear insight into our country's situation.

Being far away from home for these last five years, you are no doubt handicapped, and the imperialists have availed themselves of this drawback to make distorted propaganda.

On going abroad, every worker or student hoped that his country would be one day free and independent. Our present struggle is but a continuation of our fathers' struggle during the eighty years of French domination.

Our struggle against the French colonialists and Japanese fascists has written recent bloodstained and glorious pages of history. We have seen so many of our compatriots killed by French colonialists' bombs and bullets in the South, in Nghe An, Lang Son, and Cao Bang provinces, and in many other regions of the North. In addition, many militants have died in the Poulo Condore Island prison settlements and concentration camps, which are more horrible than the ones set up by the German fascists to torture their victims.

156

During historic August last, the success achieved by the Viet Minh Front and the abdication of Emperor Bao Dai gave proof of our people's powerful forces.

Try, dear friends, to make the civilized world and particularly the French people clearly hear your Fatherland's voice. Struggle to frustrate the ignominious slanders unleashed by the French colonialists.

In order to oppress our people once more, the French colonialists have killed women and children. They have asked for the help of the British, Indian, and Japanese forces, using airplanes, tanks, cannons, and warships. But however modern an army is, it is powerless before the determined attitude of a whole people.

Wherever they go, they will find scorched earth and the hatred of a people who are only waiting for an opportunity to drive them out of the country.

Never before have we been so closely united as today, displaying the strong spirit of a people who would rather die as free men than live as slaves.

We do not hate the French people at all. We know that having struggled against the Germans, and maintained a firm spirit during the darkest days of their history, the French people will feel our pains and sacrifices more than any other people. They will intervene with their Government to stop the bloodshed, and save honest people's lives.

Never should it be for the interests of a handful of administrators and militarists or capitalists that the French people should waste French lives.

Show yourselves worthy of your brothers and sisters who are fighting in the South to safeguard our national independence.

SPEECH DELIVERED IN
THE FIRST DAYS OF THE
RESISTANCE WAR IN SOUTH VIET-NAM
(November, 1945)

Compatriots!

During the Second World War, the French colonialists twice sold out our country to the Japanese. Thus they betrayed the allied nations, and helped the Japanese to cause the latter many losses.

Meanwhile they also betrayed our people, exposing us to the destruction of bombs and bullets. In this way, the French colonialists withdrew of their own accord from the Allied ranks and tore up the treaties they had earlier compelled us to sign.

Notwithstanding the French colonialists' treachery, our people as a whole are determined to side with the Allies and oppose the invaders. When the Japanese surrendered, our entire people single-mindedly changed our country into a Democratic Republic and elected a provisional Government which is to prepare for a national congress and draw up our draft Constitution.

Not only is our act in line with the Atlantic and San Francisco Charters, etc., solemnly proclaimed by the Allies, but it entirely conforms with the glorious principles upheld by the French people: Liberty, Equality, and Fraternity.

It is thus clear that in the past the colonialists betrayed the Allies and our country, and surrendered to the Japanese. At present, in the shadow of the British and Indian troops, and behind the Japanese soldiers, they are attacking the South of our country.

They have sabotaged the peace that China, the United States, Britain, and Russia won at the cost of scores of millions of lives. They have run counter to the promises concerning democracy and liberty that the allied powers have proclaimed. They have of their own accord sabotaged their fathers' principles of liberty and equality. In consequence, it is for a just cause, for justice of the world, and for Viet-Nam's land and people that our compatriots throughout the country have risen to struggle, and are firmly determined to maintain their independence. We do not hate the French people and France. We are energetically fighting slavery, and the ruthless policy of the French colonialists. We are not invading another's country. We only safeguard our own against the French invaders. Hence we are not alone. The countries which love peace and democracy, and the weaker nations all over the world, all sympathize with us. With the unity of the whole people within the country, and having many sympathizers abroad, we are sure of victory.

The French colonialists have behaved lawlessly in the South for almost one-and-a-half months. Our southern compatriots have sacrificed their lives in a most valiant struggle. Public opinion in the great countries—China, the United States, Russia, and Britain—has supported our just cause.

Compatriots throughout the country! Those in the South will do their utmost to resist the enemy. Those in the Center and the North will endeavor to help their southern compatriots and be on the alert.

The French colonialists should know that the Vietnamese people do not want bloodshed, that they love peace. But we are determined to sacrifice even millions of combatants and fight a long-term war of resistance in order to safeguard Viet-Nam's independence and free her children from slavery. We are sure that our war of resistance will be victorious!

Let the whole country be determined in the war of resistance!

Long live independent Viet-Nam!

DECLARATION OF
THE POLICY OF THE
PROVISIONAL COALITION GOVERNMENT
(January 1, 1946)

With a view to winning complete independence and bringing about a close cooperation between the various political parties to further strengthen the Government, it is now named the Provisional Coalition Government. At this moment, if the parties unite together, the Government can overcome difficulties. All the Vietnamese people want the Provisional Government to hold office until the election of the National Assembly, which will change it into a definite Government. Meanwhile, the Provisional Coalition Government will discuss the following practical questions:

HOME POLICY

Political objectives: to carry out satisfactorily the general elections throughout the country; to unify the various administrative organs according to democratic principles.

Economic objectives: to endeavor to develop agriculture; to encourage cultivation and stock-breeding in order to check famine.

Military objectives: to unify the various armed forces under the command of the Government. Parties are not allowed to have armies of their own.

Cultural objectives: to give aid to various cultural organs.

In short, in home policy, the Government must exert itself politically to unify the country, and intensify production in order to cope with famine and foreign invasion.

FOREIGN POLICY

Objectives: to induce other countries to recognize Viet-Nam's independence; to have friendly relations with foreign residents of Viet-Nam, particularly the Chinese. With regard to the Frenchmen, we only fight the colonialists. As for those who do not seek to prejudice our independence, we will protect their lives and property.

Such is the policy of the Provisional Coalition Government of the Democratic Republic of Viet-Nam. I hope that the entire people will support it to enable the Government to succeed.

Long live independent Viet-Nam!

APPEAL TO THE
PEOPLE TO GO TO THE POLLS
(January 5, 1946)

Tomorrow will be January 6, 1946.

It will take our people to a new path.

It will be a happy day for our compatriots, because it is the day of the general election, the first day in Vietnamese history on which our people will begin to enjoy their democratic rights.

Tomorrow our people will show to the southern fighters that while in the military field they are using weapons to oppose the enemy, in the political field we are using our votes to consolidate our forces.

Tomorrow our compatriots will show to the world that the Vietnamese people are determined to: unite closely, fight the colonialists, and regain independence.

Tomorrow they will freely choose and elect worthy people to represent them in the management of State affairs.

Candidates are many, and the number of deputies is limited. As a matter of course, tomorrow there will be people elected and others not elected.

Those elected must do their utmost to defend national independence and to make their compatriots happy. They must always bear in mind and put into practice the words: Family interests should be forgotten for the sake of national interests; private interests should be forgotten

162

for the sake of common interests; we must be worthy of our compatriots and our Fatherland.

Those who are not elected should not be discouraged. The zeal they have shown on behalf of the country and the people must always be maintained. Whether within the National Assembly or without, they will try to be useful to the country. If this time they fail, should they continue to prove their talents and virtues, then surely they will be elected by their compatriots next time.

Tomorrow all voters will not fail to go to the polls. Tomorrow everybody will enjoy the rights granted to independent and free citizens.

LETTER SENT TO THE CONGRESS OF THE SOUTHERN NATIONAL MINORITIES, HELD IN PLEIKU IN APRIL, 1946

(April 19, 1946)

Dear compatriots of national minorities,

Your Congress has opened today. This is a very cheerful family gathering.

I regret that I cannot come to attend the Congress on account of the long distance. I am far from you, yet my heart and that of the Government is always by your side.

Compatriots of the Kinh majority people or of the Tho, Muong or Man, Djarai or Ede, Sedan or Bana, and other minorities are all Viet-Nam's children, all are blood brothers and sisters. Alive or dead, in happiness or in misfortune, we stand close to one another. Whether we have enough to eat, or whether we are in want, we must help one another.

Formerly we were far from each other, firstly because we lack connections, secondly because there were people who sowed discord and division among us.

Today Viet-Nam is our common country. In the National Assembly there are deputies of all nationalities. In the Government there is a Department for National Minorities, which takes charge of all affairs concerning them.

Our country and Government are common to all of us. Hence, all nationalities must unite closely in order to safeguard our Fatherland and support our Government.

We must love, respect, and help each other in order to secure our common happiness and that of our offspring.

Rivers can dry up, mountains can wear away, but our solidarity will never decrease. We are determined to assemble our forces with a view to maintaining our freedom and independence.

I wish the Congress much success.

REPLY AT THE LUNCHEON
GIVEN BY PRIME MINISTER BIDAULT
(July 2, 1946)

The reception given me by the French people and Government has moved me to my innermost heart. Please convey to the French Government and people the sincere thanks of the Vietnamese people for the sympathy and friendliness the French people and Government have expressed to me. Before officially greeting the French Government, I had the opportunity to visit the Basque provinces, a very beautiful region of France. The contact with the Basques taught me many lessons. While maintaining their peculiarities, dialect, and customs, the Basque people continue to be French citizens. Though France has many provinces which differ from each other, it remains unified and indivisible. In the future, the French Union will astonish the world with its solidarity and unity. The French Union that we will establish on a democratic basis can be set up only under a good omen. It is here in Paris, a heroic and generous city which proclaimed the principles of liberty, equality, and fraternity, a city which has the tradition to champion the equality of other peoples, it is in this very city that I solemnly declare that Viet-Nam will join this humanitarian organization.*

* *Ho's willingness to adhere to the French Union was not as much dictated by opportunism as may be supposed. In July, 1954, after it had won the war, the D.R.V.N. reiterated its offer to join the Union, but France, then playing the South Vietnamese "card," failed to respond. One might well wonder what the Viet-Nam situation wauld have been (after all, Cyprus stayed in the Commonwealth after a guerrilla war with Britain) had the offer been accepted.* —Ed.

166

Paris is the city which discovered the eternal ideals for the 1789 Revolution; it has remained loyal to its ideals in the bloodshed between the democratic and fascist blocs.

Paris has made no small contribution to the concord of Viet-Nam and France within the French Union including free and equal nations which cherish the same democratic ideals and are all for freedom. It is here in Paris that Viet-Nam will step forward to the path of independence. I am convinced that it will not be long before independent Viet-Nam plays its worthy role in the Pacific. No doubt many difficulties are awaiting the Fontainebleau Conference which has the responsibility to lay down the foundation for the relations between new France and new Viet-Nam. But sincerity and mutual confidence will level all obstacles. Have we not done away with aggressive imperialism and narrow chauvinism which are no longer fit for the present world? We are all stimulated by the same spirit. The Confucian philosophy and the Western philosophy alike uphold an ethic principle which is "Do as you would be done by." I believe that in those conditions, the forthcoming conference will achieve satisfactory results.

Mr. Prime Minister, I believe that the sincere and friendly cooperation between our two countries will be a great example for the world to realize that with mutual confidence, free and equal nations can always solve the most difficult problems. Ladies and gentlemen, I beg to propose a toast in honor of the Prime Minister and members of the French Government.

PROCLAMATION TO THE
PEOPLE UPON RETURN FROM
FRANCE AFTER NEGOTIATIONS
(October 23, 1946)

Compatriots throughout the country,

I left for France over four months ago. Today I am back home. I am very happy to see the Fatherland and you again. I have the following statements to make:

On my way to France, during my stay in France, and on my way back from France, the French Government, to show its desire to co-operate with Viet-Nam, received me ceremoniously. Out of sincere friendship for our people, the French people received me fraternally.

On your behalf, I have the honor to thank the French Government and people.

In my absence, thanks to the clearsighted leadership of Acting President Huynh, the care and help of the Assembly, the efforts of the Government, and the unity and common effort of the people, many difficult questions were settled and much progress made in constructive work.

I thank the Government, the National Assembly, and all our compatriots.

I think constantly of our compatriots living abroad who have made many sacrifices in the struggle and are always faithful to their Fatherland, notwithstanding the hardships they have endured.

Thanks to the understanding of French personalities in the North and Center of Viet-Nam, most of the difficulties arising between the Vietnamese and the Frenchmen have lately been settled.

I hope that from now on cooperation between the two peoples will be closer.

My thoughts are also with the Chinese and other foreign residents who all bear in mind the sentence, "Brother countries, like passengers on the same boat, must help each other."

At various places, when I met friends of Chinese and Indian nationalities, we were very happy to see each other and to show our friendliness. Now, coming back to Viet-Nam, I witness the same sight.

Answering the kind invitation of the French Government, I went to France with the purpose of solving the question of Viet-Nam's independence and the unification of the North, Center, and South. Due to the present situation in France, these two questions have not yet been settled. We have to wait. But I dare to vouch that sooner or later Viet-Nam is sure to be independent, and its three parts, the North, the Center, and the South, will be unified.

What did the Delegation and I do during the months we spent in France?

We took Viet-Nam's flag to France. The French Government and people and foreign residents there looked on our flag with respect.

We drew greater attention from the French Government and people and made them understand the question of Viet-Nam better than before. We also drew the attention of the world and made it understand the question of Viet-Nam better than before.

We caused a great many Frenchmen to become friends of the Vietnamese people and approve of Viet-Nam's independence and sincere Vietnamese-French cooperation on an equal footing.

We further heightened the position of the Vietnamese youth, women's, and workers' organizations because respective international organizations have recognized our organizations as members.

The Vietnamese-French Conference has not ended yet. It will resume next May, but the September 14 *modus vivendi* has, firstly, permitted the Vietnamese and French to carry out their business easily, and secondly, it has paved the way for the next Conference to be conducted in a friendly manner.

What have we to do from now until January?

1. The Government and people must be singleminded in their efforts at organization and must work for a closer unity, economic development, national reconstruction, and realization of a new mode of life in all aspects. Men or women, old or young, intellectuals or peasants, producers or traders, everyone must endeavor to work. We must show to the French Government and people and to the world at large that the Vietnamese people are already in possession of all the required conditions to be independent and free, and that the recognition of our freedom and independence is a necessity.

2. The French in France are very friendly toward us. So the Vietnamese in Viet-Nam should also be friendly toward the French people.

Toward the French Army we must be correct.

Toward the French residents, we must be moderate.

Toward the Frenchmen who sincerely want to cooperate with us, we will sincerely cooperate, and that is advantageous to both parties.

All this is to show to the world that we are a civilized people, to get a greater number of Frenchmen to support us, and to further strengthen their support so that the provokers who intend to divide us may find themselves with no pretext, and our unity and independence will soon succeed.

3. Compatriots in the South and the southern part of Central Viet-Nam! The North, Center, and South are part and parcel of Viet-Nam. We have the same ancestors, we are of the same family, we are all brothers and sisters. Our country has three parts, which are the North, the Center, and the South. They are just like three brothers in the same family. They are just like three regions of France: Normandy, Provence, and Beauce.

No one can divide the children of the same family. No one can divide France. Likewise, no one can divide Viet-Nam.

During the past year, in waging the Resistance War, our compatriots have seen their property destroyed, have sacrificed their lives, or were imprisoned and exiled. But their patriotism remains unshakable. This iron will will never be forgotten by the entire people, the Fatherland, and the Government.

I respectfully bow to the memory of the martyrs, and sympathize with the compatriots who are suffering and making sacrifices.

So long as the Fatherland is not yet unified and our compatriots are still suffering, I can neither eat with an appetite, nor sleep in peace. I solemnly promise you that with your determination and that of the entire people, our beloved South will surely come back into the bosom of our Fatherland.

The French Government has acknowledged the holding of a referendum by our southern compatriots to decide on the fate of the South. In the September 14 *modus vivendi,* the French Government agreed to implement the main points concerning the South as follows:

1. Political prisoners and those arrested for taking part in the resistance are to be released.

2. Our southern compatriots are to have freedom of organization, of meeting, of the press, of movement, etc.

3. Both parties are to stop fighting.

The French Government will undoubtedly respect its signature and implement the above clauses.

Now, what must our southern compatriots have to do?

1. The Vietnamese army, like the French army, must simultaneously stop fighting.

2. Our compatriots must carry out political actions in a democratic way.

3. Close unity must be realized with no discrimination as to political parties, social classes, and creeds. Unity means strength. Division means weakness.

4. Acts of reprisal are forbidden. Toward those who went astray, our compatriots must display a generous policy. We must let them hear the voice of reason. Everybody loves his country. It is only for petty interests that they forget the great cause. If we use the right words, they will certainly listen to us. Violent actions are absolutely forbidden. This is what you have to do at present to create a peaceful atmosphere, paving the way democratically to reach the unification of our Viet-Nam.

APPEAL TO THE ENTIRE PEOPLE
TO WAGE THE RESISTANCE WAR
(December 20, 1946)

Compatriots all over the country!

As we desired peace, we made concessions. But the more we made concessions, the further the French colonialists went because they are resolved to invade our country once again.

No! We would rather sacrifice all than lose our country. We are determined not to be enslaved.

Compatriots! Rise up!

Men and women, old and young, regardless of creeds, political parties, or nationalities, all the Vietnamese must stand up to fight the French colonialists to save the Fatherland. Those who have rifles will use their rifles; those who have swords will use their swords; those who have no swords will use spades, hoes, or sticks. Everyone must endeavor to oppose the colonialists and save his country.

Armymen, self-defense guards, and militiamen!

The hour for national salvation has struck! We must sacrifice even our last drop of blood to safeguard our country.

Even if we have to endure hardship in the Resistance War, with the determination to make sacrifices, victory will surely be ours.

Long live an independent and unified Viet-Nam!

Long live the victorious Resistance!

MESSAGE TO THE VIETNAMESE PEOPLE, THE FRENCH PEOPLE, AND THE PEOPLES OF THE ALLIED NATIONS
(December 21, 1946)

We, the Vietnamese Government and people, are determined to struggle for our independence and national unification, but we are also ready for friendly cooperation with the French people. We therefore signed a Preliminary Agreement on March 6, 1946, and the *modus vivendi* on September 14, 1946.

But the French reactionary colonialists lack sincerity and regard those agreements as mere pieces of waste paper.

In the South they continue to arrest, massacre, and provoke the Vietnamese patriots. They oppress honest Frenchmen who advocate sincerity, and have set up a puppet Government in order to divide our people.

In the southern part of Central Viet-Nam they continue to terrorize our compatriots, attack the Vietnamese army, and invade our territory.

In the North, they provoke clashes to occupy Bac Ninh, Bac Giang, Lang Son, and many other localities. They blockade the port of Haiphong, thus making it impossible for the Chinese, Vietnamese, other foreigners, and also the French residents to carry out their business. They try to strangle the Vietnamese people and wreck our

173

national sovereignty. At present they use tanks, aircraft, cannons, and warships to massacre our compatriots, and occupy the port of Haiphong as well as other provinces lying along the rivers.

That is not all. They have gone so far as to mobilize their naval, land, and air forces and send us many ultimatums. They have massacred old people, women, and children in Hanoi, the capital, itself.

On December 19, 1946, at 8 P.M., Hanoi was attacked.

The French colonialists' actions aimed at invading our country are glaring and undeniable.

The Vietnamese people are now facing two alternatives: either to stay with hands bound and heads bowed as slaves again, or to struggle to the end to win back freedom and independence.

No! The Vietnamese people cannot accept foreign domination being imposed on them again.

No! The Vietnamese people never want to be enslaved again. They would prefer to die than lose their independence and freedom.

French people! We have affection for you and sincerely want to cooperate with you within the framework of the French Union because we have a common ideal which is freedom, equality, and independence.

It is the reactionary French colonialists who have blemished France's honor and are seeking to divide us by provoking a war. As soon as France acknowledges our independence and unification and calls back home the bellicose French colonialists, friendly relations and cooperation between the peoples of Viet-Nam and France will be restored immediately.

French soldiers! There is no grudge or rancor between us. It is for the sake of their selfish interests that the reactionary colonialists provoke clashes. Profits will be theirs, death yours, and medals of victory will be conferred on the militarists. But for you and your families, there is only suffering and poverty. Think it over and think again. Can you be content with sacrificing your bones and blood and your lives for the reactionaries? In joining us you will be treated as friends.

Peoples of the Allied powers! After the recent World War, peace was restored by the democratic countries. However, the French reactionaries trampled underfoot the Atlantic and San Francisco Charters. They are waging an aggressive war in Viet-Nam. They must bear the whole responsibility. The Vietnamese people ask you to intervene.

Compatriots! The Resistance War will be long and fraught with sufferings. Whatever sacrifices we have to make and however long the Resistance War will last, we are determined to fight to the end, until Viet-Nam is completely independent and unified. We are 20 million against 100,000 colonialists. Our victory is firmly guaranteed.

On behalf of the Government of the Democratic Republic of Viet-Nam, I give the following orders to the Armymen, self-defense guards, militiamen, and compatriots in the three parts of Viet-Nam:

1. If the French troops attack us, we must fiercely counterattack them with all the weapons at our disposal. All Vietnamese people must stand up to safeguard their Fatherland.

2. We must protect the lives and property of foreign residents and treat the prisoners of war well.

3. Those who collaborate with the enemy will be punished. Those who help and defend their country will be rewarded.

Compatriots!

The Fatherland is in danger. All of us must rise up!

Long live independent and united Viet-Nam!

Long live the successful Resistance War!

LETTER TO THE FRENCH
GOVERNMENT, NATIONAL ASSEMBLY,
AND PEOPLE

(January 7, 1947)

On behalf of the Vietnamese Government and people, I solemnly declare to you that:

1. The Vietnamese people are not fighting France and the French people. The Vietnamese people still feel friendship and admiration for France and the French people and have confidence in them.

2. The Vietnamese people sincerely wish to cooperate with the French people like brothers on a basis of sincerity and equality.

3. The Vietnamese people want only independence and national unity within the framework of the French Union, a union created on the basis of free consent.

4. The Vietnamese people want only peace, a genuine peace to build their country with the cooperation of honest French friends.

5. The Vietnamese people guarantee not only to respect France's economic and cultural interests in Viet-Nam but also to help these interests to develop further for the benefit of both countries.

6. The Vietnamese people have been dragged into an atrocious self-defense war by the policy of violence and aggression of the representatives of France in Indochina. These representatives are seeking every possible means to divide our people, divide our Fatherland,

infringe upon our national sovereignty, prevent us from demanding our independence, and sabotage the sincere cooperation between the peoples of Viet-Nam and France.

7. In order to reestablish peace, we only need to (a) return immediately to the situation before November 20 and December 17, 1946, and genuinely stop hostilities throughout Viet-Nam; (b) immediately carry out the work that various committees have mapped out to implement the September 14, 1946, *modus vivendi.* These committees must hold their meetings in Saigon or Hanoi, but not in Da Lat; (c) immediately resume the negotiations begun at Fontainebleau in order to find a long-term solution to the question of relations between Viet-Nam and France.

Many towns and villages have been destroyed, thousands of Vietnamese women, children, and old people have been massacred by air attack and cannon. Many young French and Vietnamese soldiers have been killed or wounded. Ruins are heaping upon ruins, much blood has been shed.

The French Government and people need make only one gesture to stop this calamity: that is, to recognize Viet-Nam's independence and unification; peace and order will then be restored immediately. The Vietnamese people are waiting for this gesture.

Long live new France!

Long live independent and unified Viet-Nam!

Long live Viet-Nam–France friendship!

APPEAL TO THE COMPATRIOTS
TO CARRY OUT DESTRUCTION,
TO WAGE THE RESISTANCE WAR*
(February 6, 1947)

Compatriots who love our country,
Why must we wage the Resistance War?

Because if we do not wage the Resistance War, the French will occupy our country once more. They will enslave our people once more. They will force our people to be their coolies and soldiers, and to pay them every kind of taxes. They will suppress all our democratic freedoms. They will plunder all our land and property. They will terrorize and massacre our brothers, sisters, and relatives. They will burn down or destroy our houses, pagodas, and temples. You will realize this by seeing what they have done in Hanoi and Haiphong.

Because we do not want to be buffaloes and horses to the French,

---

* As a result of this scorched-earth appeal, all European-type dwellings and installations were destroyed in one massive wave of countrywide vandalism within all the areas under D.R.V.N. control. As a British specialist was to observe about a similar phenomenon in the Viet-Cong areas of South Viet-Nam (and including Amercan-wrought destruction as well): "Social leveling makes the burden of the 'protracted war' a little lighter to bear. The less one has to lose the less hardship one will feel." (Dennis J. Duncanson, "How and Why the Viet Cong Holds Out," Encounter, December, 1966.)—ED.

because we must protect our country, we must fight the French colonialists.

To fight we must carry out destruction. If we do not do so, the French will. If our houses are solid enough to be used as bases, they will mobilize tanks and vessels to attack us, and they will burn or plunder all our property. This is why we must carry out destruction before the French can make use of our property. Suppose we want to keep sluices, roads, and houses for our own use, we can't, because the French will occupy all or destroy all.

Now we must carry out destruction to stop them, to prevent them from advancing, and from using our roads and houses.

For the sake of the Fatherland we must make sacrifices and endure hardships for a certain time. When the Resistance comes out victorious, we will pool our forces for construction and repair work and this will not be difficult at all.

On the battlefront the fighters are sacrificing their lives for the Fatherland without regret; why do we regret a section of road, a sluice, or a house which the French can use to attack our Fatherland?

You all love your country, no doubt you will have no heart to regret so.

Therefore, I earnestly call on you to exert all your efforts to carry out destruction work. We must destroy roads widely and deeply so that the French cannot use them. A pick stroke into the roads has the value of a bullet shot by our soldiers at the enemy.

I solemnly promise to you that after victory, I will endeavor to repair everything with you. We will build more beautiful roads, bridges, and sluices and better houses worthy of a free and independent nation.

Long live our victorious Resistance War!

Long live independent Viet-Nam!

LETTER TO COMRADES
IN NORTH VIET-NAM
(March 1, 1947)

Comrades in North Viet-Nam,

I do not have time to meet you to take part in the criticism, review, and discussion of public affairs. I am very sorry that the circumstances do not allow me to do so. Thus, I am sending you a few words and hope that you will pay attention to them:

1. Now that our nation is at the crossroads, to die or to live, to perish or to exist, each comrade and the whole organization must devote all their heart and strength to turn the entire people in one direction aiming at one goal: to drive out the French colonialists and bring unity and independence to the country.

That is why each comrade and the whole organization must be clearsighted, clever, careful, resolute, industrious, and single-minded.

2. This long Resistance War is the national revolution at a high level. At present, each comrade's thoughts and deeds have great importance for the whole country. The negligence of a man can bring a major affair to failure. Little errors can bring about disastrous results.

Therefore, we must absolutely get rid of the following shortcomings:

a) *Localism.* Heeding only the interests of one's own locality without taking into account the interests of the whole country. Taking care only of the organ where one is working. Owing to these shortcomings, there may occur things that seem of minor importance at first glance but that are in reality harmful to the common plan. To take an example: to grasp as many cadres and materials as possible for one's locality, unwilling to let the higher authorities move the cadres and materials to where they are needed.

b) *Sectarianism*. To listen to those who are on good terms with oneself even when they are wrong, and to make use of them even when they have no ability. To discard those who are at variance with oneself even when they are gifted, and refuse to listen to them however right they might be. This is a very harmful shortcoming. It deprives the organization of cadres and unity, and always brings the work to failure. This is a very dangerous habit.

c) *Militarism and bureaucracy*. To behave like a small king when in charge of a region. To be arrogant and high-handed. To belittle one's superiors and abuse one's authority and weigh heavily upon one's subalterns. To frighten the people by a haughty bearing. This despotic state of mind has brought about much ill-feeling and discord, and dug the gap between the higher and the lower levels, the organizations and the people.

d) *Narrow-mindedness*. We must bear in mind that everyone has his strong and weak points. We must make use of his strong points and help him to correct his shortcomings. To use people is like using wood. A skilled worker can make use of all kinds of wood whether it is big or small, straight or curved. Narrow-mindedness leads to petty deeds and it results in many enemies and few friends. A narrow-minded man receives little assistance from the others. And a narrow-minded organization cannot thrive.

e) *Formalism*. Questions are not considered for their practical results or urgency, but only for showing off. For example, at present, military training aims only at handling guns, daggers, hand grenades, turning to account topographical conditions, cleverly moving in the dark and reconnoitering; in a word, to train everybody for guerrilla warfare. But in many localities time is devoted only to training on parade. This is like practicing music for putting out a fire.

In other places, the forms of propaganda are limited to writing slogans, hanging flags and banderoles, embellishing the information houses, and setting up tribunes for form's sake, but they never go to the people to give them explanations, to help them thoroughly understand the policies of the organization.

f) *Paper work.* Love of red tape. To sit in one's office and send out orders without going to the spot to check the carrying out of the work and to map out plans for the good implementation of the instructions and resolutions of the organization. They are not aware whether the instructions and resolutions sent by the higher levels to the localities can be carried out or not. This style of work is very harmful. It prevents us from closely following the movement and form grasping the real situation. Therefore, many of our policies are not carried out thoroughly.

g) *Indiscipline, lax discipline.* In some war-stricken regions, a number of comrades have, of their own initiative, left their localities and gone to work in other places without decision of the higher levels of their organization. Thus, these comrades have not only shown a weak spirit, doing what is easy or to their liking and giving up what is difficult or not to their liking, but also they disregard the discipline of the organization and throw disorder in the ranks of the organization.

In many places, the comrades who committed errors were not punished adequately. There were comrades who have been demoted in one place but kept their former rank when going to another, or demoted only for form's sake but in reality kept their former position.

There were comrades who deserved punishment but for personal reasons were only criticized or given a warning for form's sake. In other places there were also people who went so far as to screen the others' mistakes and forgive one another, deceive the higher levels, and conceal their mistakes from the organization. Such ways of carrying out discipline not only prevent the guilty from correcting their mistakes but also make them trifle with discipline. Worse still, lax discipline will provide occasions for the reactionary elements to sneak into our ranks to sabotage our organization.

h) *Selfishness, debauchery.* There are comrades who still suffer from megalomania. They are out for a position in some committee or chairmanship. Others indulge in good food and fine clothing, try to turn public property into their own, abuse their authority or job to indulge in trading transactions and get rich, think more of their private business than public affairs. Revolutionary virtues and public opinion are of no significance to them.

There are comrades who are conceited and self-complacent, believing that as former political detainees or members of the Viet Minh Front, they are more competent than anyone else, and matchless. It is true that the imperialists' jails are schools for them, and the Viet Minh Front is an organization of patriots who devote themselves to national salvation. But it is certain that outside the Viet Minh there are still many able, talented people whom the Viet Minh has not yet succeeded in organizing. Besides, if the political prisoners and members of the Viet Minh Front are the best, does it mean that all those who have not had the honor to be in jail or those who have not joined the Viet Minh Front have no talent and are of no use at all?

Each of us must be modest. The more veteran and talented we are the greater must be our modesty. We must have a yearning for progress and keep in mind our teacher's words: "To learn, to learn, and to learn." Conceit and self-complacency will but hinder our progress.

Some comrades are still in the habit of thinking that "When one man is mandarin his whole family will profit." They give positions to their friends and relatives without heeding the disastrous results caused to the organization, provided that theirs get positions.

Although you have in general many qualities, such as perseverance, thoroughness, resourcefulness, and initiative, these are invaluable qualities which serve as bases for the development of other virtues. But in this period of great difficulties and heavy tasks, those qualities are not enough. Only if you make use of this good basis resolutely to correct the above-mentioned shortcomings are we certain to come to complete success.

3. You must do your utmost to carry out the following points:

a) Our organization must be militarized. Mind and deeds must be in absolute harmony. Our organization is the vanguard unit and if we are at variance when launching an assault we'll have no hope of victory. Not only must our organization be single-minded but the army, the people, and the administration also should be of one mind.

b) The right men must be chosen for the leading organs, with defined power and responsibility, close connection with one another, close cooperation.

Abuse of power, pluralism, conflict, showing off, and jealousy regarding responsible posts must be absolutely avoided.

At the moment, the question of leading organs is of utmost importance. Great care should be taken to appoint members of these organs, but once they are appointed, there must be absolute obedience. Only when the inferiors obey their superiors can things go smoothly.

c) Liaison and communications between provinces and zones and between Trung Bo, Nam Bo, and Bac Bo must be firmly maintained. Communications being the circulation of everything, if communications are cut off there would be great difficulties for all things. Good communications will make everything easy.

I hope that you will devote all your revolutionary spirit to overcome your shortcomings, develop your qualities, unite your efforts, strengthen inner solidarity and broaden your ranks, reorganize your work to lead the whole people enthusiastically to wage the Resistance War to a glorious victory.

LETTER TO THE VIETNAMESE
PEOPLE AFTER THE MEETING WITH
PAUL MUS, REPRESENTATIVE OF THE
FRENCH HIGH COMMISSIONER BOLLAERT*
(May 25, 1947)

Compatriots, armymen, militiamen, and self-defense guards throughout the country.

Up to now, our entire people have waged the Resistance War for five months. Our southern compatriots have waged the Resistance War for twenty months.

The French have shed much blood, our people have made no less sacrifices.

For the sake of humanity and peace, for the maintenance of the sympathy with France, our Government has proposed to the French Government to find ways and means to stop war by negotiations on the basis of our people's aspirations for unity and independence.

But the French colonialist militarists are used to atrocity, in-

---

* *Professor Paul Mus, one of France's most respected Viet-Nam scholars, served as a paratroop captain in the French Army. Sent to Indochina as an adviser to the French High Commissioner, he advocated negotiations with Ho Chi Minh. In May, 1947, he carried a French peace plan to Ho. Against Mus's objections, the plan contained a demand that Ho surrender all his foreign advisers to the French, a condition that was clearly unacceptable. Ho refused, and the war continued until France was defeated in 1954.*—ED.

humanity, and impoliteness. They hold our Army and people in contempt. They put forth arrogant and unacceptable conditions.

They asked us (1) to surrender them all our weapons, (2) to give the French Army freedom to move everywhere in our country, etc.

This means that they want us to surrender. They want to strangle our Fatherland. They want us to give them a free hand to burn down villages, plunder our property, massacre our people, rape women, and destroy temples, pagodas, and churches. This means that they want all our compatriots and our offspring to kneel down and bow our heads and be their everlasting slaves.

Compatriots! Armymen, militiamen, and self-defense guards!

We are determined not to let our mothers, fathers, and relatives be killed by them. We are determined not to let our wives and sisters be violated by them. We are determined not to let our churches, villages, and our people's property be plundered by them. We are determined not to be enslaved.

Therefore, on behalf of the Government, I call on all my compatriots to make every effort in taking part in the Resistance and help the Army to fight the enemy.

I order that all armymen, militiamen, and self-defense guards be determined to fight, to go forward and kill the enemy.

Each citizen must be a fighter. Each village must be a fortress. We must be determined to sacrifice ourselves in struggle in order to smash the colonialist militarists and reconquer unity and independence.

Compatriots! Fighters!

Our Fatherland is calling on us. Victory is awaiting us. March forward, march forward!

The long-term Resistance will certainly win!

Long live united and independent Viet-Nam!

MESSAGE TO THE COMPATRIOTS THROUGHOUT THE COUNTRY ON THE SECOND ANNIVERSARY OF INDEPENDENCE DAY

(September 2, 1947)

On the second anniversary of Independence Day, together with our compatriots, the Government and I review the work done in order to think of tasks to come.

Our Difficulties

a) *Economic difficulties*. The Government came into existence after our country had been oppressed and exploited for eighty years, at a time when our people were driven to poverty, our resources exhausted, and our economy in ruins. There were, in addition, broken dikes and floods. More than 2 million people died of starvation.

b) *Military difficulties*. Hardly had the Government been set up for a few weeks when the French aggressors occupied Nam Bo and unleashed the war.

c) *Political difficulties*. After less than one month of existence, the Government strove to save the compatriots in the North from starvation and gave help to the compatriots in the South in their struggle against the invaders, while there was a group of people who boasted to be revolutionaries but did not cooperate with the Government. They disturbed the people and sabotaged order, wishing to provoke the civil war.

In short, the Government carries the burden while there is worry at home and danger from outside, with all kinds of difficulties.

Reconstruction of the Country

However, with the support of the whole people and confident in the glorious destiny of the Fatherland, the Government made great efforts to overcome all difficulties. and hardships and scored a few achievements.

a) *In the economic field.* Together with the people, the Government repaired the dikes, increased production, abolished the poll tax, reduced taxes, saved people from starvation, and improved the people's living standard. The Government still has to build independent finance for the country.

b) *In the military field.* By its own strength, the Government set up a national army, trained millions of militiamen and self-defense guards for the defense of the Fatherland against the foreign aggressors.

c) *In the political field.* In spite of the reactionaries' schemes of sabotage, our Government and people completed the free general elections. It was the first time in our history that the people enjoyed democratic freedoms and rights, electing their represen.atives to take care of public affairs. Besides, the National Assembly intended to issue our first Constitution.

d) *In the educational field.* Owing to the encouragement of the Government, the clearsightedness of the cadres of mass education, and the compatriots' enthusiasm, in addition to the building up of new secondary and higher education, the training of specialists and gifted people, and the development of the arts, we smashed to pieces the French colonialists' policy of obscurantism. In two years, more than 4 million people of both sexes were taught to read and write and there were villages and communes which had completely wiped out illiteracy. This was a glorious achievement especially at a time when we were short of everything. Had the French colonialists not provoked the war, we would certainly have won greater achievements in these two years.

Resistance War for National Salvation

We are peace-loving people, and our Government wishes its people to live in peace and work peacefully. We want to cooperate in friendship with the French people for the benefit of both sides. That is why we signed the March 6 Agreement and the September 14 *modus vivendi.*

But the French reactionary colonialists broke their word: they meant to occupy our country and enslave us once more. They launched a war, founded a puppet government in order to divide our people and occupy our country.

Facing that barbarous aggression, our Government, army, and people have united together into a bronze wall, determined to defend the Fatherland.

Thanks to our solidarity and unbending spirit, after two years of Resistance in the South and nine months of Resistance throughout the country, the enemy forces are more exhausted with every passing day while the more we fight the stronger and more enthusiastic we become.

Experience of other countries and of our national history shows us that: The American Revolution for national liberation was successful after eight years of struggle; the French Revolution lasted five years, the Russian Revolution six years, and the Chinese Revolution fifteen years.

Our forefathers fought against foreign aggression for five years under the Tran dynasty and ten years under the Le dynasty before winning victory.

Therefore, if France sincerely recognizes the unity and independence of our country, our Government and people are ready to cooperate with her, but if the French colonialists maintain their policy of strength and plot to divide us, we are resolved to continue the Resistance War until we win unity and independence.

On this glorious and solemn day, on behalf of the Government, I call on all the compatriots, all the combatants, the compatriots in the occupied zones, Vietnamese residents abroad, to put their trust in the glorious destiny of the Fatherland, in our solidarity and fighting spirit. We should clench our teeth to endure hardships and fight with all our strength. However long the Resistance War may be, it is worth it, as it will smash the yoke of slavery of more than eighty years and bring about freedom for thousands of years to come. The officers and men on the battlefront, the compatriots in the rear, all should unite closely and strive to put into practice the four words Industriousness, Thriftiness, Probity, and Righteousness, and our Resistance War will win.

On behalf of the Government and compatriots, I convey fraternal greetings to the Asian brother peoples, the French people, and the brother peoples of the French colonies.

The whole people closely unite together!

Overthrow the French reactionary colonialists!

Long live the friendship between the Vietnamese and French peoples!

Long live the fraternal feelings of the Asian great family!

The Resistance War will win!

Long live united and independent Viet-Nam!

TWELVE RECOMMENDATIONS
(April 5, 1948)

The nation has its root in the people.

In the Resistance War and national reconstruction, the main force lies in the people. Therefore, all the people in the army, administration, and mass organizations who are in contact or live with the people must remember and carry out the following twelve recommendations.

Six forbiddances:

1. Not to do what is likely to damage the land and crops or spoil the houses and belongings of the people.

2. Not to insist on buying or borrowing what the people are not willing to sell or lend.

3. Not to bring living hens into the mountain people's houses.

4. Never to break your word.

5. Not to give offense to people's faith and customs (such as to lie down before the altar, to raise the feet over the hearth, to play music in the house, etc.).

6. Not to do or speak what is likely to make people believe that we hold them in contempt.

Six permissibles:

1. To help the people in their daily work (harvesting, fetching firewood, carrying water, sewing, etc.).

2. Whenever possible, to buy commodities for those who live far from markets (knives, salt, needles, thread, pen, paper, etc.).

3. In spare time, to tell amusing, simple, and short stories useful to the Resistance, but not betraying secrets.

4. To teach the population the national script and elementary hygiene.

5. To study the customs of each region so as to be acquainted with them in order to create an atmosphere of sympathy first, then gradually to explain to the people to abate their superstitions.

6. To show to the people that you are correct, diligent, and disciplined.

STIMULATING POEM

The above-mentioned twelve recommendations
Are feasible to all.
He who loves his country,
Will never forget them.
When the people have a habit,
All are like one man.
With good armymen and good people,
Everything will be crowned with success.
Only when the root is firm, can the tree live long,
And victory is built with the people as foundation.

APPEAL FOR
PATRIOTIC EMULATION
(August 1, 1949)

Lately I have been too busy with the Resistance War and have rarely had opportunities to talk to you, compatriots and fighters. So today I first of all convey my affectionate greetings to you: elders; personalities; political, administrative, and technical cadres; compatriots at home and abroad and in the enemy-occupied area; young people and pioneers. I convey my affectionate greetings to you: all officers and men in the army, militia, and guerrilla forces; our workers in the workshops of the Ministry of National Defense.

Today is the first day of a new drive of patriotic emulation, so I will only speak of emulation.

Since the August Revolution, the world has been struck with wonder and admiration for us, for three reasons. First, we brought our revolution to success, broke the colonialists' fetters, overthrew feudalism, and set up a democratic republic.

Second, not only can we lead the Resistance War, but we are sure of victory.

Third, we are carrying out patriotic emulation while fighting.

We began to compete with one another in June last year. The emulation drive has three aims: to wipe out famine, ignorance, and foreign invasion. Despite the lack of means and experience and the widespread destruction wrought by the French, we scored many good results after a year of emulation.

It is thanks to our compatriots, who did their utmost to increase production, that despite some difficulties we were able to stave off famine. Other countries experienced more difficulties than we in wartime.

It is thanks to our compatriots' enthusiastic support and the mass education fighters' devotedness that several provinces such as Quang Ngai, Ha Tinh, Hung Yen, and Thai Binh have almost wiped out illiteracy. Other provinces are striving to keep pace with the former. This is a glorious achievement when compared with the fact that we had less than half a million pupils under the colonialist regime in 1941.

It is thanks to the entire people's full support, the heroism of the army, the militia, and the guerrilla fighters, and the workers' efforts in turning out weapons that we have won many glorious victories from North to South. The colonialists themselves had to admit that our army has made much progress and the French Army is unable to defeat it.

Apart from these main endeavors, our compatriots practiced emulation in many other respects, and the achievements they scored are no less glorious. Here are some examples.

People's organizations and individuals competed in sponsoring the army and militia, namely in the province of Ha Tinh, which collected tens of millions of dongs for them.

Old women emulated with one another in joining the Association of Fighters' Mothers.

The entire people competed in buying Resistance bonds, in contributing Resistance duties and taxes. Women, though exempt, also emulated with one another in affording their contribution.

Old men and women emulated in organizing guerrilla units.

The youth emulated in enlisting.

Office workers emulated in improving the style of work.

Pioneers emulated in studying and helping grown-up people. Many of them sent me money in contribution to the Resistance funds.

Vietnamese nationals abroad and compatriots in the enemy-occupied area also emulated according to their abilities.

In brief, everybody emulated, every task was accomplished with emulation and success. On this occasion, on behalf of the Government I thank and congratulate our compatriots and fighters.

The more achievements we score, the clearer we see our shortcomings. Here are the main shortcomings for us to set right:

In many places, our people, particularly our cadres, do not clearly grasp the significance of the patriotic emulation movement. This results in the following shortcomings:

To misrepresent emulation as something different from daily activities. In truth these are the basis for emulation. For instance, hitherto we have been eating, dressing, living. Now we must emulate in eating, dressing, and living according to the rules of hygiene in order to prevent diseases. Hitherto we have been tilling the land. Now we must emulate in fertilizing the soil and increasing production. This is the way we must emulate in everything.

To misrepresent emulation as a temporary job. In truth it must be continuous. We must emulate to lead the Resistance War to victory, to build the country successfully.

In many instances, emulation plans are not appropriate to the circumstances nor to the locality. In some places, they are too ambitious to be achieved. In other places, emulation is at first carried out so intensively that it cannot be continued after some time for lack of strength. In still other places, each organization and each branch has its own plans, but their plans do not harmonize with each other. As a result, contradiction prevails, the people are up to their ears in work, unable to carry out all these plans and at a loss as to the plan to follow.

Experiences of success or of failure are numerous but they are not exchanged between different localities for the benefit of all. In certain places, emulation committees only work according to orders from the higher level ones. Thus an instruction issued by the central committee reaches the village committee through the regional, provincial, and district committees without inquiries as to whether it suits each locality.

These are our main shortcomings which we are determined to set right. The essential point is clearly to explain to everyone how patriotic emulation is beneficial to him, to his family, to his village, and to his country. Once everyone has thoroughly understood this, all difficulties can be settled and all shortcomings set right.

At present, as the Resistance War has reached the stage of pushing forward the struggle and preparing for the general counteroffensive, the patriotic emulation movement must also be aimed at this goal. Therefore, the emulation program at this stage still deals with the elimination of famine, ignorance, and foreign invasion, but at a higher tempo.

In the cultural field, in the places where illiteracy has been wiped out, people must emulate in further study. In other places, people must emulate in eradicating illiteracy. Writers and artists must emulate in creative work. Technicians must emulate in making discoveries. In the economic field, emulation must be carried out in supplying the people and army with enough food, clothes, and commodities to fight the enemy. In the military field, the People's Army, the militia, and guerrilla fighters must emulate in training cadres and reorganizing the army. Workshops must emulate in turning out weapons in great quantity, quickly, and well.

Moreover, we must emulate in every task that is beneficial to the national welfare and the people's livelihood and related to the Resistance and national construction. Emulation must be undertaken by the whole people and in all fields.

In patriotic emulation, virtues such as Industriousness, Thrift, Probity, and Righteousness must be highlighted.

The slogan for patriotic emulation at present is: All for victory. Victory over the colonialists. Victory over ignorance. Victory over famine. Victory over our defects.

I am sure that with the experiences in emulation we gained last year, and with the enthusiasm of our compatriots and fighters, patriotic emulation will undoubtedly score great success just as a protracted Resistance War will end in great victory. I hope that our compatriots and fighters will strive to go forward!

Furthermore, our compatriots and fighters must also keep in mind that the French colonialists suffered many defeats last spring. Their plot to use the puppets to hoodwink our people also failed. Therefore, this autumn and winter, they are striving to muster up their forces and launch rash and sudden attacks in an attempt to reverse the situation by force. We will meet with more difficulties than before. I always say: The nearer we are to victory the more difficulties we will meet with. I hope that all our compatriots and fighters will eagerly emulate and overcome all difficulties to win victory.

Our country will be genuinely independent and unified.

Our people will be really prosperous and strong.

DECLARATION OF THE GOVERNMENT OF THE DEMOCRATIC REPUBLIC OF VIET-NAM TO THE GOVERNMENTS OF THE COUNTRIES ALL OVER THE WORLD*
(January 14, 1950)

After the August, 1945, Revolution had overthrown the domination of the Japanese and French imperialists in Viet-Nam, the Democratic Republic of Viet-Nam was established. On September, 1945, the Provisional Government of the Democratic Republic of Viet-Nam read its Declaration of Independence to the Vietnamese people and the world. On March 3, 1946, the Vietnamese National Assembly elected the Government of Viet-Nam.

On September 23, 1945, the French colonialists attacked South Viet-Nam. After that, France signed with Viet-Nam on March 6, 1946, the Preliminary Agreement, and on September 14, 1946, the

* After this declaration was issued, the governments of the People's Republic of China, the Soviet Union, and the other People's Democracies successively recognized the Government of the Democratic Republic of Viet-Nam and established diplomatic relations with it. Since then the Democratic Republic of Viet-Nam has officially sided with the socialist camp headed by the Soviet Union. This was a most important political success which created conditions for the other successes of the Vietnamese people's resistance.

197

modus vivendi. But the French colonialists have carried on their unjust war in defiance of the peaceful aspirations of the French people. They have set up the puppet Bao Dai Government and used it as a tool to invade Viet-Nam and deceive the world.

Determined to safeguard their national independence from the French colonialists, the Vietnamese people and army are fighting heroically and are nearing final victory. Throughout these years of resistance, Viet-Nam has won the sympathy and support of the people of the world. The Government of the Democratic Republic of Viet-Nam declares to the Governments of the countries of the world that it is the only lawful Government of the entire Vietnamese people. On the basis of common interests, it is ready to establish diplomatic relations with the Governments of all countries which respect the equality, territorial sovereignty, and national independence of Viet-Nam in order to contribute to safeguarding peace and building world democracy.

ANSWERS TO QUESTIONS PUT BY THE PRESS REGARDING U.S. INTERVENTION IN INDOCHINA

(July 25, 1950)

Question: What is, Mr. President, the present situation of the U.S. imperialists' interventionist policy in Indochina?

Answer: The U.S. imperialists have of late openly interfered in Indochina's affairs. It is with their money and weapons and their instructions that the French colonialists have been waging war in Viet-Nam, Cambodia, and Laos.

However, the U.S. imperialists are intensifying their plot to discard the French colonialists so as to gain complete control over Indochina. That is why they do their utmost to redouble their direct intervention in every field—military, political, and economic. It is also for this reason that the contradictions between them and the French colonialists become sharper and sharper.

Question: What influence does this intervention exert on the Indochinese people?

Answer: The U.S. imperialists supply their henchmen with armaments to massacre the Indochinese people. They dump their goods in Indochina to prevent the development of local handicrafts. Their pornographic culture contaminates the youth in areas placed under their control. They follow the policy of buying up, deluding, and dividing our people. They drag some bad elements into becoming their tools and use them to invade our country.

Question: What measure shall we take against them?

Answer: To gain independence, we, the Indochinese people, must defeat the French colonialists, our number-one enemy. At the same time, we will struggle against the U.S. interventionists. The deeper their interference, the more powerful are our solidarity and our struggle. We will expose their maneuvers before all our people, especially those living in areas under their control. We will expose all those who serve as lackeys for the U.S. imperialists to coerce, deceive, and divide our people.

The close solidarity between the peoples of Viet-Nam, Cambodia, and Laos constitutes a force capable of defeating the French colonialists and the U.S. interventionists. The U.S. imperialists failed in China, they will fail in Indochina.

We are still laboring under great difficulties but victory will certainly be ours.

INSTRUCTIONS GIVEN AT THE CONFERENCE REVIEWING THE SECOND LE HONG PHONG MILITARY CAMPAIGN*

(1950)

About this review conference, I have some opinions:

At this conference, there are officers who directly took part in the campaign and are back here to review both their achievements and shortcomings. There are also cadres and officers from the various interzones, army units, and public services who did not take part in the campaign but who are here to learn experiences. To make criticism and self-criticism, to review our work, and to learn from our experiences are very good things which should be developed into a style of work in the army, administration, and mass organizations. In this review, I want to draw your attention to some points.

1. Heighten discipline. Discipline must be observed at all levels. Critical reviews must be made at all levels, from lower levels upward and from higher levels downward. We must help all the men and offi-

---

* The Cao Bang–Bac Can–Lang Son campaign. In the course of this campaign, between September and November, 1950, the newly Chinese-trained People's Army units destroyed piecemeal 7,000 French troops stationed along the Chinese border. By gaining full control of the Sino-Vietnamese border area, the Communists assured themselves of an unlimited source of weapons and supplies, and the French lost all chances of winning (or even stalemating) the Indochina War.—ED.

cers of the army to understand thoroughly the necessity for this work. Only then can we achieve success.

2. *Strictly carry out orders from higher levels.* Orders from higher levels must be unconditionally and strictly carried out. There is a Chinese proverb saying that "military orders are as firm as mountains," that is, whenever an order from a higher level is issued, it must be carried out at any cost. Don't misunderstand democracy. When no decision is yet taken, we are free to discuss. But when a decision is taken, we should not discuss any longer. Any discussion then could be only discussion on the ways and means to carry out the decision quickly and not to propose that it should not be carried out. We must prohibit any such act of unruly freedom.

3. *Love the soldiers.* The officers must love the men under their command. As regards sick armymen or invalids, the officers must look after them and inquire into their health. The commanders and political commissars must be the brothers, sisters, and friends of the soldiers. So long as they are not so, they have not yet fulfilled their tasks. Only when officers are close to soldiers, like the limbs of the same body, can the soldiers love the officers like their kith and kin. Only so can the instructions, orders, and plans from higher ranks be actively and strictly implemented by the armymen. We must congratulate and reward all armymen who have achieved meritorious services, promote all progressive officers and men, especially those who have a long service in the army.

4. *Respect the people.* We must respect the people. There are many ways of showing respect to the people. It is not sufficient to greet people in a polite manner. We must not waste the manpower and property of the people. When mobilizing the people, we must see to it that their contributions do not exceed the requirements in order to avoid waste. We must avoid anything which is prejudicial to the people's life. To know how to assist the people is also to respect them. Help them to harvest crops and organize literary classes for local militia and armymen.

5. *Take good care of public property and war booty.* Public property is the fruit of the collective labor of the people. The army must preserve and take good care of it and must not waste it. Put an end to such acts as selling the rice contributed by the people, damaging tools, and wasting ammunition.

War booty is also public property. It belongs to the nation, not to the enemy. Munitions, medicine, equipment, and food are the sweat and blood of our people. Our soldiers had to shed blood to recover them. We must prize and take good care of them, and not waste them or make them our personal property. When looking after them, we must arrange them neatly and protect them carefully against rain and sun.

6. *Sincerely make criticism and self-criticism.* In your reports to the conference, you must pay attention to this point. When making criticism and self-criticism, we must sincerely expose our shortcomings. If we make mistakes but don't want to expose them, that is like a patient who refuses to tell his disease to the doctor. When we do a lot of work it is difficult for us to avoid making mistakes. So we use the method of criticism and self-criticism to help one another in correcting our errors; we are determined to correct them in order to make progress together. Besides exposing our shortcomings, we must also report our achievements in order to develop them. In order to achieve good results in criticism and self-criticism, cadres at all levels, especially high-ranking cadres, must *be exemplary before anyone else.*

Many experiences, good and bad alike, may be drawn from this campaign. We must review them, popularize them and learn from them. They may be summed up in the following main points:

1. The leadership of the Central Committee is clearsighted. The leading committees at all levels have also adopted correct lines of leadership. The various organs of the army, mass organizations, and administration have united, closely coordinated their actions, and adopted a unified plan of work.

2. Our soldiers are very zealous and heroic. This has been amply proved by the examples of the man who had his broken arm chopped off to facilitate his movement in the assault, of another man who rushed into an enemy stronghold with a charge of dynamite in his hands, or of many others who did not eat anything for three or four days but continued to fight with all their ardor and heroism, and other examples.

3. Our people are very good. Never before have such big contingents of women of the Kinh, Man, Tho, Nung, and other nationalities volunteered to carry supplies to the front as in the recent campaign. Hardship, privation, and danger could not lessen their ardor, cheerfulness, and heroism. That is really admirable. This is partly thanks to Comrade Tran Dang Ninh and other cadres of the Viet Bac

Interzone who have correctly implemented the policies of the Party and the Government and partly to the ardent patriotism and self-sacrificing spirit of our compatriots.

4. The enemy was subjective and underestimated his adversary. He did not think that we were so powerful or could make such rapid progress. That is why he did not take appropriate measures of defense, and exposed his weaknesses.

These are major experiences which must be pointed out in the reviewing report.

I also draw your attention to the following points:

1. Concerning propaganda work. In practice, the enemy has been making much more propaganda for us than we have ourselves. We have not concentrated all means and mobilized all our abilities for propaganda. That is why our information is still very slow and does not reach broad masses. The campaign closed on October 15, yet until October 30, the people and cadres in many localities did not yet know anything or only knew very little of it. Or if they had heard about it, they did not know how to popularize the news. Our propaganda among the prisoners of war and enemy troops, as well as abroad, is still very weak. We did not know how to make excerpts from enemy newspapers which expressed anger at the colonialist military commanders, politicians, and administrative authorities who only cared for having a good time and disputed about personal interests while their soldiers died on the battlefields "without a wreath being laid or a tear being shed for them." We have failed to capitalize on this material to write leaflets for agitation among the enemy's ranks, give explanations to the prisoners of war, and make propaganda among the population in enemy-held areas.

2. Let us not indulge in subjectivism and underestimate the enemy. Do not indulge in naïve subjectivism and think that from now on victory will always be ours and there will be no more difficulties or failure. This victory is only a preliminary success. We still have to make great efforts and win many more victories like this or even greater ones before we can switch over to a general counteroffensive. From now to the day of complete victory, we shall meet with many difficulties and perhaps shall go through many failures. In a war, to win a victory or suffer a defeat are common things. The essential is that we must win final victory. We must help all officers and men and the people to bear that firmly in mind so that they will not be self-complacent when winning and disappointed when losing, but instead will always make utmost efforts to overcome difficulties and hardships and advance toward final victory.

Do not underestimate the enemy. The enemy is pulling himself in, not to lie still, but actually to leap forward again. He is striving to win time and prepare to hit back. In the meantime, they will seek to bomb and strafe the areas under our control with the aim of intimidating us, as was the case in Ha Giang, Tuyen Quang, and Bac Giang recently.

3. We must win time. We too must win time in order to make preparations. That is a condition for defeating the opponent. In military affairs, time is of prime importance. Time ranges first among the three factors for victory, before the terrain conditions and the people's support. Only by winning time can we secure the factors for defeating the enemy. It is precisely to win time that this conference should be a short one. The reports must be concise and raise the main and necessary problems. Don't be wordy. This would only waste time and bring no result at all.

4. Lastly, we must keep absolute secrecy. Secrecy is a very important thing. Everybody must keep secrecy. We must seek every means to keep secret all activities and in all circumstances: in an inn, in our talks, and in our work, we must observe secrecy. It is not sufficient for the army and public offices alone to keep secrecy. We must teach the people to keep secrecy if we want to keep our work in complete secrecy. If we succeed in keeping secrecy, that is already one step toward our success.

From all the questions I raise above, this conference should try to solve some. After the conference, if you decide to solve the remaining ones, we will surely succeed in our future battles.

The Party, Government, and people call upon all officers and men to carry out these recommendations.

POLITICAL REPORT READ AT THE SECOND NATIONAL CONGRESS OF THE VIET-NAM WORKERS' PARTY, HELD IN FEBRUARY, 1951

The International Situation in the Past Fifty Years

The first month of 1951 was the closing of the first half and the opening of the second half of the twentieth century. It is a moment of great importance in the history of mankind.

Quicker and more important changes occurred in the past fifty years than in many previous centuries added together.

The cinema, wireless telegraphy, television, and even atomic energy were discovered in the course of these fifty years. Mankind has made a big stride in harnessing nature. Also in this period, passing from free competition to monopoly, capitalism has turned into imperialism.

In these fifty years, the imperialists unleashed two world wars, the most terrible in history. It was in these wars that the Russian, German, Italian, and Japanese imperialists were defeated; the British and French imperialists lost ground; and the U.S. capitalists became the leading imperialists, the leading reactionaries.

Most important of all was the successful Russian October Revolution. The Soviet Union, a socialist country, was established, spreading over one-sixth of the area of the globe. Nearly one-half of the human race has embarked on the path of New Democracy. The oppressed peoples one after another rose up against imperialism and for independence and freedom. The Chinese Revolution was successful. The workers' movement in the imperialist countries grew stronger.

In the same period, in Viet-Nam, our Party, which is now twenty-one years old, was born. We have been independent for six years. Our long-term Resistance War has moved strongly forward and is now five years old.

In a word, many events of great importance occurred in the first half of the twentieth century, and we can venture to say that with the efforts of the revolutionaries, greater and more glorious changes will take place in the second half of this century.

The Birth of Our Party

After World War I, to make up for their heavy losses, the French colonialists invested more capital to do business in our country, grasping more wealth and exploiting more labor power of our people. Meanwhile, the successful Russian Revolution and the boiling Chinese Revolution were exerting deep and extensive influence. As a result, the Vietnamese working class, which was growing up, was enlightened; it began to struggle and needed a vanguard team, a general staff to lead it.

On January 6, 1930,* our Party came into being.

After the success of the Russian October Revolution, Lenin promoted the setting up of the Communist International. Since that time, the international proletariat and the world revolution have become a great family, and our Party is one of its youngest members.

Marx, Engels, Lenin, and Stalin are the common teachers for the world revolution. Comrade Mao Tse-tung has skillfully "Sinicized" the ideology of Marx, Engels, Lenin, and Stalin, correctly applied it to the practical situation of China, and has led the Chinese Revolution to complete victory.†

Owing to geographical, historical, economic, and cultural condi-

---

* The Third National Congress of the Viet-Nam Workers' Party passed a resolution correcting the date of the founding of the Indochinese Communist Party to February 3, 1930. (*This was made necessary by the fact that even the D.R.V.N. itself would alternately cite the opening [January 6] or the closing [February 3] of the Hong Kong Conference as the founding date of the ICP [see p. 127n].*—ED.)

† *This definition of Mao's role is particularly relevant today with regard to North Viet-Nam's attitude toward the Sino-Soviet dispute.*—ED.

tions, the Chinese Revolution exerted a great influence on the Vietnamese revolution, which had to learn and indeed has learned many
experiences from it.

Thanks to the experiences of the Chinese Revolution and to Mao
Tse-tung's thoughts, we have further understood the ideology of
Marx, Engels, Lenin, and Stalin and consequently scored many successes. This the Vietnamese revolutionaries must engrave on their
minds and be grateful for.

As the French colonialists were carrying out a policy of savage
persecution, our Party was born in very difficult circumstances. However, immediately after its founding, our Party led a fierce struggle
against the French colonialists, which climaxed in the days of the
Nghe An Soviet. This was the first time our people held local power
and began to implement, though over a small area, democratic policies.

The Nghe An Soviet failed, but it had a great influence. Its heroism
has always been intense in the heart of the masses of the people and
paved the way for future victories. From 1931 to 1945, always under
the leadership of our Party, the revolutionary movement in Viet-Nam
rose, then ebbed, then rose again. These fifteen years can be divided
into three periods: (1) 1931–35, (2) 1936–39, and (3) 1939–45.

The Period from 1931 to 1935

From 1931 to 1933, the French colonialists pursued a policy of
frantic persecution. Many Party cadres and people we.e arrested and
killed. Almost all Party and mass-organizations were in disintegration. As a result, the revolutionary movement temporarily ebbed.

Thanks to the loyalty and devotion of the remaining comrades, the
determination of the Central Committee, and the assistance of the
brother Parties, from 1933 onward the revolutionary movement
again rose gradually.

At that time, the Party strove, on the one hand, to consolidate its
underground organizations and, on the other, to combine underground work with legal activity, propaganda, and agitation in the
press and in the municipal councils, regional councils, etc.

In 1935, the Party held its First Congress at Macao. The Congress
assessed the situation in the home country and in the world, reviewed
the work done, and mapped out a program for the coming period.
But the policies worked out at the Macao Congress were not in

keeping with the revolutionary movement in the world and in the home country at that time (they advocated distribution of land to the agricultural workers, did not realize the antifascist task and the danger of fascist wars, etc.).

The Period from 1936 to 1939

In 1936, at the First Party Congress, comrades Le Hong Phong and Ha Huy Tap rectified these errors and worked out new policies in line with the resolutions of the Seventh Congress of the Communist International (setting up the Democratic Front, semilegal and semi-illegal activity of the Party).

At that time, in France, the Popular Front was in power. Our Party launched a movement for democracy and set up the Indochinese Democratic Front.

The movement of the Democratic Front was fairly strong and widespread. The people struggled openly. This was our strong point. But our weak point was: The Party did not give close leadership, therefore in many localities our cadres were narrow-minded, tending to keep within the law, were complacent with partial successes, and neglected the consolidation of the Party's underground organization. The Party did not clearly explain its standpoint on the question of national independence. A great number of comrades unprincipledly cooperated with the Trotskyites. When the Popular Front in France collapsed and World War II broke out, the movement of the Democratic Front in our country was also repressed by the colonialists, and our Party was thrown into confusion for a time.

However, this movement has also given our Party and the present National Front invaluable experiences. It has taught us that whatever conforms to the people's aspiration will receive support from the masses, who will wholeheartedly struggle for it and as such is a real mass movement. It has also taught us to avoid at all costs subjectivism, narrow-mindedness, etc.

Period from 1939 to 1945

The great events in this period in our country and in the world occurred only ten years ago. Many people witnessed them and they are still fresh in the memory of many of us. I shall recall only some principal ones:

1. In the world. In 1939, World War II broke out. At first, it was an imperialist war between the German, Italian, and Japanese fascist imperialists on the one side and the British, French, and American imperialists on the other.

In June, 1941, the German fascists attacked the Soviet Union, the fortress of the world revolution, and the latter had to fight back and to ally with the British and Americans against the fascist camp. Henceforward, the war was waged between the democratic camp and the fascist camp.

Owing to the enormous forces of the Red Army and the Soviet people, and Stalin's correct strategy, in May, 1945, Germany was crushed and in August, 1945, Japan surrendered. The democratic camp won complete victory.

In this victory, the Soviet Union was the most successful in the military field as well as in the political and spiritual fields.

Thanks to the success of the Soviet Union, the countries in Eastern Europe, which were bases or integral parts of fascist Germany, have become new democracies.

Thanks to the success of the Soviet Union, semicolonial countries such as China and colonial countries such as Korea and Viet-Nam have driven or are driving out the aggressive imperialists to wrest back freedom and independence.

Thanks to the victory of the Soviet Union, the movement for national liberation in other colonies is rising very high.

The United States was successful in the financial field. While the other countries were pouring their forces into the war and were devastated by it, the United States made big profits.

After the war, the German, Italian, and Japanese fascists were annihilated. The British and French imperialists were going downhill. The Soviet Union very quickly rehabilitated and developed its work of socialist construction. But treading in the steps of Germany, Italy, and Japan, the U.S. has now become the ringleader of the fascist imperialists.

2. In our country. After the outbreak of World War II, the Party Central Committee held the November, 1939, session and worked out its policies: to set up a united front against the French colonialists and the imperialist war and to prepare for an insurrection; to withdraw the slogan "To Confiscate the Landlords' Land To Distribute to the Tillers" in order to draw the landlord class into the National United Front.

After France's capitulation to fascist Germany, Japan encroached upon French power in Indochina and used the French colonialists as their henchmen to repress the revolution in our country. In that period, our people launched three uprisings, in Bac Son, Nam Ky, and Do Luong.

In May, 1941, the Party Central Committee held its Eighth Session. The main question was to assess that the revolution facing Viet-Nam was a revolution for national liberation, and to set up the Viet Minh Front. The main slogan was: "To Unite the Entire People, Oppose the Japanese and the French, and Wrest Back Independence; To Postpone the Agrarian Revolution." The name Viet-Nam Doc Lap Dong Minh (League for the Independence of Viet-Nam) was very clear in meaning, practical, and in full keeping with the aspirations of the entire people. Besides, the simple, practical, and complete program of the Front comprises ten points, as a propaganda song relates:

Ten policies are mapped out
Which are first useful to the country, second, benefiting the people. . . .

These ten points include points common to the whole nation and those dealing with the struggle for the interest of workers, peasants, and all strata of the population.

As a result, the Viet Minh Front was warmly welcomed by the people, and thanks to the efforts made by the cadres to keep close to the people, it developed very rapidly and very strongly. As the Front developed strongly, the Party also grew up. The Party also helped the progressive intellectuals to found the Viet-Nam Democratic Party in order to attract young intellectuals and civil servants and to accelerate the disintegration of the Dai Viet.*

In the world, the Soviet Union and the Allies scored successive victories. In our country, the Japanese and the French were in conflict. Under the Party's leadership, the Viet Minh Front grew fairly strong. In this situation, the Standing Bureau of the Central Committee held its enlarged session in March, 1945. The main resolution was to speed up the anti-Japanese movement and to prepare for the general insurrection. At that time, the French colonialists' power already had fallen into the hands of the Japanese fascists.

In May, 1945, Germany capitulated. In August, Japan surrendered. The Soviet Union and the Allies won complete victory.

* *A pro-fascist political party still active in South Viet-Nam in 1967.*—ED.

Early in August, the Party held its Second National Congress at Tan Trao to decide on the plan of action and to take part in the National People's Congress convened by the Viet Minh Front. The People's Congress was also held at Tan Trao in the same month.

The National People's Congress approved the plan put forth by the Viet Minh and the order for general insurrection and elected the Viet-Nam National Liberation Committee, which would later become the Provisional Government of our country. Because the Party's policies were correct and were carried out in good time and in a flexible way, the August General Insurrection was successful.

From the August Revolution Up to Now

Thanks to the clear-sighted and resolute leadership of our Party and the solidarity and enthusiasm of the entire people within and without the Viet Minh Front, the August Revolution was successful.

Not only the toiling classes and people but also the oppressed people in other countries can be proud that this is the first time in the revolutionary history of colonial and semicolonial peoples in which a party only fifteen years of age has led the revolution to success and seized power throughout the country.

On our part, we must bear in mind that our success was due to the great victory of the Soviet Red Army which had defeated fascist Japan, to the friendly assistance of international solidarity, to the close unity of our entire people, and to the heroic sacrifice of our revolutionary predecessors.

Our comrades, like Tran Phu, Ngo Gia Tu, Le Hong Phong, Nguyen Thi Minh Khai, Ha Huy Tap, Nguyen Van Cu, Hoang Van Thu, and thousands of others, placed the interests of the Party, the revolution, their class, and nation above and before everything else. They had deep confidence in the great forces and glorious future of their class and nation. They willingly sacrificed everything, even their lives for the sake of their Party, their class, and nation. They fertilized the Revolution tree with their blood and bones and, as a result of it, the tree of Revolution has now bloomed and borne good fruit.

All of us must follow these examples of heroism and selflessness to be genuine revolutionaries.

The August Revolution overthrew the centuries-old monarchy, broke the chains of the nearly one-hundred-year-old colonial rule, brought back power to the people, and built the basis for an independent, free, and happy Democratic Republic of Viet-Nam.

This is an extremely great change in the history of our country. Thanks to the successful August Revolution we have become a member of the great democratic family in the world. The August Revolution has exerted a direct and very great influence on the two brother Cambodian and Laotian nations. After the success of the August Revolution, the Cambodian and Laotian peoples also rose up against the imperialists to claim independence.

On September 2, 1945, the Government of the Democratic Republic of Viet-Nam declared to the world that Viet-Nam had the right to be independent, and put into practice democratic freedoms in the country. Mention should be made here that some comrades, members of the Viet-Nam National Liberation Committee who, having been elected by the National People's Congress, should have taken part in the Provisional Government but of their own accord withdrew to give the place to patriotic personalities outside the Viet Minh Front. This is a selfless, magnanimous gesture of men who do not care for position, who put the interests of the nation, of the national union above individual interests. This is a praise-worthy, honorable gesture that we must imitate.

The Difficulties of the Party and Government

As soon as the people's power came into existence, it met with great difficulties.

Due to the policy of ruthless exploitation by the Japanese and the French, within only half a year (end of 1944 and beginning of 1945) more than 2 million people in the North died of starvation.

We were independent for hardly one month when the British troops entered the South. They allegedly came to disarm the Japanese army, but were in reality an expeditionary corps helping the French colonialists in their attempt to reoccupy our country.

The Kuomintang troops entered the North under the same pretext, but actually they had three wicked aims: (1) to annihilate our Party, (2) to smash the Viet Minh Front, and (3) to help the Vietnamese reactionaries overthrow the people's power in order to set up a reactionary government under their sway.

In the face of that grave and pressing situation, our Party did everything possible to keep itself in existence, to work and develop, to give discreet and more effective leadership in order to have the time gradually to consolidate the forces of the people's power and to strengthen the National United Front.

At that time the Party could not hesitate: Hesitation meant failure. The Party had to make quick decisions and take measures—even painful ones—to save the situation. The greatest worry was about the Party's proclamation of voluntary dissolution. But in reality it went underground. And though underground, the Party continued to lead the administration and the people.

We recognize that the Party's declaration of dissolution (actual withdrawal into the underground) was a good measure. In spite of many a big difficulty, the Party and the Government guided our country through dangerous rapids and implemented many points in the program of the Viet Minh Front: holding the General Elections to elect the National Assembly and chart the Constitution; building and consolidating the people's power; annihilating the Vietnamese reactionaries; building and strengthening the people's army and arming the people; elaborating labor laws; reducing land rent and interest rates; building people's culture; broadening and consolidating the national united front (setting up of the All Viet-Nam Union).

Mention should be made of the Preliminary Agreement of March 6, 1946, and the *modus vivendi* of September 14, 1946, because they were considered as ultrarightist and caused much grumbling. But in the opinion of our comrades and compatriots in the South, they were correct. Indeed they were, because our comrades and compatriots cleverly availed themselves of this opportunity to build up and develop their forces.

Lenin said that even if a compromise with bandits was advantageous to the revolution, he would do it.

We needed peace to build our country, and therefore we made concessions to maintain peace. Although the French colonialists broke their word and unleashed war, nearly one year of temporary peace gave us time to build up our basic forces. When the French deliberately provoked war, we could no longer put up with them, and the nation-wide war broke out.

The Long-term Resistance War

The enemy schemed a lightning war. As they wanted to attack swiftly and win swiftly, our Party and Government put forth the slogan "Long-term Resistance War." The enemy plotted to sow dissension among us, so our slogan was "Unity of the Entire People."

Therefore, right from the start, our strategy prevailed over the enemy's.

To wage a long-term resistance war, there must be an adequate supply of arms and munitions to the army, of food and clothing to the troops and the people. Our country is poor and our technique low. The cities and towns which have some industry are occupied by the enemy. We tried to offset our material deficiencies by the enthusiasm of the entire people. So the Party and the Government promoted the patriotic emulation. Emulation covers all fields, but it is aimed at three main points: doing away with famine, wiping out illiteracy, and annihilating the foreign invaders.

Our workers emulated in manufacturing weapons for our troops, who enthusiastically trained themselves and magnificently scored feats of arms. The recent victories were proof of this. Our people ardently emulated and got satisfactory results. Our country is economically backward, we have been waging the Resistance War for almost five years and still can withstand it without suffering too many privations. This is a fact. The majority of our population are freed from illiteracy. This is a glorious achievement lauded by the world. I suggest that our Congress should send affectionate thanks and congratulations to our troops and compatriots.

But our organization, supervision, exchange, and summing up of experiences are still weak. This is our shortcoming. From now on, we strive to overcome them and the emulation movement will certainly bring about many more and better results.

The military aspect is the key one in the Resistance War.

At the beginning of the Resistance War our army was young. Though full of heroism, it lacked weapons, experience, officers, everything.

The enemy army was well known in the world. They had navy, infantry, and air forces. Moreover, they were supported by the British and American imperialists, especially by the latter.

The difference between our forces and the enemy's was so great that there were at the time people who likened our Resistance War to a "locust fighting an elephant."

It was so if things were seen from the material side, in their actual conditions and with a narrow mind. We had then to oppose airplanes and cannons with bamboo sticks. But guided by Marxism-Leninism, our Party did not look only at the present but also at the future and had firm confidence in the spirit and forces of the masses, of the nation. Therefore we resolutely told the wavering and pessimistic people that "Today the locust fights the elephant, but tomorrow the elephant will be disemboweled."

Practical life has shown that the colonialist "elephant" is being disemboweled while our army has grown up into a powerful tiger.

At the beginning, the enemy was the stronger and we the weaker. However, we doggedly waged the Resistance War, scored many successes, and firmly believed in our final victory because our cause is just and our troops courageous, our people united and undaunted, and because we are supported by the French people and the world democratic camp, and also because our strategy is correct.

Our Party and Government foresaw that our Resistance War has three stages. In the first stage, from September 23, 1945, to the closing of the Viet Bac campaign, in autumn-winter, 1947, all we did was to preserve and increase our main forces. In the second stage, running from the end of the Viet Bac campaign 1947 up to the present, we have actively contended with the enemy and prepared for the general counteroffensive. The third stage is the general counteroffensive.

Because they did not grasp this point of the policy of the Party and the Government, a number of comrades got wrong ideas. Some said that the slogan for general counteroffensive was put forth too early. Others wanted to know the date of the general counteroffensive. Still others believed that the general counteroffensive would certainly be launched in 1950, etc.

These wrong conceptions were harmful to our work. We must first of all keep in mind that the Resistance War will be long and hard, but we will win.

The Resistance War must be long because we have a small population and a small territory and our country is poor. Long and all-round preparations have to be made by our whole nation. We must always bear in mind that compared to us the French invaders are quite strong, and, in addition, they are assisted by the British and Americans.

They are a "thickpeel-mandarin"; we must have time to "sharpen our nails" to tear them to pieces.

We must also understand that each stage is linked up with another, the second succeeds the first and produces seeds for the third. Many changes occur in the course of one stage to another. Each stage also has changes of its own.

It is possible to examine the general situation in order to divide it into big stages, but it is not possible to cut off completely one stage from the other like cutting bread. The length of each stage depends on the situation in the home country and in the world, and on the changes between the enemy forces and ours. We must understand that the long-term Resistance War is closely connected with the preparations for general counteroffensive. As the Resistance War is long, there must also be long preparations for the general counteroffensive. It depends on the changes between the enemy forces and ours, and also on the changes in the international situation whether the general counteroffensive will come early or late.

In all circumstances, the more careful and complete the preparations, the more favorable will be the general counteroffensive and the more certain our success.

The slogan "To Prepare Strongly for the General Counteroffensive" was put forth early in 1950.

Did we make preparations during that year?

Yes, we did. The Government issued the general mobilization order and launched the movement for patriotic emulation. As is well known, the troops and the people have been striving to make preparations and have obtained good results.

Did we pass to the general counteroffensive in 1950?

Yes, we did and are passing to it. The big diplomatic successes scored early in 1950 and the victories won on the battlefronts at the end of that year were proof of this.

Have we launched the general counteroffensive?

We have been preparing to switch over to the general counteroffensive, which is not yet actually being carried out. We must fully grasp the meaning of the words, "To Prepare To Pass Strongly Over to. . . ."

Once the preparations are complete we will launch the general counteroffensive. The more complete the preparations, the quicker will come the hour for launching the general counteroffensive and the more favorable will it be.

We should avoid precipitation, rashness, and impatience. The troops, the people, the cadres, everybody and every branch must strive to make complete preparations. When our preparations are completed we will launch the general counteroffensive and it will certainly be successful then.

Correction of Mistakes

Our Party has scored many achievements but has also committed no less mistakes. We must sincerely practice self-criticism in order to correct them. Efforts must be devoted to the correction of our mistakes so that we shall be able to make progress.

Before speaking of our mistakes, we must recognize that our Party cadres, especially those in the temporarily occupied zones, are very heroic and devoted and, in spite of all hardships and dangers, always keep close to the people, cling to their work without fear and complaints, and are always ready to sacrifice their lives. They are model fighters of the nation, the meritorious sons and daughters of the Party.

It can be said that since the founding of the Party, *the Party's policies as a whole were correct*. If they were not correct, how can we score such big achievements now? But we also have big shortcomings and mistakes, as follows:

As their ideological studies are lacking, the ideology of many Party cadres and members is not sound and their theoretical level low. As a result, in the carrying out of the policies of the Party and the Government there occurred erroneous tendencies, either "leftist" or "rightist" ones (as in the implementation of the policies on land, on the Front, national minorities, religion, administration, etc.).

Our organizational work is still weak, so it often cannot ensure correct implementation of the policies of the Party and the Government.

Therefore, ideological study and raising of the theoretical level and readjustment of organization are urgent works for the Party.

Besides, there still are among the leading organs at all levels widespread and grave mistakes in style of work, planning, and manner of guiding. These are subjectivism, bureaucracy, commandism, narrowmindedness, and arrogance.

Subjectivism manifests itself in the idea that the long-term Resistance War can become a short-term Resistance War.

Bureaucracy shows in fondness for red tape, divorce from the masses of the people, lack of investigation and study of control and supervision of the implementation of the work, and reluctance to learn the experiences of the masses.

Commandism reveals itself in the tendency to rely on the administration to force the people to do things, without taking care to agitate and explain to the people, to make them work on their own initiative and own accord.

Narrow-mindedness is apparent in harshness toward non-Party people or overlooking them, unwilling to discuss with them or ask their opinion.

And arrogance is revealed as follows:

1. To rest on past laurels and consider oneself as the "savior" of the people and the "beneficiary" of the Party, asking for position and honor. Unable to do big work and unwilling to do the small. Arrogance is very harmful to the solidarity within as well as without the Party.

2. To abuse one's position as Party member to disregard even discipline and the higher levels of the people's organization or administration.

The comrades who have committed this mistake have not understood that each Party member must be exemplary in observing discipline, not only Party discipline but also that of the people's organizations and that of the revolutionary power.

The Central Committee shares in the responsibility for these mistakes committed by the Party members because it has not yet paid enough attention to supervisory work. Although ideological training has been given, it has not been widespread and adequate enough. Inner democracy has not been broadly practiced. Criticism and self-criticism have not yet become a daily habit.

However, all these have been partly corrected. The recent critical reviews and movement for criticism and self-criticism have yielded good results in spite of a few deviations.

Stalin said that a revolutionary party needs criticism and self-criticism just as a human being needs air. He also said that close supervision can help avoid many grave mistakes.

From now on, the Party must try to give widespread ideological education in order to raise the political standards of the Party members. A collective style of work must be promoted. The relations between the Party and the masses must be strengthened. The observance of discipline, understanding of principles, and Party spirit of every Party member must be highlighted. The Party must widen the movement for criticism and self-criticism within the Party, the State organs, the people's organizations, in the press, and among the people. Criticism and self-criticism must be conducted regularly, in a practical and democratic way, from the high level downward and from the low level upward. Lastly, there must be close supervision by the Party.

If we succeed in doing so, there would be less errors and quicker progress.

New Situation and New Tasks

1. New situation. As is well known, the present world is divided into two distinct camps: the democratic camp and the antidemocratic camp.

The democratic camp is headed by the Soviet Union, including the socialist countries, and the new democracies in Europe and in Asia. It also embraces the oppressed nations which are struggling against aggressive imperialism and the democratic organizations and personalities in the capitalist countries.

The democratic camp is a powerful camp which is growing in strength. The following points are evidence of this:

Let us glance at the world map: From Eastern Europe to Eastern Asia, the U.S.S.R. and the new democracies form an immense bloc of 800 million people. In this bloc the nations are united, having the same goal and without any antagonisms. It is the symbol of progress and of the bright future of mankind. This is an extremely powerful force.

At the Second Congress of the Peace Front held in the Polish capital in November, 1950, the representatives of 500 million peace fighters in eighty-one countries pledged their determination to safeguard world peace and to oppose imperialist wars. This is the United Front of the peaceful and democratic world. This is a very powerful force whose strength is growing with every passing day.

The antidemocratic camp is headed by the United States. Immediately after the end of World War II, the United States became the ringleader of imperialists and world reactionaries. Britain and France are its right and left hands and the reactionary governments in the East and the West its henchmen.

Aspiring to world hegemony, the United States brandishes dollars in one hand to lure the world people and an atomic bomb in the other to menace them. The Truman Program, the Marshall Plan, NATO, and the Southeast Asia program are all U.S. maneuvers aiming at preparing a third world war.

But the U.S. ambition has encountered an enormous resistance: the great force of the Soviet Union, the movement for democracy and peace, and the movement for national liberation which have been seething all over the world.

At present, the U.S. policy in Asia is to assist the reactionaries such as Chiang Kai-shek, Syngman Rhee, Bao Dai, etc., to help the British imperialists repress the resistance forces in Malaya and the French colonialists crush the Resistance War in Viet-Nam, while the United States itself wages an aggressive war against Korea and occupies Taiwan in an attempt to undermine the Chinese Revolution.

In Europe the United States has, through the Marshall Plan and NATO, seized control over the Western countries in the military, political, and economic fields and at the same time has been striving to arm them, compelling them to supply men to be used as cannon fodder as in the plan for setting up in Western Europe seventy divisions under an American Commander-in-Chief.

However, the U.S. camp has many weaknesses.

Besides the strength of the democratic camp, the U.S. camp is threatened by another force: the economic crisis.

There are many contradictions in the U.S. camp. For example, the United States wants Western Germany to set up an army of ten divisions but has been opposed by the French. Britain covertly opposes the United States because it is contending for oil fields in the Near East and for influence in the Far East.

The people, especially the toiling sections in the countries "aided" by the United States, hate it for encroaching upon their economic interests and independence of their countries.

The United States is too greedy. It schemes to set up bases all over the world. It helps every reactionary group and every reactionary government. Its front extends beyond measure, consequently its forces thin out. Clear proof of this is that the United States, together with forty of its vassal countries that have invaded Korea, are suffering defeats. The United States helped the reactionary clique in China, the Kuomintang headed by Chiang Kai-shek, but Chiang was defeated. The United States helps the French colonialists in Viet-Nam, yet the Vietnamese Resistance War is winning.

In short, we can foretell that the reactionary imperialist camp will certainly be defeated and the camp of peace and democracy victorious.

Viet-Nam is a part of the whole democratic camp. It is at present a stronghold against imperialism, against the antidemocratic camp headed by the United States.

Since the beginning of the Resistance War, Britain and the United States have helped the French colonialists. And since 1950, the United States has openly intervened in our country. At the end of 1950, Britain and France prepared to set up a "united" front to put their forces together against the Resistance War in Malaya and in Viet-Nam.

Thus, the international situation is closely related to us. The success of the democratic camp is also ours, and our success is also a success for the democratic camp. Therefore, at present our main slogan is: *"to annihilate the French colonialists and to defeat the U.S. interventionists in order to win unity and complete independence and to safeguard world peace."*

2. New tasks. The comrades of the Central Committee will report on the important questions such as the political program, the constitution, the military question, the administration, the National United Front, the economic question, etc. My report will only mention some main tasks among our new ones: (a) to bring the Resistance War to complete victory; and (b) to found the Viet-Nam Workers' Party.

Efforts must be made to develop forces for the troops and the people constantly to win success after success in order to advance to the general counteroffensive. This task aims at some main points:

1) *To build and develop the army.* Efforts must be made to intensify the building and strengthening of the political and military work in our army. The political consciousness, the tactics and technique, and the self-imposed discipline of our troops must be heightened. Our army must become a genuine people's army.

Simultaneously, the militia and guerrilla units must be developed and strengthened in organization, training, guidance, and combativeness. The militia and guerrilla forces must become a vast and solid iron net spread all over the country so that wherever the enemy goes he will be enmeshed.

2) *To develop patriotism.* Our people are ardent patriots. This is our invaluable tradition. Today, as in the past, every time the Fatherland is invaded their patriotism boils over in a wave of great violence that sweeps away all dangers and difficulties and drowns all the traitors and aggressors.

Our history has many great resistance wars which are proof of our people's patriotism. We can be proud of the glorious historical pages of the eras of the Trung sisters, Lady Trieu, Tran Hung Dao, Le Loi, Quang Trung, etc. We must engrave on our mind the achievements of our national heroes because they are the symbols of a heroic nation.

Our fellow countrymen of today are worthy of their forefathers. Our white-headed elders as well as our children, our compatriots residing abroad and in the provisionally occupied areas, in the plains, on the highlands, all are imbued with an ardent love for the country and hatred for the aggressor. The fighters on the battle front went hungry for days on end in order to pursue the enemy and annihilate him. The public employees in the rear went hungry for the sake of the troops. The women advised their husbands to enlist in the army, while they themselves volunteered to help in the transport service. The sponsoring mothers love and take care of the troops as of their own children. The workers and peasants of both sexes emulate to increase production, not shrinking from hardships so that they can contribute their part to the Resistance War, and the landlords gave their land to the Government. Though different in action, all these lofty acts are similar in their ardent patriotism. Patriotism is like other valuables. Sometimes it is visible to the naked eye when exhibited in a shop window or crystal vases. But there are times it is discreetly hidden in a trunk or suitcase. Our duty is to try to bring all these hidden valuables into exhibition. I mean that every effort must be made to explain, popularize, organize, and give leadership so that the patriotism of all of us finds expression in the work benefiting the country and the Resistance War.

Genuine patriotism is altogether different from the chauvinism of the reactionary imperialists. It is part and parcel of internationalism. It was thanks to patriotism that the army and the people of the Soviet Union crushed fascist Germany and Japan and safeguarded the socialist Fatherland, thereby helping the working class and the oppressed peoples of the world. It was thanks to patriotism that the Chinese Liberation Army and people destroyed the traitorous Chiang Kai-shek clique and drove out the American imperialists. It was also thanks to patriotism that the Korean troops and people together with the Chinese Volunteer Army routed the American imperialists and their henchmen. It is also thanks to patriotism that our troops and people have for many long years endured untold suffering and hardships and have been determined to smash the colonialist aggressors and the Vietnamese traitors, and to build an independent, unified, democratic, free, prosperous, and strong Viet-Nam, a new democratic Viet-Nam.

3) *To step up patriotic emulation.* First, the troops must emulate to exterminate the enemy and score feats of arms, and second, the people must emulate to increase production. We must devote ourselves heart and soul to the speeding up of these two works.

In the great work of Resistance War and national construction, the Lien Viet,* the Viet Minh,† the Trade Union, the Peasants' Association, and other people's organizations have great influence. We must help them develop, strengthen, and work positively.

Concerning land policy, in the free zones we must strictly carry out reduction of land rent and interest rates, confiscating lands appropriated by the French and the Vietnamese traitors to temporarily distribute them to the poor peasants and the families of armymen, with a view to improving the livelihood of the peasants, heightening their spirit, and fostering their force for the Resistance War.

Concerning economy and finance, our economic basis must be safeguarded and developed to fight the enemy economy. There must be an equitable and rational tax system. Expenses must balance income in order to ensure supplies for the army and the people.

The cultural work must be sped up to train the New Man and new cadres for the Resistance War and national construction. All vestiges of colonialism and the servile influence of imperialist culture must be systematically rooted out. Simultaneously, the fine traditions of the national culture must be developed and must assimilate what is new in the progressive culture of the world with a view to building a Vietnamese culture having a national, scientific, and popular character.

* Viet-Nam National United Front.
† League for the Independence of Viet-Nam.

When we are victorious, the provisionally occupied areas will be liberated one after the other. Therefore, preparations must be made to consolidate the newly liberated areas in all aspects.

The life and property of the foreign residents who abide by the Vietnamese law will be protected. Chinese residents should be encouraged to take part in the Resistance War. If they volunteer to do so, they will enjoy every right and duty of a Vietnamese citizen.

We are waging our Resistance War, the brother Cambodian and Laotian nations are also waging theirs. The French colonialists and the American interventionists are the common enemy of our three nations. Consequently, we must strive to help our Cambodian and Laotian brothers and their resistance wars, and arrive at setting up a Viet-Nam–Cambodian–Laotian Front.

We are successful in our Resistance, thanks partly to the sympathy of the brother countries and of the peoples of the world. Therefore, we must strengthen the friendship between our countries and the brother countries, between our people and the people of other countries in the world.

To carry out these points, we must have a legal party appropriate to the situation in the world and at home in order to lead our people's struggle to victory. This party is the Viet-Nam Workers' Party.

As regards its composition, the Viet-Nam Workers' Party will admit the most enthusiastic and most enlightened workers, peasants, and intellectuals.

As regards theory, it adheres to Marxism-Leninism.

As regards organization, it adopts the system of democratic centralization.

As regards discipline, it has an iron discipline which is at the same time a self-imposed discipline.

As regards its law of development, it makes use of criticism and self-criticism to educate its members and the masses of the people.

As regards its immediate goal, the Viet-Nam Workers' Party unites and leads the entire people to wage the Resistance War to complete victory. To win back national unity and complete independence, it leads the entire people to implement new democracy and to create conditions for the advance to socialism.

The Viet-Nam Workers' Party must be a great, powerful, steady, pure, and thoroughly revolutionary Party.

The Viet-Nam Workers' Party must be the clear-sighted, determined, and loyal leader of the working class and other working people, of the Vietnamese people, to unite and lead the people in carrying out the armed resistance to complete victory so as to achieve new democracy.

At the present stage, the interests of the working class and other working people, and of the nation, are one. It is precisely because it is the Party of the working class and working people that the Viet-Nam Workers' Party must be the Party of the Vietnamese people.

The first task, the most urgent task of our Party today, is to lead the Resistance War to victory. The other tasks must be connected with it. Our work is very great. Our future is very glorious. But we have to experience many difficulties. The war has its own difficulties. Victory, too, has its own difficulties.

For example, the mind of the cadres, Party members, and people is not yet tempered well enough to cope with all developments at home and abroad.

It is possible that the American imperialists will give the French invaders greater assistance, and therefore the latter will act more frenziedly.

We are getting more and more work, but the number of cadres is insufficient and our cadres lack ability and experience.

We have to solve the economic and financial problem rationally and beneficially to the people, etc.

We do not fear difficulties. But we must foresee and clearly see difficulties and be prepared and ready to overcome them.

With the solidarity and unity of mind, the determination and indomitable spirit of our Party, Government, and entire people, we will certainly overcome all difficulties in order to gain complete victory.

The October Revolution was victorious. The building of socialism in the Soviet Union has been successful. The Chinese Revolution has been successful. These great successes have opened the way to success for our revolution and that of many other countries in the world.

We have a great and powerful Party. It is great and powerful thanks to Marxism-Leninism, to the constant efforts of all our Party members, and to the love, confidence, and support of our army and people as a whole.

We have the most clear-sighted and worthy elder brothers and friends of mankind—comrade Stalin and comrade Mao Tse-tung.

That is why I am convinced that we will fulfill the following heavy but glorious tasks:

To found a most powerful party, the Viet-Nam Workers' Party,

To carry out the Resistance till complete victory,

To build a new democratic Viet-Nam,

To contribute to the defense of democracy in the world and a lasting peace.

CLOSING SPEECH AT
THE PUBLIC APPEARANCE OF
THE VIET-NAM WORKERS' PARTY*
(March 3, 1951)

Dear representatives,

You have welcomed the report by comrade Truong Chinh on the founding of the Viet-Nam Workers' Party. You are the representatives of the National United Front, that is, of the entire people. Your opinion is that of the entire people. Therefore, you have welcomed and esteemed the Viet-Nam Workers' Party, we are confident that the entire people will also favor it.

Comrade Truong Chinh has given a detailed report on the policy, platform, organization, etc. of the Viet-Nam Workers' Party. On behalf of the Party, I convey to you its heartfelt thanks and sum up the following.

The goal of the Viet-Nam Workers' Party can be thus summarized: to unite the entire people and serve the Fatherland.

The task of the Viet-Nam Workers' Party is resolutely to lead the entire people to bring the resistance to victory and the rehabilitation to success.

*The Viet-Nam Workers' Party (Dang Lao-Dong) made its first public appearance on March 3, 1951, at the Unification Congress to merge the Viet Minh and the Lien Viet. It is the official Communist Party of Viet-Nam. Its present southern branch is known as the People's Revolutionary Party (PRP). —ED.

The policy of the Viet-Nam Workers' Party in the military, political, economic, cultural fields, etc., has been clearly stated in its Manifesto and Platform. This policy can be put into a few words: to make our Viet-Nam independent, unified, democratic, prosperous, and strong.

I wish to add a few points to avoid any eventual misunderstanding. First, in religious matters, the Viet-Nam Workers' Party advocates strict observance of freedom of belief for everybody. Second, with regard to the friendly parties, organizations within the National United Front, the Viet-Nam Workers' Party advocates close unity, lasting unity, and mutual progress.

The Viet-Nam Workers' Party is the Party of the working class and toiling people, that is, the workers, peasants, and brain workers most resolute, ardent, pure, wholeheartedly devoted to serving the Fatherland and the people. Those whom wealth cannot suborn, poverty cannot upset, and violence cannot subdue.

About a revolutionary man and a revolutionary Party, the great Chinese writer Lu-Hsun has this couplet:

> He stares disdainfully upon a thousand athletes,
> And bows to serve as a horse to children.

"Thousand athletes" means powerful enemies, like the French colonialists and the American interventionists, or difficulties and hardships.

"Children" means the peaceful masses of people, or deeds beneficent to the State and the people.

The Viet-Nam Workers' Party does not fear any enemy, however fierce it may be; any task, however heavy or perilous it may be; but the Viet-Nam Workers' Party is ready to serve as buffalo, horse, or faithful servant to the people.

However, the Viet-Nam Workers' Party is an organization of individuals who, as such, are liable to make mistakes. Therefore, the Viet-Nam Workers' Party waits for and welcomes any frank criticism by friendly parties and organizations, prominent personalities, and the entire people so as to make constant progress.

Lastly, we pledge that the Viet-Nam Workers' Party will resolutely fulfill its task of bringing the resistance to victory and the rehabilitation to success.

ADDRESS ON THE OCCASION
OF THE INAUGURATION OF THE
CONGRESS TO MERGE THE VIET
MINH AND LIEN VIET
(March 3, 1951)

I am very glad to have the honor of winding up the inauguration ceremony of this Unification Congress Viet Minh–Lien Viet.

First of all, on behalf of the Presidium, I send my greetings to our fighters, cadres of the Viet Minh–Lien Viet Front, my condolences to our compatriots in the temporarily occupied zone and abroad.

Today's happiness is common to our entire people, to this Congress, but my own is understandable and indescribable as well. A man who has struggled with you for many years for the entire people's unity today sees a forest of unity in full bloom with an eternal future.

What makes me happier is that not only the entire Vietnamese people are united, but the Cambodian and Laotian peoples are also united. The news of the unity of these two brother nations is personally brought by the Cambodian and Laotian delegates.

Thus, the Vietnamese people are united, the Cambodian people are united, and the Laotian people are united. Let us strive for Vietnamese–Cambodian–Laotian unity.

With the common will of our three brother nations, we will overcome all difficulties and hardships, smash the aggressive French colonialists, smash the American interventionists and any other invader.

You will thoroughly discuss and clear-sightedly fix the platform and statute of the National United Front in this Congress. I only point out some points for your study.

1. The Front must make steady progress on the road of democracy.

2. The activities of the Front must center on a cardinal task to avoid useless waste of force. This cardinal task is patriotic emulation.

3. The parties, organizations, and prominent personalities within the Front must closely unite, cordially help one another, sincerely learn from one another's merits, and criticize one another's shortcomings to progress together.

This Congress is composed of representatives of all strata, religious beliefs, nationalities, old and young peoples, men and women, a mutually loved great family. After the Congress, this bloc of unity and cordiality will no doubt develop and consolidate among the entire people. This bloc of great unity will embrace the people of the friendly countries, of France, and of peace-and-democracy-loving people throughout the world.

This prodigious force will help us not only bring the resistance to victory and the rehabilitation to success, but also contribute to the defense of world peace and democracy.

Venerables, delegates, brothers and sisters,

At the beginning of last year, we won a great political victory, the recognition of our Government by the Soviet Union, China, and the people's democracies which led to the great victory at the Border and in the Midland.

At the beginning of this year, we won a new great political victory, the founding of the Viet-Nam Workers' Party and the Viet Minh–Lien Viet unification. With this trend, we will score greater military victories.

Long live the unity of the entire people!

Long live the Viet-Nam National United Front!

Long live the Vietnamese–Cambodian–Laotian great unity!

The Resistance will certainly be victorious!

The camp of peace and democracy will certainly be victorious!

THE IMPERIALIST AGGRESSORS CAN NEVER ENSLAVE THE HEROIC VIETNAMESE PEOPLE*

I avail myself of the short New Year's holiday to write these lines.

More fortunate than other peoples, we, the Vietnamese people, like our friends the Chinese and the Korean peoples, enjoy two New Year's festivals every year. One New Year's Day is celebrated according to the Gregorian calendar and falls on the first of January. On that day, which is the official New Year's Day, only government offices send greetings to one another. Another New Year's Day, the Tet, is observed according to the lunar calendar, and this year falls on a day of the closing week of January. This traditional New Year's Day, celebrated by the people, usually lasts from three to seven days in peacetime.

In our country, spring begins in the first days of January. At present, a splendid springtime prevails everywhere. The radiant sunbeams bring with them a merry and healthy life. Like an immense green carpet, the young rice plants cover the fields, heralding a coming bumper harvest. The birds warble merrily in evergreen bushes. Here winter lasts only a few days and the thermometer rarely falls to 10 degrees above zero. As far as snow is concerned, generally speaking it is unknown to our people.

* Published in the review *For a Lasting Peace, for a People's Democracy*, April 4, 1952, under the pen name Din.

232

Before, during the Tet festival, pictures and greetings written on red paper could be seen stuck at entrance doors of palaces as well as tiny thatched huts. Today these greetings and pictures are replaced by slogans urging struggle and labor, such as: "Intensify the Emulation Movement for Armed Struggle, Production, and Economic Development!," "The War of Resistance Will Win!," "Combat Bureaucracy, Corruption, and Waste!," "The National Construction Will Certainly Be Crowned with Success!"

During the Tet festival, people are clad in their most beautiful garments. In every family the most delicious foods are prepared. Religious services are performed in front of the ancestral altars. Visits are paid between kith and kin to exchange greetings. Grown-ups give gifts to children; civilians send presents to soldiers. In short, it can be said that this is a spring festival.

Before telling you the situation of Viet-Nam, may I send you and all your comrades my warmest greetings!

Collusion Between the Aggressors

Let us review Viet-Nam's situation in 1951.

After their defeat in the China–Viet-Nam border campaign in October, 1950—the greatest reverse they had suffered in the whole history of their colonial wars, which involved for them the loss of five provinces at one time (Cao Bang, Lang Son, Lao Cai, Thai Nguyen, and Hoa Binh)—the French colonialists began the year 1951 with the dispatch of General de Lattre de Tassigny to Viet-Nam.*

They resorted to total war. Their maneuver was to consolidate the Bao Dai puppet government, organize puppet troops, and redouble spying activities. They set up no man's lands of from 5 to 10 kilometers wide around areas under their control and strengthened the Red River delta by a network of 2,300 bunkers. They stepped up mopping-up operations in our rear, applied the policy of annihilation and wholesale destruction of our manpower and potential resources by killing our compatriots, devastating our countryside,

---

* *Jean de Lattre de Tassigny, Commander in Chief of the French Forces, Far East, and the French High Commissioner in Indochina in 1950–52, temporarily regained the initiative in the Indochina War. He died of cancer while still in command, being made Marshal of France on his deathbed. His only son, Lieutenant Bernard de Lattre, was killed in North Viet-Nam.*—ED.

burning our rice fields, etc. In a word, they followed the policy of "using Vietnamese to fight Vietnamese and nursing the war by means of warfare."

It is on orders and with the assistance of their masters, the American interventionists, that the French colonialists performed the above-mentioned deeds.

Among the first Americans now living in Viet-Nam (of course, in areas under French control) there are a fairly noteworthy spy, Donald Heath, ambassador accredited to the puppet government,* and a general, head of the U.S. military mission.†

In September, 1951, de Lattre de Tassigny went to Washington to make his report and beg for aid. In October, General Collins, Chief of Staff of the U.S. Army, came to Viet-Nam to inspect the French Expeditionary Corps and puppet troops.

In order to show their American masters that U.S. aid is used in a worthwhile manner at present as well as in the future, in November, de Lattre de Tassigny attacked the chief town of Hoa Binh province. The result of this "shooting offensive," which the reactionary press in France and in the world commented on uproariously, was that the Viet-Nam People's Army held the overwhelming majority of enemy troops tightly between two prongs and annihilated them. But this did not prevent de Lattre de Tassigny and his henchmen from hullabalooing that they had carried the day!

At the very beginning of the war, the Americans supplied France with money and armaments. To take an example, 85 per cent of weapons, war materials, and even canned food captured by our troops were labeled "Made in U.S.A." This aid had been stepped up all the more rapidly since June, 1950, when the United States began interfering in Korea. American aid to the French invaders consisted of airplanes, boats, trucks, military outfits, napalm bombs, etc.

Meanwhile, the Americans compelled the French colonialists to step up the organization of four divisions of puppet troops, with each party footing half the bill. Of course, this collusion between the

* *Donald Heath was the first U.S. Ambassador accredited to Viet-Nam.—* ED.

† *Brigadier General Francis Brink, who committed suicide in 1952 while on a trip to Washington. A large American officers' hotel in Saigon is named after him.—*ED.

French and American aggressors and the puppet clique was fraught with contradictions and contentions.

The French colonialists are now landed in a dilemma: either they receive U.S. aid and be then replaced by their American "allies," or they receive nothing and be then defeated by the Vietnamese people. To organize the puppet army by means of pressganging the youth in areas under their control would be tantamount to swallowing a bomb when one is hungry: A day will come when at last the bomb bursts inside. However, not to organize the army on this basis would mean instantaneous death for the enemy because even the French strategists have to admit that the French Expeditionary Corps grows thinner and thinner and is on the verge of collapse.

Furthermore, U.S. aid is paid for at a very high price. In the enemy-held areas, French capitalism is swept aside by American capitalism. American concerns like the Petroleum Oil Corporation, the Caltex Oil Corporation, the Bethlehem Steel Corporation, the Florida Phosphate Corporation, and others monopolize rubber, ores, and other natural resources of our country. U.S. goods swamp the market. The French reactionary press, especially *Le Monde,* is compelled to acknowledge sadly that French capitalism is now giving way to U.S. capitalism.

The U.S. interventionists have nurtured the French aggressors and the Vietnamese puppets, but the Vietnamese people do not let anybody delude and enslave them.

People's China is our close neighbor. Her brilliant example gives us a great impetus. Not long ago the Chinese people defeated the U.S. imperialists and won a historical victory. The execrated Chiang Kai-shek was swept from the Chinese mainland, though he is more cunning than the placeman Bao Dai. Can the U.S. interventionists, who were drummed out of China and are now suffering heavy defeats in Korea, conquer Viet-Nam? Of course not!

Atrocious Crimes of the U.S. Interventionists

Defeated on the battlefield, the French colonialists retaliated upon unarmed people and committed abominable crimes. The following are a few examples:

As everywhere in the enemy-controlled areas, on October 15, 1951, at Ha Dong, the French soldiers raided the youths even in the streets and press-ganged them into the puppet army. And there as everywhere, the people protested against such acts. Three young girls stood in a line across the street in front of the trucks packed with the captured youngsters to prevent them from being sent to concentration camps. These courageous acts were worthy of heroine Raymonde Dien.* The French colonialists revved the engines and, in a split second, our three young patriots were run over.

In October, 1951, the invaders staged a large-scale raid in Thai Binh province. They captured more than 16,000 people—most of whom were old people, women, and children—and penned them in a football field surrounded by barbed wire and guarded by soldiers and dogs. For four days, the captives were exposed in the sun and rain, ankle-deep in mud. They received no food and no drinking water. Over 300 of them died of exhaustion and disease.

The relatives and friends who brought food to the captives were roughly manhandled, and the food was thrown into the mud and trampled under foot. M. Phac, a surgeon of seventy who tried to save the victims' lives, was shot dead on the spot, as were a number of pregnant women.

Incensed by these barbarous acts, the townsfolk staged a strike and sought ways and means to help the internees. The determination of the population compelled the French colonialists to let the food in, but on order of Colonel Charton of the French Expeditionary Corps, it was declared a donation from the United States.

On October 28, 1951, Le Van Lam, twenty-seven, from Ha Coi, a puppet soldier who had been saved from drowning by an old fisherman at Do Son, said after he had recovered consciousness: "On October 27, the French embarked me, as well as 100 other wounded men, on board a steamer, saying they would send us to Saigon for medical attention. In the night, when the ship was in the offing, they threw us one by one into the water. Fortunately, I managed to snatch at a piece of floating wood and swam landward. I was unconscious when I was saved."

The following is the confession of Chaubert, a French captain captured at Tu Ky on November 25, 1951: "The French High

---

* On February 13, 1950, Raymonde Dien, a member of the French Communist Party, lay across a railway track to prevent the movement of a train carrying armaments and tanks to the French forces in Indochina. She was sentenced by a French court to one year's imprisonment, but, owing to the pressure of public opinion, was released in November, 1950.—ED.

POEMS FROM PRISON DIARY*

HARD IS THE ROAD OF LIFE

Having climbed over steep mountains and high peaks,
How should I expect on the plains to meet greater danger?
In the mountains, I met the tiger and came out unscathed.
On the plains, I encountered men, and was thrown into prison.

I was a representative of Viet-Nam
On my way to China to meet an important personage.
On the quiet road a sudden storm broke loose,
And I was thrust into jail as an honored guest.

I am a straightforward man, with no crime on my conscience,
But I was accused of being a spy for China.
So life, you see, is never a very smooth business,
And now the present bristles with difficulties.

* Hanoi: Foreign Languages Publishing House, 1959.

THE LEG IRONS

With hungry mouth open like a wicked monster,
Each night the irons devour the legs of people:
The jaws grip the right leg of every prisoner:
Only the left is free to bend and stretch.

Yet there is one thing stranger in this world:
People rush in to place their legs in irons.
Once they are shackled, they can sleep in peace.
Otherwise they would have no place to lay their heads.

LEARNING TO PLAY CHESS

To wear away the time, we learn to play chess,
In thousands, horses and infantry chase each other.
Move quickly into action, in attack or in retreat.
Talent and swift feet give us the upper hand.

Eyes must look far ahead, and thoughts be deeply pondered.
Be bold and unremitting in attack.
Give the wrong command, and two chariots are rendered useless.
Come the right moment, a pawn can bring you victory.

The forces on both sides are equally balanced,
But victory will come only to one side.
Attack, retreat, with unerring strategy:
Then you will merit the title of great commander.

the free zones exist everywhere, but they are not safe. Children go to their classrooms—in fact, there are only single classrooms and not schools in the strict meaning of the word—with the same vigilance that their fathers and brothers display in guerrilla fighting. At present, there are in South Viet-Nam 3,332 classrooms, with an attendance of 111,700 pupils.

The liquidation of illiteracy is actively undertaken. In the first half of 1951, there were in Zone III, Zone V, and Viet Bac Zone 324,000 people who were freed from illiteracy and 350,000 others who began learning. During the same period, illiteracy was wiped out in 53 villages and 3 districts (one district is composed of from 5 to 10 villages). People's organizations opened 837 classes attended by 9,800 public employees. The Party, National United Front, Government, the General Confederation of Labor, and the Army have periodically opened short-term (about one week) political training courses.

In short, great efforts are being made in mass education.

Development and Strengthening of International Relations

In 1951, the relations between the Vietnamese people and foreign countries were developed and strengthened.

For the first time, in 1951, various delegations of the Vietnamese people visited great People's China and heroic Korea. Through these visits, the age-old friendship between our three countries has been strengthened.

The delegation of Vietnamese youth to the Youth Festival in Berlin, the delegation of the Viet-Nam General Confederation of Labor to the Congress of the World Federation of Trade Unions in Warsaw, and the delegation to the World Peace Conference in Vienna have returned to Viet-Nam filled with confidence and enthusiasm. At various meetings and in the press, members of these delegations told the Vietnamese people of the tremendous progress they had witnessed in the people's democracies and the warm friendship shown by the brother countries to the Vietnamese people who are struggling for national independence and freedom.

Those delegates who had the chance of visiting the Soviet Union are overjoyed because they can tell us of the great triumph of socialism and the ever-growing happiness enjoyed by the Soviet people. Upon returning from the Youth Festival, Truong Thi Xin, a young woman worker, said, "The youth in the Soviet Union received us most affectionately during our stay in their great country."

The talks held by these delegates are living lessons most useful for the inculcation of internationalism.

"Peace in Viet-Nam!" and "Withdraw Foreign Troops from Viet-Nam!" were the claims formulated in a resolution passed by the plenary session of the World Peace Council held in Vienna, claims which have given great enthusiasm to the Vietnamese people.

The Interventionists Suffer Defeat After Defeat

Last year was a year of brilliant victories for our People's Army, and a year of heavy defeats and losses in men and materials for the invaders. According to incomplete figures and excluding the China–Viet-Nam border campaign in October, 1950, during which the French Army lost more than 7,000 men (annihilated and captured), in 1951 the enemy lost 37,700 officers and men (P.O.W.'s included). He will never forget the Vinh Yen–Phuc Yen campaign (North Viet-Nam) in January last year, during which he received a deadly blow from the Viet-Nam People's Army. He will not forget the strategic points of Quang Yen (Road Number 18), Ninh Binh, Phu Ly, and Nghia Lo in North Viet-Nam, where our valiant fighters crushed him to pieces in March, May, June, and September. But the most striking battle was waged in December in the Hoa Binh region, which left to the enemy no more than 8,000 men alive. Our heroic militiamen and guerrillas who operate in the north, center, and south of Viet-Nam have caused heavy losses to the enemy. From the outbreak of the war of aggression unleashed by the French, their Expeditionary Corps has lost 170,000 men (killed, wounded, and captured), while the Vietnamese regular army and guerrilla units have grown stronger and stronger.

Guerrilla warfare is now being intensified and expanded in the enemy-controlled areas, especially in the Red River delta. Our guerrillas are particularly active in the provinces of Bac Giang, Bac Ninh, Ha Nam, Ninh Binh, Ha Dong, Hung Yen, and Thai Binh.

Early in October, 1951, fourteen enemy regiments carried out a large-scale raid in the districts of Duyen Ha, Hung Nhan, and Tien Hung. From October 1 to October 4, our guerrillas waged violent battles. In three points (Cong Ho, An My, and An Binh), 500 French soldiers were annihilated. All these victories were due to the heroism of our soldiers and guerrillas and to the sacrifice of the entire Vietnamese people. In each campaign, tens of thousands of voluntary workers of both sexes helped the armymen. As a rule, they worked in very hard conditions, in pelting rain, on muddy and steep mountain tracks, etc.

Thousands of patriots have left the enemy-controlled areas to take part in the above-mentioned task. It is worth mentioning here that the youth have set up many shock units.

The following example will illustrate the great patriotism and initiative of our people:

In the Hoa Binh campaign, our army had to cross the Lo River. French troops were stationed along the right bank, while their boats continually patrolled the river. In these conditions how could the crossing be made without the enemy's noticing it?

But the local population managed to find a way. In a locality some dozen kilometers from the Lo River, they called in a great number of craft and, through roundabout paths, carried them to the spot assigned at scheduled time. As soon as our troops had crossed the river, the inhabitants carried their craft back so as to keep secrecy and avoid enemy air raids.

Here I wish to speak of the women who support the soldiers. Most of them are old peasants; many have grandchildren. They help our officers and men and nurse the wounded as if they were their own sons. Like "goddesses protecting our lives," they take care of those of our fighters who work in enemy-controlled areas. Their deeds are highly esteemed and appreciated.

As is said above, the French colonialists are compelled to set up puppet troops in order to offset the losses suffered by the French Expeditionary Corps. But this is a dangerous method for the enemy.

First, everywhere in the enemy-held areas, the population struggles against the enemy's raiding and coercing the youth into their army. Second, the people so mobilized have resorted to actions of sabotage. Take an example: Once, the Quisling governor of Tonkin, styling himself "elder of the youth," paid a visit to the officers' training school of second degree at Nam Dinh. On hearing this news, the cadets prepared in his honor a "dignified" reception by writing on the

school wall the slogans "Down with Bao Dai!" and "Down with the
Puppet Clique!," while Bao Dai's name was given to the lavatory.

During this visit, the cadets made so much noise that the governor
was unable to speak. They put to him such a question as, "Dear
elder! Why do you want to use us as cannon fodder for the French
colonialists?" A group of cadets contemplated giving him a thrashing,
but he managed to take French leave like a piteous dog.

Many units of the puppet army secretly sent letters to President
Ho Chi Minh, saying that they were waiting for a propitious occasion
to "pass over to the side of the Fatherland" and that they were ready
to "carry out any orders issued by the Resistance, despite the danger
they might encounter."

Complete Failure of the French Colonialists

As soon as de Lattre de Tassigny set foot in Viet-Nam early in
1951, he boasted of the eventual victories of the French troops.

After his defeat and disillusion at the beginning of 1952, he realized that he would soon meet with complete failure.

The fate of the French colonialists' policy brought misgivings to
the most reactionary circles in France.

In the October 22, 1951, issue of *Information* Daladier, one of the
"criminals" in the Munich affair, wrote:

Delving into the real reason of our desperate financial situation, we
shall see that one of the underlying causes was lack of ripe consideration of our policy over Indochina. . . . In 1951, an expenditure of as
much as 330,000 million francs was officially reserved for the Indochinese budget. Due to the constant rise in the prices of commodities
and increase in the establishments of the French Expeditionary Corps,
which number 180,000 at present, it should be expected that in 1952
this expenditure will increase by 100,000 million francs. We have the
impression that the war in Indochina has caused exceedingly grave
danger to our financial as well as military situation. . . . It is impossible to foresee a rapid victory in a war which has lasted five years
and is in many ways reminiscent of the war unleashed by Napoleon
against Spain and the expedition against Mexico during the Second
Empire.

In its issue of December 13, 1951, the paper *Intransigeant* wrote:

France is paralyzed by the war in Indochina. We have gradually lost
the initiative of operation because our main forces are now pinned
down in the plains of North Viet-Nam. . . . In 1951, 330,000 million

francs were earmarked for the military budget of Indochina, while according to the official figures, our expenditure amounted to over 350,000 million. A credit of 380,000 million francs will be allotted to the 1952 budget, but in all probability the mark of 500,000 million will be reached. Such is the truth. . . . Whenever France tried to take some action, well, she immediately realized that she was paralyzed by the war in Indochina.

In its issue of December 16, 1951, *France Tireur* wrote:

General Vo Nguyen Giap's battalions, which are said to have been annihilated and to have a shattered morale, are now launching counter-offensives in the Hanoi region. . . . It is more and more obvious that the policy we have followed up to the present time has failed. Today it is clear that it has met with complete failure.

The following excerpt is from a letter sent to his colleagues by Captain Gazignoff of the French Expeditionary Corps, captured by us on January 7, 1952, in the Hoa Binh battle:

Taken prisoner a few days ago, I am very astonished at the kind and correct attitude of the Viet-Nam People's armymen toward me. . . . The Vietnamese troops will certainly win final victory, because they struggle for a noble ideal, a common cause, and are swayed by a self-imposed discipline. It is as clear as daylight that the Viet-Nam People's Army will crush the French Expeditionary Corps, but it is ready to receive any of us who will pass over to its side.

French officers, noncommissioned officers, and men who want to go over to the Viet-Nam People's Army will be considered as friends and will be set free.

The Vietnamese People Will Win

In 1952, Viet-Nam will embark on a program which includes the following points: to buckle down to production work and consolidate the national economy; to struggle and annihilate the enemy's forces; to intensify guerrilla warfare; to expose by all means the enemy's policy of "using the Vietnamese to fight the Vietnamese, and nursing the war by means of warfare"; to closely link patriotism to internationalism; energetically to combat bureaucracy, corruption, and waste.

The patriotism and heroism of the Vietnamese people allow us to have firm confidence in final victory.

The Vietnamese people's future is as bright as the sun in spring. Overjoyed at the radiance of the sun in spring, we shall struggle for the splendid future of Viet-Nam, for the future of democracy, world peace, and socialism. We triumph at the present time, we shall triumph in the future, because our path is enlightened by the great Marxist-Leninist doctrine.

SPEECH OPENING
THE FIRST IDEOLOGICAL
REMOLDING COURSE ORGANIZED
BY THE PARTY CENTRAL COMMITTEE
(May 11, 1952)

On behalf of the Central Committee I welcome you to this first ideological remolding course, which paves the way for the ideological remolding of the whole Party.

Why have we to carry out the ideological remolding of the Party?

Our Party has led our class and people successfully to carry out the August Revolution and has liberated our people from colonial rule and monarchical regime to set up people's power.

At present, our Party's task is to unite and lead our class together with the people to wage the Resistance War and build the country. This is a heavy and glorious task which can be performed only by our Party—the Party of the working class and of the toiling people.

Our Party possesses Marxism-Leninism, which is the most revolutionary and most scientific ideology. Its line and policies are correct. Its bases exist all over the country. Its cadres and members are unconditionally devoted and tested through heroic struggles.

But owing to difficult conditions, a great number of our cadres and members have not yet received adequate training. That is why they have a low ideological and political level and many deviations. This is obvious in such mistakes as unclarity on the policy of long-term resistance war and self-sufficiency, no clear-cut discrimination between enemies and friends, arrogance, bureaucracy, grave corruption, and libertinage, etc.

As a leading Party, our Party must be strong, pure, and exemplary. The whole Party must be united in mind and deed to be able to fulfill the tasks entrusted to it.

The aim of the ideological remolding of the Party is to raise the ideological and political level of the Party cadres and members to enable them to act in full keeping with the proletarian viewpoint and standpoint.

If the Party ideological remolding campaign is successfully carried out, it will develop our success in the military, political, and economic fields, etc.

It is through this campaign that the Party tempers, readjusts, and strengthens its ranks to keep up the long Resistance War until victory. This is the significance of the ideological remolding of the Party.

The campaign must have a focus: ideological readjustment before readjustment of organization. The ideological remolding course must be organized for Party cadres first.

Therefore, the task of the comrades attending this first ideological remolding course is to devote themselves to study, to be frank in making self-criticism and criticism, to gain more experiences and revolutionary virtues. When this course is over you must emulate with one another to help the Central Committee carry out the ideological remolding of the whole Party and the whole army and improve mass work.

The cadres decide everything. You are all high-ranking cadres and are assuming important responsibilities. The success or failure of the work depends for the most part on your ideology, virtues, attitude, and style of work.

The Central Committee earnestly hopes that during this course you will strive to emulate with one another in studying and tempering yourselves to become model cadres, worthy of the expectation and trust of the Party, the Government, the army, and the people, to become most able fighters in building the Party and helping it bring the Resistance War and national construction to success.

We are revolutionaries. We have determination. Moreover, we receive assistance from the brother parties, so however great may be the difficulties, we are resolute to fulfill our task. I hope that you will make every effort and will attain success.

TEACHING AT THE MEETING OF
OFFICERS FOR THE PREPARATION
OF THE MILITARY CAMPAIGN
IN THE NORTHWEST*
(September 9, 1952)

Yesterday it rained heavily and all the streams were flooded. Arriving at a brook with a strong current and seeing a group of compatriots sitting on the other side waiting for the water to subside, I said to myself, "Shouldn't I cross the stream at once so as not to keep you waiting." So a few other comrades and I took off our clothes and, groping our way with sticks, we succeeded in wading across the brook. On seeing my success, the group of compatriots also made up their mind to cross the stream. This is an experience for you, comrades. Whatever we do—big or small—if we are determined we shall be successful and shall imbue other people with the same determination.

Now I speak of the military campaign.

The Party Central Committee and the Party General Committee of

* The Northwest military campaign was launched on October 14, 1952, in the direction of the Laotian border, by a force of three People's Army divisions. The French lost the bulk of North Viet-Nam's uplands, including the valley of Dien Bien Phu, which they decided to retake one year later. For details of French military operations, see Fall, Street Without Joy (3d rev. ed.; Harrisburg, Pa.: The Stackpole Co., 1963).—ED.

the Army have carefully weighed the advantages and difficulties of the coming campaign and are determined that this campaign must be carried out successfully. It is not enough that only the Central Committee has determination. You must weigh and clearly see for yourselves the advantages and difficulties in order to be imbued with this determination. It is not enough that the Central Committee and you are determined, we must act in such a way that this determination permeates every soldier. This determination from the Central Committee must reach the rank and file through you. It must become a monolithic bloc from higher to lower ranks and from lower to higher ranks. To have determination does not mean to speak glibly of it, but to have deep confidence. When meeting with advantages we must be determined to develop them and when encountering difficulties we must be determined to overcome them. Everyone in the army must be deeply imbued with determination.

In this meeting, the Party General Committee of the Army has disseminated in detail the Central Committee's resolutions, and you have debated them. The significance and objectives of the military campaign are: to annihilate the enemy's manpower, to win over the people, and to liberate territory. The main task is *to annihilate the enemy's manpower.*

You have discussed the advantages and difficulties. When meeting with an advantage, if we are not determined to develop it, it may likely turn into difficulty. When meeting with a difficulty, if we are determined to overcome it, it will become an advantage. In truth, nothing is easy and nothing is difficult. For example, it is easy to break off a branch. But if we are not determined and do it half-heartedly, we may not be able to break it off. It is difficult to carry out the revolution and to wage the Resistance War, but with our determination we will be successful.

Determination does not lie in the meeting place and in words, but in work and deeds. We must have determination to promote a valiant fighting style. We must have determination to oppose all negative, wavering, and selfish acts and false reports.

We must be determined to fight, to endure hardships and difficulties, to overcome them, and be determined to implement the policies of the Central Committee and the Government. In other words, in our behavior, mind, deeds, and fighting, in everything—big or small—we must be determined to win success.

The army is strong when it is well fed. The comrades in the commissariat must have determination to supply the troops with adequate food and weapons.

On their side, the troops must be determined to light-heartedly endure privations, to strive to give a hand to the commissariat if necessary.

Food and weapons are sweat and tears of our compatriots, blood and bones of our troops, so we must value, spare, preserve, and properly use them.

War booty is not a gift from the enemy. It is thanks to the sweat and tears of our compatriots and the blood and bones of our troops that we can capture it. Prior to its capture, it belongs to the enemy, after it, it is ours. Therefore, concerning war booty, we distribute to our compatriots what ought to be distributed, hand over to the Government what should be, and what should be used as reward for the troops must be given in an equitable and rational way. Corruption and waste must be absolutely avoided.

The Government has issued policies concerning the national minorities; you and the troops must implement them correctly. This is a measure to win over the people, frustrating the enemy's scheme of "using Vietnamese to harm Vietnamese." We must so do that each fighter becomes a propagandist. You must behave in such a way that the people welcome you on your arrival and give you willing aid during your stay and miss you on your departure. This would be a great success.

You must be aware that only a small part of enemy troops are Europeans and Africans while the majority are puppet troops. A great number of the latter are press-ganged into the army by the French. If you cleverly carry out the work of agitation among the puppet troops, this would be a way to annihilate enemy manpower.

Our units are helped by civilians moving with them. You must educate and take good care of the volunteer workers, explain our policies to them, and encourage them to work light-heartedly. A close friendship and solidarity must prevail between the troops and the volunteer workers, so that the latter are unwilling to go home, and like to stay on and help the troops. This is one of the factors for victory. If you fail to do so, we shall meet with many difficulties.

It is thanks to good education, correct policies, and strict discipline that the troops are strong. That is why discipline must be strict. There are two points in discipline that call for attention: punishment and reward.

Up to now, punishment and reward have been insufficient, and that is a big mistake. There must be units mentioned in dispatches and awarded with medals. After you have proposed someone for a medal, the proposal has immediately to be made public. The Government, the High Command, and I are ready to reward those who score achievements. On the other hand, those who have wrongly carried out the orders or made false reports must be punished severely.

The units must emulate with each other and the cadres between themselves to promote the movement for valiant fighting.

We must bear in mind that the revolutionary troops, first of all, the Party members, do not shun difficulties but must overcome them. We must learn the spirit of the Soviet Red Army and of the Chinese Liberation Army: When carrying out some difficult task, the unit which is entrusted with it prides itself on this honor, whereas those which are not appointed feel quite unhappy to find that they have not yet the capacity required.

You can learn from this attitude. I am convinced that thanks to the leadership of the Party and the Government you will be able to take it up.

Divisional commanders down to group leaders must share joy and hardships with the soldiers, take care of, help, and treat each other like blood brothers. This is a tradition of the Soviet Red Army and of the Chinese Liberation Army that our soldiers must learn as well. To succeed in so doing is tantamount to partially triumphing over the enemy before fighting him.

The units must emulate with each other to do as I advise you. Are you determined to emulate with each other?

You are determined, so you must by all means score successes in your fighting. I am waiting for news of victory from you. I promise a reward to the troops in the period from September 2 to December 19. It is a small reward but of great value because I have made it myself. There are other rewards beside this one for the units that are the first to perform feats of arms.

Heroes are not only the troops who exterminate the enemy and perform feats of arms but also the supply men who strive to serve the troops. In each of you exists heroism in the bud, you must develop it.

If you fulfill your task, I shall always be cheerful and in good health.

As is known to some of you, on the setting up of our army, our men were equipped with only a few commodities and the few rifles they got were bought in contraband. We obtained great achievements notwithstanding, and the August Revolution was victorious.

Now that we have numerous troops, good generals, and everyone has determination, we will certainly be successful.

EIGHT-POINT ORDER ISSUED BY THE GOVERNMENT OF THE DEMOCRATIC REPUBLIC OF VIET-NAM*
(October 1, 1952)

For a long time, the French colonialists and Vietnamese kings and their courts outrightly oppressed and exploited our fellow countrymen in the highland. Today the Government sends its troops to wipe out the French invaders, the puppet troops, and the traitors to the country in order to free our compatriots from the enemy's yoke and to help them build a free and happy life.

The eight-point order below is issued by the Government for public servants, armymen, and the population at large.

1. Protection of the people's lives and property. All the population, regardless of social classes, creeds, and occupations, ought to keep order, wholeheartedly support the people's power, and obey the Government law and military orders. The people's administration and army are duty-bound to unite closely with the population and protect their lives and property. The traitors to the country, spies, pirates, rioters, or wreckers will be severely punished.

2. Protection of the people's occupations and professions. The administration and the army shall guarantee security and order for

* This order was issued when People's Army troops entered the Northwest Region.

253

the people. Honest people who engage in farming, handicraft, trade, etc., can go on with their business. People who have taken refuge in another place because their villages were concentrated by the enemy or who have evacuated to the resistance zones are urged to return to their native villages and attend to their former business.

3. Confiscation of the property of the French invaders and traitors to the country. All property belonging to the French invaders and traitors will be confiscated and disposed of by the people's administration. Their land will be allotted to poor or landless peasants.

Public employees serving in the post and telecommunications service, treasury, factories and workshops, plantations, storehouses, etc., left by the French and puppet administration should take care of machines, tools, materials, accounting books, in order to hand them over to the people's power. Whoever wishes to resume his work will be employed by the Government according to his ability.

4. Protection of temples, pagodas, churches, schools, hospitals, and other social and cultural establishments. Those who have worked in these establishments will continue their work as usual. The administration and people's army will protect them. The administration, army, and people's organizations shall respect the religious beliefs, customs, and habits of the population.

5. Reward of meritorious people and punishment of guilty people. Traitors to the country and great despots shall be punished.

The Government will be lenient toward those who have previously been coerced by the enemy into their ranks but who do not now oppose the people's power and army. Those who help the people's power and army to annihilate the enemy and suppress the traitors shall be rewarded.

Those who indulge in sabotage and theft, abscond with public property and money or official documents and refuse to hand them back to the people's power and army shall be punished.

6. Maintenance of order and security. Remnants of the French troops and pirates are obliged to surrender to the people's administration or army. The Government will be lenient toward those who surrender of their own will with all their weapons.

Those who refuse to surrender or conceal weapons shall be punished. Those who harbor the colonialists and the puppet men or give free hand or assistance to the pirates shall be prosecuted.

Those who distinguish themselves in helping the people's power and army to capture the remnants of the colonial troops and the pirates or who call on them to surrender shall be rewarded.

7. *Organization of the people, especially the peasants.* The people must be organized in order to help one another in production, to improve their livelihood and also, to assist the people's power and army to gradually carry out work profitable to the local population.

8. *Protection of the lives and property of foreign residents.* Foreign residents will live and work peacefully and keep order. They ought to respect the Government law and order of the Viet-Nam People's Army. Security agents and spies of the colonialists or those who act against the Resistance in Viet-Nam or who help or harbor the colonialists and the traitors shall be punished according to the law issued by the Vietnamese Government.

The discipline of the people's army is strict; the soldiers buy and sell at fair price, and do not take so much as a needle or thread from the population.

Compatriots! Be calm and go on with your work; keep order and discipline, give assistance to the soldiers, support the people's power, keep secrets for the army, cadres, and Government offices; don't listen to the propaganda of the enemy and puppet administration.

REPLIES TO A
FOREIGN CORRESPONDENT*

(November 26, 1953)

Question: The debate in the French National Assembly has proved that a great number of French politicians are for a peaceful settlement of the conflicts in Viet-Nam by direct negotiations with the Vietnamese Government. This desire is spreading among the French people. Do your Government and you welcome it?

Answer: The war in Viet-Nam was launched by the French Government. The Vietnamese people are obliged to take up arms and have heroically struggled for nearly eight years against the aggressors, to safeguard our independence and the right to live freely and peacefully. Now, if the French colonialists continue their aggressive war, the Vietnamese people are determined to carry on the patriotic resistance until final victory. However, if the French Government has drawn a lesson from the war they have been waging these last years and want to negotiate an armistice in Viet-Nam and to solve the Viet-Nam problem by peaceful means, the people and Government of the Democratic Republic of Viet-Nam are ready to meet this desire.

Question: Will a cease fire or an armistice be possible?

* In early November, 1953, a Swedish correspondent cabled a questionnaire to President Ho Chi Minh on the situation of the war in Viet-Nam and the prospects of the peaceful settlement of the Viet-Nam problem.

Answer: A cessation of hostilities is possible, provided that the French Government ends its war of aggression in Viet-Nam. The French Government's sincere respect for the genuine independence of Viet-Nam must be the basis of the armistice.

Question: Would you agree to a neutral country mediating to organize a meeting between you and the representatives of the High Command of the other side? May Sweden be entrusted with this responsibility?

Answer: If there are neutral countries which try to speed up a cessation of hostilities in Viet-Nam by means of negotiations, they will be welcomed. However, the negotiation for an armistice is mainly the concern of the Government of the Democratic Republic of Viet-Nam and the French Government.

Question: In your opinion, is there any other way to end the hostilities?

Answer: The war in Viet-Nam has brought havoc to the Vietnamese people and at the same time caused countless sufferings to the French people; therefore, the French people are struggling against the war in Viet-Nam.

I have constantly showed my sympathy, affection, and respect for the French people and the French peace fighters. Today not only is the independence of Viet-Nam seriously jeopardized, but the independence of France is also gravely threatened. On the one hand, the U.S. imperialists egg on the French colonialists to continue and expand the aggressive war in Viet-Nam, thus weakening them more and more through fighting, in the hope of replacing France in Indochina; on the other, they oblige France to ratify the European defense treaty that is to revive German militarism.

Therefore, the struggle of the French people to gain independence, democracy, and peace for France and to end the war in Viet-Nam constitutes one of the important factors to settle the Viet-Nam question by peaceful means.

REPORT TO THE
NATIONAL ASSEMBLY OF THE
DEMOCRATIC REPUBLIC OF VIET-NAM*

On behalf of the Government, I joyfully welcome you, who have come to attend this extraordinary session of the National Assembly.

I send my affectionate greetings to the deputies who cannot come on account of their Resistance work.

On behalf of the Government, I pay tribute to the deputies who have heroically sacrificed their lives for the Resistance and the Fatherland.

On behalf of the Government, I also welcome the delegates of the National United Front, coming to greet the National Assembly.

For these eight years, our entire people have been carrying out the greatest task, which is to conduct the Resistance War. From now on, we have another central task, which is land reform. We must endeavor to speed up the Resistance War in order to vouch for the success of land reform. We must exert all our efforts to implement land reform in order to secure complete victory for the Resistance War.

At this extraordinary session, the National Assembly will hear the report on the work done for the Resistance War during these last

* The Third Session of the National Assembly of the Democratic Republic of Viet-Nam, held December 1–4, 1953, performed a significant act with regard to the development of the Vietnamese Resistance and revolution: the passage of the Agrarian Reform Law, based on reports by President Ho Chi Minh and Pham Van Dong.

years, and will discuss the policies on land reform and approve the land-reform laws.

Our country is a part of the world. Its situation has an influence on the world, and the situation of the world also concerns our country. For this reason, before reporting on the Resistance work and the policies on land reform, I shall briefly report on the situation in the world and in our country.

World Situation

We can say plainly that with every passing day our camp is growing stronger and stronger and the enemy camp weaker and weaker.

The Soviet Union, a bulwark of world peace and democracy, is strongly marching forward from socialism to Communism. The happiness dreamt of by mankind for so many centuries is gradually being realized in one-sixth of the world.

To safeguard world peace, the Soviet Union also possesses A-bombs and H-bombs, but it has time and again proposed their banning.

With the wholehearted assistance of the Soviet Union, the East European people's democracies are doing their utmost to build socialism.

China has gained a great victory in fighting the United States and helping Korea, and has successively scored many great achievements in the first year of the Five-Year Plan in construction work.

The great successes achieved by the Italian Communist Party and the French Communist Party in various elections, the mammoth strikes (August and September, 1953) in these two countries, the struggle waged by the toiling class in various countries, and the movement for national liberation in Malaya, the Philippines, North Africa, Central Africa, Guiana, etc., have proved that the struggle waged by the people throughout the world is developing.

The Peace Conference of Asia and the Pacific (held in October, 1952) and the Conference of the World People for the Safeguarding of Peace (held in November, 1952) have upheld the tremendous strength of the world camp of peace and democracy.

During the recent period, the greatest success gained by the world camp of peace and democracy was the cessation of hostilities in Korea. Putting up the most heroic struggle, the Korean Army and people, hand in hand with the Chinese volunteers, annihilated more than 1 million soldiers of the United States and its satellites. Acting as pincers, the forces of democracy and world peace have forced them to come to an armistice in Korea.

Last October, the Third World Congress of Trade Unions, on behalf of more than 88 million workers in seventy-nine countries, passed a resolution that December 19, 1953, will be "the day of solidarity with the heroic Vietnamese people, and of struggle for the cessation of the aggressive war in Viet-Nam." This is warm internationalism, positive class feelings; it gives our people more enthusiasm to conduct the Resistance War, and gives us more confidence in final victory.

This is the summary of the situation of our camp.

What about the imperialist camp headed by the United States? The United States and sixteen countries of its camp (including Great Britain and France) have suffered an ignominious defeat in Korea. From the end of the nineteenth century until today, the United States has many times used wars to enrich itself and occupy a leading position. This is the first (but not the last) time they suffered a great failure, losing not only men (more than 390,500 American soldiers dead and wounded) and wealth (more than $20 billion), but also their face before other countries. The U.S. position in the United Nations is growing weaker, its camp is becoming more and more divided, and its economy is suffering an ever more acute crisis.

The capitalist countries dependent on the United States, such as Great Britain and France, are facing ever greater economic and political difficulties due to their arms-race policy, to the people's movement at home, and to the movement of national liberation in their colonies.

The present U.S. scheme is to rekindle war to rule over the whole world.

In Asia, it sabotages the convening of the political conference so as to rekindle war in Korea. It rearms Japan. It prevents China from joining the United Nations. It interferes more actively in the war in Viet-Nam, Cambodia, and Laos.

In Europe, it frustrates the unification of Germany and rearms West Germany to use it as the mainstay for the "European Army."

Our camp is becoming stronger and stronger, more united and single-minded within the front of democracy and peace headed by the Soviet Union.

Our present main goal is to relax international tensions and to solve all disputes in the world by means of negotiations.

The present task of the world people is to consolidate the achievements they have gained, to keep vigilance against the U.S. scheme, strongly push forward the world peace movement.

The world situation is favorable to us. We support the world peace movement. But we must not have the illusion that peace can be realized easily. It can be gained only through hard struggle. As the French colonialists and American interventionists pursue their aggressive war in our country, we must overcome all difficulties, practice self-sufficiency, strongly push forward the Resistance War to complete victory.

Domestic Situation of the Enemy

1. In the military field. The enemy has suffered great losses (about 320,000 men by October, 1953). The European and African effectives are thinning out with every passing day. On the main battlefields, the enemy keeps losing his initiative. Recently, he tried to work his way into the free area in the Third Interzone and into some other coastal localities in the Fourth Interzone, but he is basically on the defensive.

However, at present the enemy is still strong. We must not underestimate him.

2. The political situation. The contradictions are becoming more acute between the Americans and the French, between the French and the puppets, and between the pro-French puppets and the pro-American puppets.

In the areas temporarily occupied by the enemy, his policy of deceit and exploitation is energetically opposed by our people.

In France, the antiwar movement is gaining ground.

3. Economy and finance. War has cost the enemy an ever greater expenditure (from 1946 up to now, he has spent more than 3,000,000 million francs).

But he can still exploit rubber and coal, export a quantity of rice, collect taxes, and plunder the people's property in the enemy-occupied areas. In addition, he is given "assistance" by the Americans.

On the other hand, he is doing his utmost to destroy our production and means of transport in free areas, in guerrilla bases and guerrilla zones.

4. Culture and social welfare. In the temporarily occupied areas, the enemy makes intense propaganda by his depraved culture and hooliganism in order to poison our people, especially our youth. He misuses religions to divide our people.

His main scheme is "using Vietnamese to fight Vietnamese, feeding war by war."

What is the enemy doing and what does he intend doing at the present time?

Interfering more deeply in the war in Viet-Nam, Cambodia, and Laos, the Americans give the French and the puppets more money and weapons. They win over the Vietnamese, Cambodian, and Laotian puppets and speed up the organization of a puppet army. They force the French to make concession to the puppets, that is, to them. They have a plan to replace the French step by step, but continue to use the latter as stooges in the implementation of their war policy.

Apart from their economic exploitation and plundering, the French and American imperialists use a policy of deceit in the political field, such as declaring sham "independence" and "democracy" and holding fraudulent elections; pretending to carry out land reform to deceive the peasants in temporarily occupied areas; setting up "yellow" trade unions to mislead the workers; and advancing a fable of peace to blindfold the French people and the people over the world, and to deceive our people.

Meanwhile, General Navarre feverishly mustered his mobile forces to attack us, sow trouble in our rear, develop the commando activities, and speed up intelligence warfare.

In short, the French and Americans are making efforts to implement their scheme, that is, to extend the war by means of "using Vietnamese to fight Vietnamese, feeding war by war."

We must not be subjective and underestimate the enemy. We must always be vigilant and ready to frustrate his schemes. But we can say that his activities do not prove that he is strong but that he is weak. He is afraid of our long-term resistance policy. He is afraid of the world peace movement.

In order to foil the enemy schemes, we must endeavor to speed up our Resistance War. To do so, we must carry out land reform.

Our Domestic Situation

1. In the military field. From autumn-winter, 1950, up to now, we have gained great victories in seven military campaigns and have taken the initiative on the main fronts. We have liberated the greater part of the large Northwest area. The guerrilla movement has developed strongly everywhere.

The political and technical remolding drives have brought good results. Our army has grown up rapidly in effectives as well as in quality.

Many regular units, local units, and guerrilla units have scored very heroic and glorious military feats.

2. *The political situation.* The ideological remolding courses for the cadres within and without the Party have achieved satisfactory results (almost 15,800 cadres from central to village levels have attended these courses).

The National United Front has been consolidated and enlarged.

The alliance between Viet-Nam, Cambodia, and Laos has grown closer.

The diplomatic activities of our Government and people have been enlarged and have won the sympathy and support of the people of the world, especially the people of the friendly countries and of France.

3. *Economy and finance.* Our people have overcome many difficulties, have made efforts to emulate in production, have contributed greatly in manpower and wealth to the Resistance War. Our finance has been gradually stabilized. We have established commercial relations with China, which is very advantageous to our people.

4. *Culture and social welfare.* An ever greater number of toiling people have taken part in study. The number of general-education schools and the number of pupils have increased. The training of specialists has been gradually reorganized and enlarged.

This is the summary of the notable achievements of our people, Government, and Party; but we still have the following shortcoming, concerning the land policy: In former times we were biased against unity with landlords for the sake of the Resistance War, and we have not attached due importance to the peasant question and the agrarian question.

Recently our Government and Party have put right this shortcoming, and much progress has been scored. But in some localities, the policy of the central authorities has not been implemented correctly. A number of cadres think and act contrary to the policy of the Government and Party, they lack organizational concepts and do not keep discipline. Other cadres attach importance only to fighting feudalism and belittle the struggle against imperialism.

We must put right these shortcomings, and prevent "leftist" or rightist deviations.

Land Reform

Concerning this problem, I sum up the following points on the significance of land reform.

Our revolution is a people's national democratic revolution against aggressive imperialism and its mainstay, feudalism.

Our slogan during the Resistance War is, "All for the Front, All for Victory!" The more the Resistance War develops, the more manpower and wealth it requires, and our peasants have contributed the greatest part of manpower and wealth to the Resistance. We must liberate them from the feudal yoke, foster them in order fully to mobilize this huge force for the Resistance to win victory.

The key to the victory of the Resistance lies in consolidating and enlarging the National United Front, consolidating the worker-peasant alliance and the people's power, strengthening and developing the Army, consolidating the Party and strengthening its leadership in all aspects. Only by mobilizing the masses to carry out land reform can we carry out these works satisfactorily.

The enemy actively uses Vietnamese to fight Vietnamese and feeds war by war. They are doing their utmost to deceive, divide, and exploit our people. Land reform will exert an influence on and encourage our peasant compatriots in the enemy rear to struggle more enthusiastically against the enemy, in order to liberate themselves and more enthusiastically to support the Democratic Resistance Government; at the same time it exerts an influence on and disintegrates the puppet army because the absolute majority of the puppet soldiers are peasants in enemy-occupied areas.

The absolute majority of our people are peasants. Over these last years, thanks to their forces, the Resistance War has been successful. In the future, it is also thanks to the peasant forces that we will be able to gain complete victory and successfully build our country.

Our peasants account for almost 90 per cent of the population, but they own only 30 per cent of the arable land and have to work hard all the year round and suffer poverty all their lives.

The landlord and feudal class accounts for less than 5 per cent of the population, but they and the colonialists occupy about 70 per cent of the arable land, live in clover, and do nothing. This situation is most unjust. Our country has been invaded, our people are backward and poor. During the Resistance years, though the Government has carried out the policy of land rent reduction, land rent refunding, and temporary distribution of land (belonging to the French and Vietnamese traitors) and communal land to the peasants in the free areas, the key problem which is not yet solved is that the peasant masses do not have land or lack land. This exerts an influence on the peasant forces in the Resistance War and on production.

Only by implementing land reform, giving land to the tillers, and liberating the productive forces in the countryside from the feudal yoke can we do away with poverty and backwardness, strongly mobilize the huge forces of the peasants to develop production, and speed up the Resistance War to complete victory.

The goal set for land reform is to wipe out the feudal system of land appropriation, distribute land to the tillers, liberate the productive forces in the countryside, develop production, and speed up the Resistance War.

The general line and policy is to rely entirely on landless and land-poor peasants, to unite closely with the middle peasants, to rally with the rich peasants, to wipe out feudal exploitation step by step and with differentiation, to develop production, and to speed up the Resistance War.

To conform to the characteristics of the Resistance War and of the National United Front, which are to meet the needs of the peasants in land, at the same time to consolidate and develop the National United Front in a way favorable to the Resistance War and to production while implementing land reform, we must apply different kinds of treatment to the landlords according to the political attitude of each of them. This means that we must apply a policy of differentiation which consists in confiscation, requisitioning with or without compensation. We will not apply a policy of wholesale confiscation or wholesale requisitioning without compensation.

The guiding principle for land reform is to mobilize the peasants boldly, to rely on the masses, to follow the mass line correctly, and to organize, educate, and lead the peasants to struggle in a planned way, step by step, according to a proper order and under close leadership.

The dispersion of land by landlords after the promulgation of the land rent-reduction decree (July 14, 1949) is illegal (except for particular cases dealt with in the circular issued by the Prime Minister's Office on June 1, 1953).

The land confiscated or requisitioned with or without compensation is to be distributed definitely to the peasants who have no land or are short of it. The peasants have the right to ownership of the land thus distributed.

The guiding principle for land distribution is to take villages as units, to allot land to those who previously tilled it, to take into consideration the quantity, quality, and situation of the land, to give a greater share of land to those who do not have enough, to give fertile land to those who have but poor land, to give land which is situated near the village to those who have only land situated far from their houses, to give priority to the peasants who previously tilled the land to be distributed.

The die-hard elements who are determined to sabotage land reform, and the traitors, reactionaries, and despots who are sentenced to upwards of five years' imprisonment will not receive land.

The mass mobilizations launched this year are for experimental purposes and for the preparation for the land reform next year. These experimental drives have given us a number of experiences. In general, in the localities where the Party and Government policies have been firmly grasped and the mass line correctly followed (except in some localities where a number of cadres have committed mistakes and deviations), satisfactory results have been scored.

The mass mobilization has failed in localities where it was launched hurriedly by impatient local cadres without the decision of the central authorities.

Land reform is a policy applied throughout the country, but it must be carried out step by step, first in localities where sufficient conditions have been obtained and then in other localities.

After the land reform law is approved by the National Assembly, the Government will, next year, fix the date and the localities in the Free Zone in which land reform will be carried out.

The Government will deal with the regions inhabited by the national minorities, the Fifth Zone, South Viet-Nam, and the guerrilla bases later on. In guerrilla- and enemy-occupied areas, land reform will be carried out after their liberation.

In the localities where the mass mobilization is not yet launched for radical land-rent reduction, we have to wait until it is completed before carrying out land reform. We must do so in order to organize the peasants, raise their political consciousness, build their political supremacy in the villages, at the same time to train cadres, readjust the organization, and prepare political conditions for land reform.

No locality is allowed to start the mass mobilization for land reform without the decision of the Government.

Land reform is a peasant revolution, a class struggle in the countryside; it is a large-scale, hard, and complicated struggle, that is why preparations must be carefully made, plans clearly mapped out, the leadership very close, the localities judiciously chosen, the time strictly followed, and the implementation correct. These are conditions leading to success.

The experiences of other countries have taught us that a successful land reform will help us overcome many difficulties and solve many problems.

In the military field, our peasant compatriots will take part in the Resistance War more enthusiastically, thus helping the development of the Army and the mobilization of the people for voluntary labor to serve the Resistance. Our soldiers will have less worry about their families and will fight more fiercely.

In the political field, the political and economic power in the countryside will be in the hands of the peasants, the people's democratic dictatorship will be carried out genuinely, the worker-peasant alliance will be firmer, the National United Front will include more than 90 per cent of the people in the countryside and will become prodigiously great and strong.

In the economic field, liberated from feudalism and landlordism, the peasants will joyfully carry out production and practice thrift, consumption will be increased, industry and commerce will develop, and the national economy as a whole will expand.

Thanks to the development of production, the livelihood of the peasants, workers, soldiers, and cadres will be improved more rapidly.

In culture and social welfare, the large majority of the people will have enough food and clothes and, as a saying goes, "one must eat to be able to discharge one's duty," they will study more enthusiastically, thereby good customs will develop. The experiences drawn from the localities where the mass mobilization was launched show that our compatriots are very fond of study. This is a good opportunity for the intellectuals to serve the people.

As is said above, land reform is a widespread, complicated, and hard class struggle. It is all the more complicated and all the harder because we are conducting the Resistance War. But it is just because we want to speed up the Resistance War to victory that we must be determined to make land reform a success. It is a complicated and hard struggle, that is why a number of cadres (Party members or non-Party members) might commit mistakes and deviations in their thinking, in their action, and in implementing the policies on land reform. To prevent and put right these shortcomings and mistakes, we must firmly grasp the policies of the Party and Government, completely rely on the masses, and correctly follow the mass line.

The Government and the Party call on all the cadres and Party members to abide correctly by the policies of the Government and the Party, to keep discipline, to side entirely with the peasants, to lead them in their struggle, to sacrifice their private interests for the interests of the Resistance War and of the masses when there are contradictions between their private interests and the interests of the Resistance War and of the peasant masses.

We must mobilize the entire Party, entire Army, and entire people to ensure the implementation of land reform, to fulfill this great task.

With regard to the members and cadres of various democratic parties and to patriotic personalities, this is an enormous trial. We all must gain the battle in this trial, as we are gaining the battle in the immense trial that is the Resistance War against aggressive imperialism.

That is why our two central tasks in the next years are to do our utmost to fight the enemy and to carry out land reform.

We must strive to fight the enemy on various fronts, to annihilate the enemy forces as much as possible, to smash his new military schemes.

We must mobilize the masses to carry out land reform in the localities fixed by the Government.

To carry out land reform is to secure victory for the Resistance War.

To fight the enemy, to annihilate the enemy forces, is to secure success for land reform.

All other works must be subordinated to those two central tasks and serve them. In 1954, we must pay particular importance to three great works:

To combine land reform with the strengthening of the armed forces (the regular army, the local army, the militia, and guerrilla units) in all aspects: organization, training, raising of their political and technical level, and their combativeness.

To combine land reform with the training of cadres and the raising of their ideology and, with the promoting and readjustment of cadres, the readjustment of the Party bases in the countryside.

To combine land reform with the development of agricultural production, to ensure the requirements of the Resistance War and food for the people, in order to push forward the activities of the national economy.

To implement fully these two central tasks and three great works is to create more favorable conditions for the carrying out of other works, such as firmly to maintain and develop the struggle in the enemy rear, to consolidate the people's democratic power in villages, to reorganize the security service, to develop and consolidate the National United Front, to collect agricultural taxes, to develop economy and finance, to intensify propaganda, and to develop education, culture, and social welfare.

Our forces lie in millions of peasants who are ready to wait for the Government and Party to organize and lead them in order to rise up enthusiastically and smash the feudal and colonial yoke. With skillful organization and leadership, these forces will shake heaven and earth, all the colonialists and feudalists will be swept away. We can conclude that under the correct leadership of the Government and the Party, with the wholehearted assistance of the National Assembly and the Front, the successful completion of land reform will help us take a big stride and bring the Resistance War and national construction to victory.

CONGRATULATORY LETTER TO ARMYMEN, WAR SERVICE WORKERS, SHOCK YOUTH, AND PEOPLE IN THE NORTHWEST AREA WHO HAVE WON BRILLIANT VICTORY AT DIEN BIEN PHU*

(May 8, 1954)

Our army has liberated Dien Bien Phu. The Government and I convey our cordial greetings to you, cadres, fighters, war service workers, shock youth, and local people who have gloriously fulfilled your tasks.

This victory is big, but it is only the beginning. We must not be self-complacent and subjective and underestimate the enemy. We are determined to fight for independence, national unity, democracy, and peace. A struggle, whether military or diplomatic, must be long and hard before complete victory can be achieved.

The Government and I will reward the officers, soldiers, patriotic workers, shock youth, and local people who have performed brilliant deeds.

---

* *There exists another version of this proclamation, dated May 13, 1954, and addressed to Ho's "nephews and nieces," to whom he awards the insignia "Combattant of Dien Bien Phu."*—ED.

APPEAL MADE AFTER
THE SUCCESSFUL CONCLUSION
OF THE GENEVA AGREEMENTS
(July 22, 1954)

The Geneva Conference has come to an end. It is a great victory for our diplomacy.

On behalf of the Government, I cordially make the following appeal:

1. For the sake of peace, unity, independence, and democracy of the Fatherland, our people, armymen, cadres, and Government have, during these eight years or so, joined in a monolithic bloc, endured hardship, and resolutely overcome all difficulties to carry out the Resistance; we have won many brilliant victories. On this occasion, on behalf of the Government, I cordially congratulate you, from North to South. I respectfully bow to the memory of the armymen and people who have sacrificed their lives for the Fatherland, and send my homages of comfort to the wounded and sick armymen.

This great victory is also due to the support given us in our just struggle by the peoples of our brother countries, by the French people, and by the peace-loving people of the world.

Thanks to these victories and the efforts made by the delegation of the Soviet Union at the Berlin Conference, negotiations were opened between our country and France at the Geneva Conference. At this conference, the struggle of our delegation and the assistance given by the delegations of the Soviet Union and China have ended in a great victory for us: The French Government has recognized the independence, sovereignty, unity, and territorial integrity of our country; it has agreed to withdraw French troops from our country, etc.

From now on, we must make every effort to consolidate peace and achieve reunification, independence, and democracy throughout our country.

2. In order to re-establish peace, the first step to take is that the armed forces of both parties should cease fire.

The regroupment in two regions is a temporary measure; it is a transitional step for the implementation of the armistice and restoration of peace, and paves the way for national reunification through general elections. Regroupment in regions is in no way a partition of our country, neither is it an administrative division.

During the armistice, our army is regrouped in the North; the French troops are regrouped in the South, that is to say, there is a change of regions. A number of regions which were formerly occupied by the French now become our free zones. Vice versa, a number of regions formerly liberated by us will now be temporarily occupied by the French troops before they leave for France.

This is a necessity; North, Central, and South Viet-Nam are territories of ours. Our country will certainly be unified, our entire people will surely be liberated.

Our compatriots in the South were the first to wage the war of Resistance. They possess a high political consciousness. I am confident that they will place national interests above local interests, permanent interests above temporary interests, and join their efforts with the entire people in strengthening peace, achieving unity, independence, and democracy all over the country. The Party, Government, and I always follow the efforts of our people and we are sure that our compatriots will be victorious.

3. The struggle to consolidate peace and achieve reunification, independence, and democracy is also a long and hard struggle. In order to carry the day, our people, armymen, and cadres from North to South must unite closely. They must be at one in thought and deed.

We are resolved to abide by the agreements entered into with the French Government. At the same time, we demand that the French Government correctly implement the agreements they have signed with us.

We must do our utmost to strengthen peace and be vigilant to check the maneuvers of peace wreckers.

We must endeavor to struggle for the holding of free general elections throughout the country to reunify our territory.

We must exert all our efforts to restore, build, strengthen, and develop our forces in every field so as to attain complete independence.

We must do our utmost to carry out social reforms in order to improve our people's livelihood and realize genuine democracy.

We further tighten our fraternal relations with Cambodia and Laos.

We strengthen the great friendship between us and the Soviet Union, China, and other brother countries. To maintain peace, we enhance our solidarity with the French people, the Asian people, and people all over the world.

4. I call on all our compatriots, armymen, and cadres to follow strictly the lines and policies laid down by the Party and Government, to struggle for the consolidation of peace and the achievement of national reunification, independence, and democracy throughout the country.

I eagerly appeal to all genuine patriots, irrespective of their social class, creed, political stand, and former affiliation, to cooperate sincerely with us and fight for the sake of our country and our people so as to bring about peace and achieve reunification, independence, and democracy for our beloved Viet-Nam.

If our people are as one, if thousands of men are like one, victory will certainly be ours.

Long live a peaceful, unified, independent, and democratic Viet-Nam.

APPEAL ON THE OCCASION OF THE CELEBRATION OF THE AUGUST REVOLUTION AND NATIONAL DAY

(September 2, 1954)

Compatriots, armymen, and cadres all over the country and Vietnamese residents abroad,

On the occasion of the ninth anniversary of the August Revolution and the National Day, on behalf of the Government I solemnly send you our cordial greetings.

During eighty years, the feudal kings and princes sold out our Fatherland and people to the French colonialists. In the course of this gloomy period, our ancestors and then our generation unremittingly struggled to regain freedom and national independence.

The great victory of the Soviet Union over the German fascists and Japanese militarists in World War II contributed to the success of our August Revolution.

What was the aim of the August Revolution?

It was to restore peace, national unity, independence, and democracy to our country and people.

The August Revolution being achieved, independence was declared on September 2. The Democratic Republic of Viet-Nam was born. General elections were held and our people throughout the country elected a National Assembly, which ratified the Constitution and chose the central government. Local administrations, from village to

274

province, were entirely appointed by the people. Since that time, national unity, independence, and democracy have begun to materialize in our country.

Our people and government long for peace to construct our country and to build a free and happy life.

But soon the bellicose French colonialists unleashed a new war in an attempt to invade our country and to enslave our people once more.

In face of this danger, our people, army, cadres, and government, closely united, resolutely waged a war of resistance which lasted nearly nine years and won many great victories.

The aim of our Resistance was to preserve and develop the achievements secured by the August Revolution, that is to say, peace, unity, independence, and democracy.

Thanks to the valiant struggle waged by our army and people, supported by the peoples of brother countries, by the French people and peace-loving people of the world, we have won the day at the Geneva Conference.

The French Government has recognized the following points, approved by member countries of the Conference:

1. Peace shall be restored in Indochina, on the basis of France's respecting the independence, sovereignty, national unity, and territorial integrity of Viet-Nam, Cambodia, and Laos.

2. The peoples of Viet-Nam, Cambodia, and Laos shall hold free general elections to reunify their country.

3. France shall withdraw its army from Indochina.

We have signed an armistice with France; peace is being restored in Viet-Nam and all over Indochina.

This great victory was made possible by the ardent patriotism, monolithic solidarity, fighting spirit, and sacrifice of our army and people from North to South, from the temporarily enemy controlled zone to the free zones.

This victory was the outcome of the August Revolution, of the Independence Day of September 2, and of the heroic Resistance waged during the past eight to nine years.

This is a victory of the people of Viet-Nam, Cambodia, and Laos, a victory of the French people and the peace-loving people of the world.

This new victory changes the situation of our country, which shifts from a state of war to a state of peace. In order to secure all-out and lasting peace, we must fight with might and main.

This situation sets new tasks for our people, army, cadres, and government. At present, our common tasks are: correct implementation of the Armistice Agreement, the struggle to maintain and consolidate peace, to achieve national reunification, independence, and democracy all over the country.

To achieve national reunification, independence, and democracy throughout the country, we must first of all preserve and strengthen peace.

To preserve and strengthen peace, it is necessary for both the Vietnamese and French sides to be sincere. On this occasion, I solemnly declare once again that:

We are resolved to respect and implement the Armistice Agreement entered into with France. We shall protect French economic and cultural interests in Viet-Nam. We are ready to resume negotiations with the French Government and to re-establish good relations with France on the basis of equality and mutual benefit.

At the same time, we trust that the French Government will also respect and implement the Armistice Agreement and fully guarantee the execution of the points mentioned in the declaration of the Geneva Conference and in the statement made by the French Government.

Maintenance and consolidation of peace require close solidarity on our part—solidarity among the entire people from North to South as in one family; solidarity with the peoples of Cambodia and Laos; solidarity with the Asian people, with the French people, and the peace-loving people of the world, in particular the Chinese and Soviet peoples.

We must unite in a monolithic bloc against the maneuvers of peace wreckers, the U.S. imperialists, the war-thirsty French clique and their henchmen.

Our people from North to South must fight for the organization of free general elections to reunify the whole country.

Independence and democracy will be achieved throughout the country if peace is maintained and consolidated and the whole country reunified.

The new development of the situation imposes upon us the following urgent tasks:

To strengthen the people's army, which is the leading force to defend the Fatherland and maintain peace.

To continue to put into practice the motto "land to the tillers" to liberate the peasantry, the overwhelming majority of our people.

In the former free zones, to carry on the work of consolidation in every field, to improve the people's livelihood, and to develop the valiant tradition of our people.

To enhance solidarity among the various nationalities in the country and gradually introduce autonomy into minority regions.

In newly liberated rural and urban areas, first and foremost to restore order and stabilize the people's living conditions, protect the lives and property of our compatriots as well as of foreign residents, including the French.

To guarantee freedom of conscience. To employ and treat well the employees and officials who formerly worked with the opposite side and who now wish to serve the country and the people.

To rehabilitate commerce, education, etc.

In the political field, to consolidate the people's power in former free zones and in newly liberated areas, develop and strengthen the patriotic organizations, raise the political and moral level of our people, and to unite our efforts to defend peace and achieve national unity, independence, and democracy throughout the country.

In the economic field, to accelerate the emulation movement in production and implement the policy of paying attention to public as well as private interests, of benefiting both employers and employees. Town and countryside will help each other. Free circulation of commodities within and without the country will be guaranteed so as to rehabilitate and expand production to contribute to economic prosperity and to improve the people's livelihood.

In the cultural field, to wipe out illiteracy, train cadres to serve national construction, protect our people's health, and to promote our good traditions.

In the regions where the French troops are temporarily stationed, our people will have to lead the political struggle to secure such democratic rights as freedom of organization, freedom of opinion, etc., to prepare free general elections for national reunification.

Our compatriots residing abroad must love one another and help each other. They must constantly support the Fatherland and strengthen the friendship between our people and those of the countries in which they live.

As far as the patriots are concerned, whatever classes they may belong to and even if they had formerly collaborated with the other side, we are ready to unite with them to defend and strengthen peace and achieve national unity, independence, and democracy all over the country.

We have carried the day, but peace is not definitely consolidated; unity, independence, and democracy are not yet achieved throughout the country. Therefore, it is necessary for us to wage a long and hard struggle to reach that goal. Meanwhile, we must always be vigilant to thwart the maneuvers which are likely to sabotage our common work.

Our tasks are many and difficult indeed, but we disposed of a powerful force, we are closely united, and resolved to fight. The progressive people in the world support us. Victory will certainly be ours.

On behalf of the people and government of the Democratic Republic of Viet-Nam, I take this opportunity of thanking the peoples and governments of brother countries, the French people's organizations, the peace and democratic organizations of the world, and the progressive personalities in the countries which had supported us during our Resistance and shared our joy when peace was restored. This internationalism is invaluable. It encouraged us through the trying days of our Resistance. It will help us to build a lasting peace.

The ever-growing movement of peace and democracy in the world was conducive to our victory. And this will be a worthy contribution to the defense of peace in Asia and in the world.

Compatriots, armymen, cadres, and Vietnamese residents abroad! March enthusiastically forward!

Long live a peaceful, unified, independent, and democratic Viet-Nam!

The peaceable and democratic forces in the world will win!

PART FOUR

Reconstruction
and Errors
(1954–60)

LENINISM AND THE
LIBERATION OF OPPRESSED PEOPLES*

On April 22, 1870, in old despotic Russia, there was born the future leader and talented teacher of the toiling masses and oppressed people throughout the world—Vladimir Ilyich Lenin.

At the end of the nineteenth and the beginning of the twentieth century, capitalism reached its highest and ultimate development—imperialism—and ushered in the era of proletarian revolution. The man who skillfully continued Marx's and Engels' great work in the new historical conditions was V. I. Lenin.

Struggling uncompromisingly with the reformists and all kinds of distortionists of Marxism, Lenin brought scientific socialism to a new stage. He enriched Marxism, the great ideological weapon of the proletariat, and greatly contributed to the formulation of the theory of proletarian dictatorship. He developed the Marxist principle on the worker-peasant alliance, the national and colonial question, proletarian internationalism, the building and strengthening of a new type proletarian party, which is the only organization capable of leading the multiform struggle of the working class and enslaved peoples. Lenin established a new theory of the socialist revolution and demonstrated the possibilities of the triumph of socialism in a single country.

Lenin helped the working people, who were suffering from imperialist oppression, to realize in a more comprehensive manner the

* Printed in *Pravda*, April 18, 1955.

law of social development, the requirements and objective conditions of the political struggle in every stage of the proletarian revolution, and the whole liberation movement. He acquainted the oppressed masses with the intricate and complex developments of our times. He gave them the miraculous weapon to fight for their emancipation—the theory and tactics of Bolshevism.

The Russian Communist Party founded by Lenin set a bright example to the world's people. Under the clear-sighted leadership of the great Lenin, the talented strategist and tactician, the Communist Party led the Russian proletariat to seize power and establish the first state of the working masses; the founding of this state ushered in a new era in the history of mankind. In the eyes of peoples loving peace and democracy, the Soviet Union is an unshakable bulwark of independence and freedom. After World War II, the mighty camp of peace, democracy, and socialism headed by the Soviet Union took shape, in opposition to imperialism.

Lenin's popularity and doctrine are closely linked to all the successes of the camp of peace and democracy which stretches from the Elbe River to the Pacific Ocean, and from the arctic pole to the tropics. This is why all the oppressed and unfortunate people regard Lenin's banner, which is now being held aloft by the Communists of all countries, as a symbol of faith and a torchlight of hope.

The heroic struggle waged by the Soviet people to build Communism is now encouraging all the peoples and showing them the way to attain a living worthy of man.

The consistent peace policy of the Soviet Government, clearly embodied in the decree signed by Lenin and promulgated immediately after the triumph of the socialist revolution, is now stimulating the broad masses of people to struggle for the defense and strengthening of peace and against the warmongers headed by U.S. imperialists.

The principles laid down by Lenin on the people's right to self-determination, peaceful coexistence, noninterference into the internal affairs of other countries—equality and relations beneficial to the parties concerned, principles which are the bases of the Soviet Union's foreign policy—are now showing the peoples of colonial and dependent countries the path of struggle for national reunification and independence.

For the Asian peoples as well as for the peoples throughout the world who are fighting for peace, independence, democracy, and socialism, Leninism is like the sun which brings with it a cheerful life. Lenin always attached great importance to the movement for national liberation waged by the Asian peoples, and regarded it as part and parcel of the struggle put up by the toiling masses throughout the world against the imperialist oppressors. Lenin made it clear that the awakening of Asia and the first struggle waged by the advanced proletariat in Europe to seize power marked a new era in world history, an era which began with the twentieth century. In 1913, V. I. Lenin wrote: "The whole of Europe takes the leading place; the entire bourgeoisie in Europe is colluding with all the reactionary forces and medieval forces in China.

"But all young Asia, that is, hundreds of millions of toiling masses in Asia, has the proletariat of all civilized countries as a firm ally. No force in the world is able to check the victory of the proletariat in the liberation of the European and Asian peoples."

Today, in the midst of the twentieth century, the "young Asia" referred to by Lenin is precisely the People's Republic of China, the People's Republic of Mongolia, the People's Democratic Republic of Korea, and the Democratic Republic of Viet-Nam. In other regions of Asia, similar young forces are rising to struggle for national liberation. These scientific previsions of the great revolutionary strategist have been substantiated so swiftly that the imperialist camp becomes anxious and fearful!

If, under the leadership of the Marxist-Leninist parties, the enslaved peoples of Asia have recorded practical successes, it is because they have followed Lenin's great teachings.

In his appeal to the revolutionaries in the East, Lenin wrote: "You have before you a task which was unknown to the Communists in the world: relying on the theory and common practice of Communism and applying them to specific conditions which do not exist in Europe, you must know how to use them in the conditions in which the peasants are the basic masses and the task is not to struggle against capitalism but against medieval vestiges."

This is an instruction most valuable for a country like ours, in which 90 per cent of the population live on agriculture, and a great deal of the vestiges of rotten feudalism and mandarinate still exists.

Under the leadership of the glorious Communist Party of China and of comrade Mao Tse-tung, its clear-sighted leader, the victory of the great Revolution in China was the triumph of Leninist thinking. It is precisely for this reason that comrade Mao Tse-tung said that the gun report of the October Revolution has brought Marxism-Leninism to China, and 600 million people are once and for all freed from the grip of imperialism.

Applying Leninism to internationalism, the Soviet Union, where socialism has triumphed, has constantly given great moral assistance to the national liberation movement in colonial and dependent countries. Particularly with her consistent peace policy and due to her great prestige all over the world, the Soviet Union has greatly helped the Korean and Vietnamese peoples to defend their fatherlands against the danger wrought by the U.S. imperialists and their allies. The diplomatic activities of the Soviet Union were a deciding factor in bringing the wars in Korea and Viet-Nam to an end.

Educated in the spirit of proletarian internationalism, the Vietnamese people highly appreciate the moral support of the peoples throughout the world, including the French toiling people who have been fighting to put an end to the war in Indochina.

Lenin bequeathed to us, as to all the Communist and workers' parties, an invaluable treasure which was his ideology: organizational principles, theory, and tactics of a revolutionary party. Leninism is a powerful ideological force which guides our Party and makes it possible to become the highest organization of the toiling masses and the embodiment of the intelligence, dignity, and conscience of our people.

Under the banner of Leninism, the Viet-Nam Workers' Party has won the confidence of our people and is considered as their vanguard party. Our Party has known how to make use of the potentialities and creative initiative of our people, who never resigned themselves to the yoke of slavery and colonialism.

Lenin embodied the unity of mind within the Party, the solidarity of its ranks, the respect of revolutionary discipline, the unshakable faith in the great cause of Communism and firm confidence in the final victory. All this is now an encouragement for the Viet-Nam Workers' Party, which has daily and hourly applied the principle of criticism and self-criticism and regarded it as the miraculous method to correct mistakes and shortcomings and to struggle against the manifestations of subjectivism and complacency. Our Party has no other interests than those of our people and our Fatherland; therefore, it attaches great importance to raising the level of its work. While doing its utmost to fulfill its tasks, our Party has constantly studied

Leninism in order to raise its combativeness, political dynamism, the unity in organization, and the ideological level of the Party members.

Our people and Party members were steeled in the flame of the long and hard struggle for national salvation and suffered untold hardship and suffering. For over eight years, our people and Party waged a heroic struggle which ended victoriously in favor of the Vietnamese people and in the re-establishment of peace in Indochina. The Geneva Agreement demonstrated that the struggle for national liberation waged by the Vietnamese people and the brother peoples of Laos and Cambodia and their lofty sacrifice and heroism have been internationally recognized. Our Party can be proud that during these years it was resolute and preserving and led the people to struggle with a great sacrificing spirit.

Today, while peace has been restored, we are continuing to fight for the correct implementation of the Geneva Agreement. According to figures already checked, we have recently been able to affirm that the other side has violated the Agreement 2,114 times, including 467 times in South Viet-Nam. Here are some shocking figures: 806 dead, 3,501 wounded, and 12,741 persons arrested groundlessly.

Last year, in September, the Viet-Nam Workers' Party passed many resolutions on our people's action aimed at strictly implementing the Geneva Agreement and opposing all maneuvers to sabotage it. Our main tasks are: to consolidate peace, complete land reform, work with might and main in order to improve our economic life, stabilize our livelihood in every respect in the territory north of the 17th parallel, and continue the political struggle waged by the entire people. We have put forth the following slogans for our struggle: to consolidate peace, achieve national reunification, gain complete independence, and popularize democracy throughout the country.

Today we are struggling to carry through these fundamental tasks. At the same time, we cannot ignore that, after the conferences held by the imperialists in Manila and Bangkok,* a new situation has

---

* At a conference in Manila in September, 1954, in the wake of the D.R.V.N.'s victory over France, the United States, Great Britain, France, Australia, New Zealand, the Philippines, Thailand, and Pakistan established the Southeast Asia Treaty Organization (SEATO). This political and military alliance, designed to provide protection specifically for Laos, Cambodia, and South Viet-Nam, has thus far not been brought into the Viet-Nam conflict. In recent years, France and Pakistan have not been active in the organization.— ED.

arisen in Asia. Today the United States has openly intervened in Indochina's affairs and has carried out many more maneuvers to torpedo the Geneva Agreement.

For the realization of their goal, the imperialists and their henchmen of all kinds are nuturing the dark scheme of permanently dividing our country, placing South Viet-Nam under their sway, checking all democratic forces, and sabotaging the 1956 general elections.

In these conditions, our struggle shifts now from the stage of armistice to that of political struggle to check the enemy's plot to rekindle war and to achieve national reunification by nationwide elections scheduled for July, 1956.

Peace, reunification, national independence, and democracy are problems which are closely linked together. If there is no consolidation of peace, there is no possibility of reunifying Viet-Nam through general elections. Inversely, if there is no national reunification by means of general elections, there is no possibility of establishing a firm basis for peace.

The recent developments and the examination of the political situation enable our Party to see clearly that the struggle for peace, independence, and democracy waged by the Vietnamese people will be a hard one, and that on this path the Vietnamese people will encounter a lot of difficulties. However, our Party is firmly confident in the final victory.

From the most powerful Leninist doctrine, we draw a great strength to fulfill our sacred task of securing peace, reunification, independence, and democracy and to win victory for socialism.

LETTER TO THE
COMPATRIOTS IN THE
THAI-MEO AUTONOMOUS REGION*
(May 7, 1955)

For one year now, the Northwest area has been completely liberated. This is owing to the close unity among all nationalities and their enthusiastic participation in the Resistance War, to the valiant struggle of our army, and to the clear-sighted leadership of the Party and Government.

Now, upon the proposal of the Party and the decision of the Government, the Thai-Meo Autonomous Region is established.

The aim of the founding of the Thai-Meo Autonomous Region is to enable the brother nationalities gradually to run all their own activities so as rapidly to develop their economy and culture and realize equality among nationalities in all respects.

*The uplands of both North and South Viet-Nam are inhabited by tribes of non-Vietnamese ethnic stock who are highly reluctant to accept lowland Vietnamese control. Ho recognized this very early, and the North Vietnamese mountain areas were rapidly given internal autonomy, with school and administrative systems, as well as militia units, in which the local languages were used and local mores preserved. This is not the case in the South. As a result, several tribal rebellions have broken out in recent years, and a non-Communist autonomy movement, FULRO (Front Unifié de Lutte de la Race Opprimée [United Struggle Front of the Oppressed Race]), has added a "three-corned" aspect to the Viet-Nam war in some areas.—ED.

The Thai-Meo Autonomous Region is an integral part of the great family of Viet-Nam, making with other brother nationalities a monolithic bloc of unity. It will always enjoy the education and leadership of the Party and Government and the assistance of other brother nationalities.

The Thai-Meo Autonomous Region is at present under a democratic regime, with the people as masters. It is completely different from the faked "Thai Autonomy" previously founded by the enemy with a view to dividing and repressing the nationalities.

Today we celebrate the anniversary of the great victory won by our army and people in Dien Bien Phu; at the same time we officially found the Thai-Meo Autonomous Region. Therefore, this is a very glorious historical day for the compatriots in the Northwest and for the whole Democratic Republic of Viet-Nam as well.

The compatriots in the Northwest have the particular honor of having their autonomous region established first. Hence, they have the particular task of striving to set an example to other autonomous regions which will be founded one after the other.

To deserve that great honor and to fulfill that lofty task, the compatriots in the Thai-Meo Autonomous Region should: ensure close unity among all nationalities, love and help one another as brothers and sisters; emulate in increasing production so that everybody will be provided with enough clothing and food; keep constant vigilance and be ready to help the army and the security service in frustrating the enemy's plots of sowing dissension and of sabotage.

As regards the cadres, there should be sincere unity between old and new cadres, between cadres of the locality and those coming on duty from other places, between army cadres and cadres of the Party and Government; they should all wholeheartedly serve the people and resolutely fight against bureaucracy, commandism, corruption, and waste.

On this occasion, the Government again earnestly calls on those Northwesterners who have gone astray to right their wrong without delay and to return to their honest life among the people. The Government and the people are always lenient with those who have repented.

The Party and the Government have confidence in the patriotic spirit and the struggle of the compatriots in the Thai-Meo Autonomous Region and hope that all of them will remain single-minded and unite their efforts to develop and improve the autonomous region day by day so as to make valuable contributions to the struggle for peace, national unity, independence, and democracy in the whole of our beloved country.

TENTH ANNIVERSARY
OF THE NATIONAL DAY OF THE
DEMOCRATIC REPUBLIC OF VIET-NAM*
(September, 1955)

On September 2 of this year the Democratic Republic of Viet-Nam became ten years old, and the Vietnamese people who are from now on free on the greater part of their territory are commemorating this glorious National Day with indescribable enthusiasm and joy.

Right from the first days of colonial aggression and for nearly one century, the Vietnamese people unceasingly struggled against the invaders, evincing extraordinary gallantry and heroism. The guerrilla activities of Truong Cong Dinh and Truong Quyen in Nam Bo (1867), the Resistance movements in 1874 and especially in 1884, the twelve-year-long struggle under the leadership of Phan Dinh Phung (1884–96), and following it, the fighting led by Hoang Hoa Tham until the eve of World War I, the movement of struggle in Trung Bo (1907), the Bien Hoa uprising (1914–15), the insurrection in Hué (1916), the Thai Nguyen uprising (1917), etc., give evidence of the fierce struggle waged by the Vietnamese people for freedom and national independence. But at that epoch the Court and the feudalists, who were still responsible for national interests, car-

* Printed in the review *For a Lasting Peace, for a People's Democracy,* December 2, 1955.

ried out the criminal policy of constant betrayal of the people's aspirations, which consequently could not materialize.

The great October Revolution had given a new impetus to the struggle of the oppressed peoples. The prompt settlement by the young Soviet power of the question of former Czarist colonies and its giving back freedom to the peoples in those places had a strong repercussion in all the colonies and semicolonies in Asia. Victorious Marxism-Leninism has pointed out to all nations the road to self-liberation. A Marxist-Leninist Party was born in Viet-Nam in February, 1930. While in the Yen Bai uprising (February, 1930) the bourgeoisie lost all its influence on the national liberation movement, the working class and the toiling peasant masses reorganized their political party, which became the only leader of the anti-imperialist revolution. In September, 1930, the first people's power was set up in three districts in North Trung Bo. This movement was repressed by imperialism with unprecedented barbarity.

However, as early as 1940, many armed uprisings were organized in North, Center, and South Viet-Nam against the French colonialists and Japanese imperialists. Although repressed, these insurrectionist movements were sparks and sparkles which, five years later, were to flare up into a revolution smashing to pieces the foreign rule in Viet-Nam.

In May, 1941, the Viet Minh National United Front was founded, and this was the broadest united bloc ever known in the national liberation movement of our country. The National Front, with the Party as its main force, mobilized and organized guerrilla groups that fought throughout World War II on the side of the Allies against fascist aggressors.

The victories of the valiant Soviet army over Hitler Germany and later over Japanese imperialism greatly contributed to the success of the General Insurrection on August 19, 1945, and on September 2 the Democratic Republic of Viet-Nam was founded.

Thus, owing to the defeat of fascism, the world situation became favorable and the August Revolution was successful because it possessed the three conditions that cannot be absent in any anti-imperialist revolution in a colonial country. These are the leadership of the working class, the setting up of a broad anti-imperialist national front, and the armed insurrection.

Thenceforward, the history of our country has opened a glorious page. The Vietnamese people were freed. The August Revolution has liberated them from the colonialists' yoke, from any other enslavement of the imperialists, and from the mandarinate.

The toiling people have for the first time become masters of themselves and of the destiny of their country. They set to work to drive away the dreadful specter of famine, which had killed 2 million people in the last months of imperialist rule (from late 1944 to 1945). They strove to heal the devastating wounds left behind by the dirty enslaving system, whose practice continued until the middle of this century of successful revolutions. The toiling people elected the National Assembly, began to build up people's power, and carried out various measures rapidly to wipe out illiteracy and ignorance left behind by the colonialists' rule.

However, the French colonialists still dreamed of the possibility of reestablishing their oppressive regime in our country. They regarded our peaceful attitude as a weakness. Encouraged by the British-American reactionary forces and in collusion with the Chiang Kai-shek clique, on September 23, 1945, they attacked the Vietnamese people in Saigon, then sought to penetrate the North. Afterwards, trampling on what they had pledged in the Preliminary Agreement of March 6, 1946, and the *modus vivendi* of September 14, 1946, the colonialists perpetrated a massacre in Haiphong, occupied Lang Son, and staged repeated provocations until December 19, when the Resistance War of our entire people against the invaders began.

In response to the appeal of the Party and the Democratic Government, our entire people rose up as one man to defend the Fatherland and the achievements of the August Revolution.

The national salvation war began in material conditions unfavorable to the Vietnamese people: famine was rife; the henchmen of French colonialism and Japanese imperialism were still swarming while the People's Army could only be set up later in the course of the fighting. Therefore, in the prevailing situation, the French Expeditionary Corps seemed to hold military supremacy, and the enemy took advantage of all our difficulties, believing that these difficulties would help them to triumph swiftly over our young army and annihilate our democratic government. But the situation developed completely contrary to their expectation and proved that they were utterly mistaken.

Backed by the U.S. reactionary circles, the enemy launched an all-out war against the Vietnamese people. But under the leadership of the Party and the Government, the Vietnamese people united their efforts and unremittingly fought the enemy. They stepped up and spread guerrilla warfare in enemy-occupied areas. They succeeded in consolidating their rear and enthusiastically built their own People's Army. In coordination with the guerrillas, the People's Army valiantly fought and annihilated the enemy troops in many campaigns: in Viet Bac in autumn–winter, 1947; on the Viet-Nam–Chinese border in the last months of 1950; in the Midland and Red River delta, in Hoa Binh, Ba Vi, and on the Da River in 1951; in South Viet-Nam in 1952; in Lai Chau in 1953; and finally, on May 7, 1954, it won the decisive victory at Dien Bien Phu. The Dien Bien Phu victory, which was won right on the eve of the opening of the Geneva Conference, exerted a great influence on the proceedings of the Conference and contributed to the signing of the Geneva Agreement guaranteeing the restoration of peace in Indochina upon the basis of recognition of the national rights of the peoples of Viet-Nam, Cambodia, and Laos.

At the same time, all political schemes of the colonialists and imperialists, namely "feeding war by war, using Vietnamese to fight Vietnamese," the "independence" and "democracy" farces to mislead our people, and the imperialist-patterned "land reform," turned bankrupt.

Throughout that period, the Party and the Government also paid attention to the building and development of the economy, finance, and culture of the Democratic Republic. First and foremost, the land reform on the principle of "land to the tiller" began to be carried out. As a result of the efforts made to maintain and expand the indispensable branches of small industries and handicrafts, our people and army were supplied with more consumer goods. Growing of rice and subsidiary crops as well as all work for the improvement of irrigation and for flood-fighting were encouraged. Transport and communications were developed to an adequate extent. The state sector in the national economy—national bank, trading concerns—came into being and grew steadily; national education, the education given to the peasantry and the army, and the struggle against illiteracy obtained extraordinary results in spite of difficult conditions.

Thus, in all military, political, and economic spheres, our young Democratic Republic has victoriously stood the tests and trials of the war in which, according to Lenin, all the virtues of a people must be given full expression.

The ardent patriotism and the ideological and political unity of our people and army around the Party and the Government helped us to weather unimaginably difficult ordeals and create political, economic, and military conditions for victory.

Their unshakable confidence in the success of their just cause inspired our people and increased their bravery.

The virtues and combativeness that our armymen, guerrillas, and cadres succeeded in learning in the particularly rich history of the national liberation movement helped our young army score historic feats of arms and tinge its banner with an eternal glory.

The bright example of the Soviet and Chinese armies and peoples continuously inspired our people and fighters and contributed to the tempering of our heroes. The French people and all peace-loving people in the world gave us invaluable support. They were on our side in the most critical moments of the Resistance War and shared joy with us when peace was restored.

The Democratic Republic has won a glorious victory because this is the victory of the oppressed over the oppressor, the victory of freedom over slavery. Our people have escaped re-enslavement, and the achievements of the August Revolution—peace, unity, independence, and democracy—are safeguarded and strengthened.

Peace has been restored in Indochina on the basis of recognition of the independence, sovereignty, unity, and territorial integrity of Viet-Nam, Laos, and Cambodia; peace has been brought to us by the 1954 Geneva Conference. It cannot be consolidated as long as our country remains partitioned by the provisional demarcation line at the 17th parallel. Moreover, the attitude of the southern authorities and their sponsors is a serious threat to peace, which has been restored for only two years.

Indeed, although the first step, i.e., the military stage stipulated in the Geneva Agreement, in general ended satisfactorily, as the whole territory of North Viet-Nam has been liberated, the second step, i.e., the stage leading to the reunification of Viet-Nam through general elections to be held in 1956, cannot as yet be started as a result of Ngo Dinh Diem's deliberate hindrance.

The southern authorities savagely massacre our compatriots and all patriotic and peace forces in the South. Within only one year, they committed more than 3,000 crimes and violations of the Geneva Agreement. At least 4,000 patriots were killed or wounded and over 19,000 arrested. In addition to these terrorist acts, the Diem administration also feverishly carried out the U.S. political line with a view to turning South Viet-Nam into a U.S. colony and military base, which would be permanently incorporated in the sphere of activity of the South-East Asian aggressive organization (SEATO). Despite these deeds, Ngo Dinh Diem shamelessly boasted of being a "fighter" for peace, democracy, and the independence of Viet-Nam.

This situation has determined the tasks of the Government of the Democratic Republic of Viet-Nam, which has set itself as primary objective the strict and correct implementation of the Geneva Agreement; that is, immediately to hold the consultative conference between the North and the South, the first step toward the holding of free general elections to reunify the country. Thus, peace and national reunification are our main demands for the time being.

Besides, we have to heal the war wounds, gradually raise the people's living standard, and build up a genuinely free and democratic new life in our country. To do so, we have, on the one hand, to rehabilitate our national economy: agriculture, handicraft, transport, and industry. Since they can enjoy peace, our people have enthusiastically entered this road. But greater efforts still have to be made to cultivate the land laid fallow, repair dikes to prevent floods, and build up an irrigation network to do away with drought and famine, as these two calamities are inseparable. On the other hand, the welfare of the Vietnamese toiling people must be raised gradually on the basis of increased labor productivity.

The above-mentioned tasks are really heavy and complicated as a result of the war, colonialism, and the feudal system. However, thanks to the assistance of the brother countries, we have greater and greater possibilities and can have confidence in a successful future. Indeed, after the talks in July between the Vietnamese Government Delegation and the leaders of the Soviet Union and of the People's Republic of China, these two countries decided to grant us aid totaling 1,530,000 million dongs* in the coming years. The other democracies also give us priceless assistance in our work of rehabilitation. This

---

* *This is in old currency, now 1,530 million dongs, or $434.2 million. According to a recent study by Albert Parry ("Soviet Aid to Viet-Nam," The Reporter, January 12, 1967), Soviet economic aid to North Viet-Nam totaled $350 million in the period 1954–64, and $74.8 million in 1965. During the latter year North Viet-Nam also received $555 million worth of arms. In a conference held in Moscow in October, 1966, the Soviet Union and its East European allies promised to provide $1 billion in goods and services to North Viet-Nam; of this amount, $800 million would come from the U.S.S.R.*—ED.

aid is carried out in the form of supply of equipment, machines, and technicians. Many economic and cultural sectors of Viet-Nam benefit by this assistance.

This selfless and unconditional aid, beneficial to the people, is completely different from the "aid" conceived by the imperialists. Through their "aid," the imperialists always aim at exploiting and enslaving the peoples. The Marshall Plan, which has gradually encroached upon the sovereignty of the recipient countries, is eloquent proof of this.

In its relations with other countries, the policy of the Democratic Republic of Viet-Nam is clear-cut and transparent: It is a policy of peace and good relationship. This policy is based on the five great principles put forth in the Sino-Indian and Sino-Burmese joint declarations, which are: mutual respect for territorial integrity and national sovereignty, nonaggression, noninterference in internal affairs, equality and mutual benefit, and peaceful coexistence. Particularly the Bandung Conference* has shown that these principles are supported by broad circles of public opinion in Asia and Africa.

We particularly urge the maintenance of peaceful relations with our neighbors, namely Cambodia and Laos. As regards France, we continue to advocate that we can establish with it preferential economic and cultural relations in conditions of complete equality and mutual benefit, first of all, and of mutual confidence and sincere cooperation.

On this tenth anniversary of the National Day, looking back to the past, we can rightfully be proud of the path traversed. But we also—and chiefly—turn to the future and are aware of what is still to be done. We still have to carry out a hard, long, and intricate political struggle. However, if we are persevering, resolute, and vigilant, if our Party and the National Front continue to apply the tested principles of criticism and self-criticism—we have every reason to believe that our Party and the National Front will continue to apply them—we will certainly win complete success.

In the past ten years, the camp of peace and democracy has made big progress. The Soviet Union has triumphed over the fascist invaders and since then has obtained many important achievements in

---

* The Afro-Asian Conference, held from April 18 to 24, 1955, in Bandung, was attended by twenty-nine Afro-Asian countries. The Conference approved a declaration on the condemnation of colonialism and worked out several measures to strengthen the economic and political relations among the Afro-Asian countries. It issued a statement on the ten principles of peaceful and friendly coexistence among these nations.

the building of Communism as well as in its policy of struggle for peace and international relaxation of tension. The people's democracies have also been strengthened in the political and economic spheres. The successful Chinese revolution has liberated 600 million people, who are advancing hand in hand to happiness. With the brotherly support of the Chinese Volunteers, the Korean people have driven back the Syngman Rhee clique and the troops under the shadow of the U.N. banner. The Vietnamese people have won victory in the war started by the French colonialists and wrested back peace at the Geneva Conference. The peace forces are growing stronger and succeed in consolidating their position. All these great achievements have brought our people a boundless confidence in the magnificent future of our Fatherland and in the certain victory of our cause.

Though still meeting with difficulties and obstacles, we are going forward with the confidence and enthusiasm of the victors!

SPEECH CLOSING THE NINTH (ENLARGED) SESSION OF THE CENTRAL COMMITTEE OF THE VIET-NAM WORKERS' PARTY

(April 24, 1956)

The ninth (enlarged) session of the Central Committee has achieved good results. After several days of intensive work, we have grasped the great significance of the Twentieth Congress of the Communist Party of the Soviet Union. This Congress has:

Analyzed the new situation prevailing in the world, and pointed out the new conditions favorable to the preservation of peace and the advance toward socialism by the Revolutionary Parties of the working class and the laboring people;

Clearly shown the Soviet Union's victorious road, giving us still greater enthusiasm and making us believe still more strongly in the invincible forces of the Soviet Union, the bastion of revolution and of world peace;

Pointed out the tasks of the Communist Party in the ideological and organizational fields. The Congress particularly emphasized the application of Marxist-Leninist principles to collective leadership and opposed the cult of the individual.

While recognizing that war may be averted, we must be vigilant to detect the warmongers' schemes; for as long as imperialism exists, the danger of war still exists.

While recognizing that in certain countries the road to socialism may be a peaceful one, we should be aware of this fact: In countries where the machinery of state, the armed forces, and the police of the bourgeois class are still strong, the proletarian class still has to prepare for armed struggle.

While recognizing the possibility of reunifying Viet-Nam by peaceful means, we should always remember that our people's principal enemies are the American imperialists and their agents who still occupy half our country and are preparing for war; therefore, we should firmly hold aloft the banner of peace and enhance our vigilance.

In speaking of the cult of the individual, we should have a balanced view with regard to Comrade Stalin. Comrade Stalin made great contributions to the Revolution, but he also made serious mistakes.

The Congress has taught us a lesson in very courageous criticism and self-criticism. This is a victory for the Communist Party of the Soviet Union and also a common victory for the brother parties.

This lesson is extremely valuable to the brother parties and to our Party. Our Party has grown up in the condition of a colonial and semifeudal country, only half of which has just been freed from the imperialist and feudal yoke. That is why bad thoughts, nonproletarian thoughts, can easily get into our Party.

The clear conclusions and the exemplary courageous criticism and self-criticism by the Congress testify to the continuous progress and successes of the Communist Party of the Soviet Union. This has increased the enemy's fears and they are intensifying their slanderous propaganda.

In speaking of our own Party, we make this special remark: We have collective leadership, but we also have a number of shortcomings because:

We are still weak in political theory and we have not fully grasped the practical situation.

We have not set forth proper Party work regulations.

Democracy within the Party has not been fully extended: Self-criticism and criticism, especially criticism from below, have not yet been developed.

To overcome these shortcomings, we have further to develop collective leadership from the Central Committee down to the Party organizations in the localities, in government organizations as well as in Party organizations.

Collective leadership should be on a par with individual responsibility.

Party work regulations should be clearly defined and the highest principle of the Party, the principle of collective leadership, should be ensured.

Democratic principles should be broadened, self-criticism and criticism, especially criticism from below, should be widespread. We should raise our theoretical level. Theory must be closely linked with the realities of the Revolution; we should always take into account the prevailing conditions and maintain close contact with the masses.

We should always remember that the most important point in our present economic plan is gradually to improve the people's living conditions.

We have to recognize that the cult of the individual exists in some measure inside and outside the Party. Although it has not yet brought serious consequence, it has already limited initiative and diminished the enthusiasm of Party members and the people.

This cult of the individual exists from the Central to the communal levels. To fight this evil, the principal means to be used is education; at the same time, we have to enhance the role of the Party, of the collectivity, and of the people.

In this session, you have sincerely criticized yourselves and criticized the Central Committee and the Political Bureau; this is very good. We are not afraid of shortcomings, because we have sufficient will and determination to correct them.

Sincere self-criticism and frank criticism is the most effective weapon to overcome shortcomings and develop qualities. Therefore, not only have we to develop criticism and self-criticism in the Party and in the government organs but also to welcome frank criticism from the people.

We are united and one-minded, we have great confidence in the Soviet Union, the socialist camp, the forces of peace in the world, in our people and our Party.

Let us boldly go forward. Victory will certainly be ours.

LETTER TO THE CADRES
FROM SOUTH VIET-NAM
REGROUPED IN THE NORTH
(June 19, 1956)

Dear cadres from the South regrouped in the North,

From May 19 to this day, I have received from you and your children many letters conveying to me your wishes of longevity. I am writing this letter to thank you all.

On this occasion, I wish to answer some of your questions.

It is often said that "North and South belong to the same family and are brothers." These words have a deep significance. They testify to the firm, unshakable solidarity of our people from North to South. Your very presence here testifies to this solidarity. Since the day you were regrouped here, you have regarded the North as your home, you have overcome all difficulties, and eagerly taken part in the construction of the North. A number of you are in the army to contribute to the consolidation of national defense. Others are in government services. Yet others are engaged in agriculture, working in factories and on construction sites. Everyone has endeavored to do his duty. Many have attained brilliant achievements and have been awarded medals. Among other such units, there is the Seventh Company, which has taken the lead in every task and has been commended eight times. It has set a good example of the Southern cadres' heroic labor.

In the name of the Party and the Government, I congratulate you all and urge you to make continuous efforts and constant progress.

Our policy is: to consolidate the North and to keep in mind the South.

To build a good house, we must build a strong foundation. To have a vigorous plant with green leaves, beautiful flowers, and good fruit, we must take good care of it and feed the root.

The North is the foundation, the root of the struggle for complete national liberation and the reunification of the country. That is why everything we are doing in the North is aimed at strengthening both the North and the South. Therefore, to work here is the same as struggling in the South: it is to struggle for the South and for the whole of Viet-Nam.

Struggle is always accompanied by difficulties. But your difficulties are our common difficulties. After fifteen years of devastating war, the newly liberated North is suffering many privations. In addition to this, the different administrative levels and responsible cadres have not paid enough attention to your material and spiritual life, have not proceeded as had been decided by the Party and the Government. There has not been sufficient supervision and continuous control on the part of the Party and the Government.

The Party and the Government have realized these shortcomings and are actively putting things right with a view to carrying out the policy which has been set forth. I hope that you will actively contribute to putting things right in a constructive manner.

From the moral aspect, if everybody understands that our political struggle will certainly be victorious but will be a long and hard struggle, then the tendency to become impatient, pessimistic, and to succumb to other cares will disappear.

The political struggle will certainly be victorious, national reunification will certainly be achieved.

As you know, the camp of socialism and people's democracy led by the Soviet Union is growing stronger and stronger. The area of peace includes countries with a total population of 1,500 million people and is continuously expanding. Recently, three African countries have recovered independence. Several small countries, such as Cambodia and Ceylon, have adopted a policy of neutrality and peace. In many countries in the U.S. camp, such as Thailand and the Philippines, there is also an anti-American movement. Thus, the United States is becoming more and more isolated. Therefore, the world situation is favorable to us.

The Americans and their agents are endeavoring to sabotage the Geneva Agreement. They refuse to hold political consultations with us or to organize in due time free general elections as has been stipulated in the Geneva Agreement; they are scheming to divide our country permanently. They are betraying the people's interests and their ranks are being torn by internal strife. That is why, despite their arrogant attitude, their strength is unstable, like that of a palace built on sand.

As to our struggle, it is a just struggle; the peace-loving peoples of the world support us. Our people from North to South (including the patriots among the religious sects and parties in the South) hate and oppose the American-Diem clique. The North is being increasingly consolidated to become a firm support, a strong base for our entire people's struggle. For these reasons, our political struggle will certainly be victorious.

The present political struggle is a stage in our national democratic revolution.

Ever since our country was first occupied by the French colonialists, our people have been struggling continuously for over eighty years. The result was the triumph of the August Revolution. Then came the Resistance War, which lasted nearly nine years. Our brilliant military victory brought about a brilliant diplomatic victory. The Geneva Agreement has recognized our country's independence, sovereignty, unity, and territorial integrity.

But the Americans and their lackeys are striving to hinder the reunification of our country. We must continue our struggle.

The Revolution and the Resistance have been victorious, thanks to our people's close unity, great enthusiasm, firm belief in victory, and extremely persevering struggle. In the present political struggle, as in the Revolution and the Resistance, our compatriots in the South are in the vanguard, closely united and struggling heroically and perseveringly.

The situation in the world and at home is favorable to us, our people are united and firmly believe in final victory. That is why our present political struggle, although long and hard, will certainly be victorious.

This letter is quite long enough, and I think you have all understood.

I wish you good health and much progress.

I send many kisses to you and to your children.

LETTER TO THE PEASANTS AND CADRES ON THE SUCCESSFUL COMPLETION OF LAND REFORM IN THE NORTH

(August 18, 1956)

Two years have passed since the victorious end of the Resistance. The northern part of our country has been completely liberated from the colonialists' shackles; now the peasants in the North are also freed from the yoke of the feudal landlords.

Nearly 10 million peasants have received land, tens of thousands of new cadres have been trained in the countryside. The organization of the Party, administration, and peasants' associations in the communes has been readjusted.

This is a great victory, which opens the way for our peasants to build a life with enough food and clothing, and brings a valuable contribution to economic rehabilitation and development and to the consolidation of the North into a solid base for the struggle to reunify our country.

This victory has been scored thanks to the correct policy of our Party and Government, the united struggle of the laboring peasants, the active support of the army and the people, and to the cadres' sacrifice and efforts.

On this occasion, on behalf of the Party and Government, I affectionately: congratulate our peasants on their victory; congratulate the land-reform cadres and the communal cadres and activists who have undergone hardships, overcome difficulties, and perseveringly struggled; congratulate the people and the army who have actively contributed to the common victory.

Land reform is a class struggle against the feudalists, an earth-shaking, fierce, and hard revolution. Moreover, the enemy has frenziedly carried out sabotage work. A number of our cadres have not thoroughly grasped the land-reform policy or correctly followed the mass line. The leadership of the Party Central Committee and of the Government is sometimes lacking in concreteness, and control and encouragement are disregarded. All this has caused us to commit errors and meet with shortcomings in carrying out land reform: in realizing the unity of the countryside, in fighting the enemy, in readjusting the organization, in applying the policy of agricultural taxes, etc.

The Party Central Committee and the Government have rigorously reviewed these errors and shortcomings and drawn up plans resolutely to correct them with a view to uniting the cadres and the people, stabilizing the countryside, and promoting production.

We have to correct such shortcomings as: not relying fully on the poor and landless peasants, not uniting closely with the middle peasants, and not establishing a sincere alliance with the rich peasants.

The status of those who have been wrongly classified as landlords or as rich peasants should be reviewed.

Party membership, rights, and honor should be restituted to Party members, cadres, and others who have been wrongly convicted.

With regard to landlords, we should abide by the eight-point regulation when dealing with them and pay attention to those landlords who have taken part in the Resistance and supported the revolution or those whose children are enrolled in the army or working as cadres.

Wherever land area and production output have been erroneously estimated, a readjustment is required.

The correction of errors should be resolute and planned. What can be corrected immediately should be dealt with without delay. What cannot be corrected forthwith should be done in combination with the checking-up operation. It is necessary to further the achievements we have made, and at the same time resolutely to right the wrongs committed.

At present, the people have become masters of the countryside;

they should therefore be closely united, enthusiastically engage in production, develop and consolidate the mutual aid teams, etc., in order to become wealthier day after day and to contribute to the enriching of our people and the strengthening of our country.

Cadres should endeavor to study general culture and politics, to set an example in work and production, and in a practical way take care of the people's living conditions.

The people should frankly criticize and help the cadres in their work. Cadres at zonal and provincial levels should give practical assistance to cadres of district and commune so that their work and production may have good results.

Unity is our invincible force. In order to consolidate the North into a solid base for the struggle to reunify our country, our entire people should be closely and widely united on the basis of the worker-peasant alliance in the Viet-Nam Fatherland Front. It is all the more necessary for veteran and new cadres of the Party and Government to assume identity of ideas, to be united and single-minded, and to compete to serve the people.

All the cadres and people should closely unite around the Party and Government, and endeavor to emulate with one another in making our democratic countryside happier and more prosperous.

REPORT TO THE MEETING OF REPRESENTATIVES OF THE HANOI PEOPLE ON THE SUCCESS OF THE SIXTH SESSION OF THE NATIONAL ASSEMBLY (FIRST LEGISLATURE)*

(February 15, 1957)

Today, as representatives of our compatriots in the capital city of Hanoi, we take upon ourselves the task of reporting on the work of the Sixth Session of the National Assembly. I am very pleased to say that this session of the National Assembly has scored great successes.

Through twenty-nine days our deputies have worked unremittingly and diligently, even at night and on Sundays.

The people throughout our country have had their mind turned toward the National Assembly. Nearly 4,000 letters and telegrams have

* The National Assembly (First Legislature) held its sixth session from December 29, 1956, to January 25, 1957. At this session agreement was reached between the National Assembly and the Government on the following tasks: land reform, economic rehabilitation, struggle for national reunification, etc. The National Assembly was unanimous in declaring that the successes achieved in all fields were great and fundamental whereas the errors and shortcomings committed in a number of works were limited and could certainly be overcome. (*But it was also the assembly that had to deal with the thorny problem of rectifying the blunders of the overly brutal land reform, which had led to an open uprising in Nghê-An province in November, 1956.*—ED.)

307

been received from all corners of the country welcoming the session. Many delegations sent by the people of the capital and other provinces came and greeted the National Assembly. An atmosphere of solidarity and enthusiasm prevailed between the National Assembly and the people.

The National Assembly has heard the Government report on the various works carried out during last year, such as struggle for national reunification, land reform, economy and finance, social and cultural affairs, budget, national defense, the question of nationalities, and foreign affairs.

The deputies have worked with a spirit of broad democracy. The various subcommittees have carried out animated but thorough debates on the questions reported by the Government. During the whole session, the deputies have read 123 reports which proved to be very useful to the forthcoming task of the Government.

The National Assembly has assessed that the policy and political lines followed by the Party and Government during the past period were in the main correct. Generally speaking, in every work we have recorded great achievements, though a number of errors and shortcomings still exist.

The National Assembly has discussed the question of national reunification. The struggle waged by our people for this purpose is long and difficult but will certainly be victorious. To achieve national reunification, all our people must unite closely, make further efforts to consolidate the North and make it a basis for national liberation. Our deputies have voiced the iron will of our people in the work of national reunification. The National Assembly has many a time warmly welcomed the firm and consistent combativeness of our compatriots in the South.

With regard to land reform, the National Assembly has affirmed that the land-reform law sanctioned at its Third Session was basically correct because it aimed at abolishing the system of feudal ownership, which has hamstrung the onward march of our people, and restituting land to millions of toiling peasants. Though serious mistakes were committed, land reform has obtained great results insofar as it has overthrown the feudal landlord class and given land to the tillers. The mistakes are now being rectified. We must resolutely correct these errors in order to make land reform a success, and to this end, we must strengthen solidarity among the rural population and grasp the Party and Government line in the countryside.

As far as economic and financial matters and the 1956 budget are concerned, the National Assembly has confirmed the great achievements scored by our people in the rehabilitation work during the past two years, especially the successes achieved in food production, which has exceeded the 1939 figure. At present, our difficulties are still great because our country suffered long imperialist domination and was devastated by fifteen years of war. We must keep firm our virtues of economy and industriousness and boost production, then certainly these difficulties will be gradually removed and our livelihood will be improved step by step.

The National Assembly has debated on the cultural and social question and agreed that many achievements have been recorded in this regard—opening of new schools and building of new hospitals. However, greater efforts should still be made.

With regard to the strengthening of national defense, the National Assembly has clearly set the task for the army and the people to safeguard peace and defend the country. Over the past two years, our armymen made great progress and are now gradually embarking on the path of modernization. Our armymen must be more zealous in their study and work; our people must heighten their spirit of strengthening national defense and helping the army.

In foreign affairs, the National Assembly has realized that since the restoration of peace, the international position of our country has been raised a great deal. We must further strengthen our solidarity with the brother countries in the socialist camp, cement friendship with peace-loving countries, especially with our neighbors and other countries in Asia and Africa. We must gain greater sympathy from the world's people and continue our struggle for the implementation of the Geneva Agreement.

At its sitting on January 22, the National Assembly wholeheartedly carried out the resolution by which it placed entire confidence in the Government. The resolution read: "The National Assembly confirms that in 1956, the work of strengthening the North and struggling for national reunification was crowned with great successes, though errors and shortcomings still existed in some work. Our successes are fundamental, and will certainly be developed. Our errors and shortcomings are few and temporary, and will certainly be removed, and are now in the process of being overcome."

The National Assembly has passed many laws, which Dr. Tran Duy Hung will presently report to you. The spirit and content of these laws have testified to the policy of broadening democracy and strengthening dictatorship. Ours is a system of people's democracy; we must broaden democracy toward the people and strengthen dictatorship vis-à-vis the people's enemy. Only by strengthening dictatorship toward the enemy can we defend our people's freedom and democracy.

To develop the democratic activities of the state and prepare favorable conditions for their constant improvement, the National Assembly has passed a resolution by which it will streamline its organization and define the competence and responsibilities of its Standing Committee. It has decided to hold supplementary elections in the localities of North Viet-Nam where the deputies are lacking and to set up a committee entrusted with the task of studying the amending of the Constitution so as to enable it to reflect the achievements recorded by the Revolution and the Resistance and fall in line with the development of our system. I have the honor to tell you that I have been appointed head of this committee. This is not only an honor for myself, but for all Hanoi citizens. I request all our compatriots, especially those in Hanoi, enthusiastically to take part in the work of amending the Constitution. I am sure that we shall have a new Constitution worthy of our people.

The National Assembly has also defined its attitude regarding major international problems.

It has approved a declaration welcoming the appeal of the Supreme Soviet of the U.S.S.R. on the banning of atomic weapons and on reduction of armament. Once again we voice the peace policy of our people and Government.

The National Assembly has warmly supported the people and the Revolutionary Workers' and Peasants' Government of Hungary, who are now struggling to strengthen their socialist system. We regard the success of the Hungarian people as our own.

This declaration testifies to the international solidarity between our country and the socialist countries headed by the Soviet Union.

The National Assembly has approved a statement by which it warmly supports the Egyptian people, who are struggling to defend their sovereignty and independence, and the Algerian people, who are valiantly fighting against French colonialism. We are confident that the struggle waged by the peoples of Asia and Africa will certainly be crowned with success.

For the implementation of the decisions sanctioned by the National

Assembly and the policies and political lines followed by the Government and to win further successes, the National Assembly has called on our compatriots throughout the country and residing abroad and on our People's Army to unite closely in their struggle, consolidate the North, maintain and extend the struggle waged in the South, and strengthen our international solidarity.

The National Assembly has appealed to our compatriots in the South to struggle perseveringly and to strengthen their will for national reunification and independence. "No force can hamper the determination of our people for unity and fraternal love."

Our regime is now developing powerfully. Our people possess a huge force; our country will certainly be united, independent, democratic, rich, and strong.

Compatriots, the Sixth Session of the National Assembly has come to a successful end. It was successful because the single-mindedness between the National Assembly and the Government has symbolized the unity and single-mindedness of our entire people. It was successful because the policies and political lines followed by our Party and Government during the past years were correct in the main; because our people were united in their efforts to implement these policies and political lines, did their best to develop their good points, and were resolved to correct their mistakes; because our deputies, the people's representatives in the National Assembly, were anxious to discuss matters in the interest of the country and the people so that our people are enthusiastic and have confidence in this session of the National Assembly.

We are duty-bound to unite and struggle in order to carry into practice the decisions of the National Assembly, implement the policies and political lines of the Party and Government, speed up the tasks set for this year, increase production, practice savings, consolidate the North, and unite the people throughout the country on the basis of the program of the Fatherland Front for the struggle for national reunification.

Our compatriots in Hanoi are entrusted with the glorious task of setting an example for the people of the whole country in strengthening solidarity, broadening democracy, and instilling the spirit of the Sixth Session of the National Assembly into our people. If our compatriots in the capital city and in the whole country are able to do so, certainly this year we shall achieve more glorious successes.

INSTRUCTIONS GIVEN AT THE MEETING FOR IDEOLOGICAL REMOLDING OF GENERAL AND FIELD OFFICERS

(May 16, 1957)

The recent Twelfth Session of the Party Central Committee has assessed that, since the restoration of peace, our army has maintained and developed its fine revolutionary tradition and has fulfilled the tasks entrusted to it by the Party and the Government. It has scored achievements in all fields and begun to set up good bases for turning it into a regular and modern army. This is the result of the clear-sighted leadership of the Party Central Committee and the Government, of the correct guidance of the Party General Committee in the army, of the warm support of the people, and of the active efforts of all the officers and men and the whole Party branch in the army. The Central Committee was warm in praise of the army as a whole. You are general and field officers who have made noteworthy contributions to these achievements. So today I praise all of you.

In this one-month-long meeting you have carefully studied the Central Committee's resolutions on the building of the army and the strengthening of national defense. You have made frank and serious criticism and self-criticism. The Party General Committee in the army has listened attentively to your ideas, accepting what is correct and explaining what is wrong, and has made first remarks on the strong and weak points of the officers. You have succeeded in distinguishing the right from the wrong in a number of important questions, are in complete agreement with the Central Committee about all questions mentioned in the resolutions, and have seen a number of your own strong and weak points. As a result of this, the proletarian-class stand and the viewpoints of each of you have been strengthened further, and the confidence in the Party's leadership raised higher, creating good conditions for the strengthening of the solidarity and single-mindedness between the high and low ranks, which is the most important condition for all success of the army. This is the good result of the democratic life, of correct criticism and self-criticism in the Party. On behalf of the Central Committee, I am very pleased to praise you for the results of the meeting.

On the way of revolutionary development, our Party and our army, just as each of us, always have strong points and cannot avoid committing mistakes. Only by ceaselessly making criticism and self-criticism to distinguish the right from the wrong, in order to develop what is right and to correct what is wrong, can we make ourselves, our Party, and our revolution advance steadfastly.

We have obtained big achievements, yet the tasks facing us are very heavy. This year, we have to carry out successfully the correction of mistakes, fundamentally achieve the economic rehabilitation of the North, and prepare ourselves to enter a new stage to consolidate the North, gradually advancing to socialism. Simultaneously, we must carry on the struggle for national reunification by peaceful means and must be prepared against all the enemy's maneuvers. For the building of the army and strengthening of national defense, we have this year, on the one hand, to continue to fulfill the plan for military training and, on the other, to prepare to implement the regular rules and regulations and study the settlement of the problem of strengthening the rear. These are very great and important tasks for the whole party, the whole army, and the whole people. In undertaking these tasks we have many advantages and shall certainly be successful, but we also have great difficulties. In face of the big revolutionary struggle in the present stage and of the complicated and heavy tasks, there are in our Party and army, besides good and active ideas which are being consolidated and developed, vague and deviated conceptions and ideas which must be overcome to enable us to step up the revolution.

To overcome all difficulties and to fulfill our immediate and heavy tasks, the most important question for our army this year is, as decided by the Central Committee, to carry out the political remolding campaign, to raise higher the political consciousness of the whole army, to make criticism and self-criticism, to overcome the vague and deviated thinking, and to bring the political and ideological level of the army nearer to the demands of the revolutionary task in general and of the task of building the army in particular. In carrying out the ideological remolding, we must firmly stick to the principle of educating and raising the proletarian ideas, overcoming wrong ideas, highlighting the good points, and correcting the weak points by patiently educating, convincing, and promoting the self-consciousness of everyone. We must succeed in strengthening the single-minded solidarity in the Party and in the army. The officers must seriously study and practice criticism and self-criticism to make progress and to set a good example to the soldiers.

I hope that you will strive to fulfill the tasks of this year. I am looking forward to the good results of this year's ideological remolding of the whole army and to the new achievements in all fields that will be scored by the army and by you.

I wish you good health and good progress and send my greetings to all the officers and men.

SPEECH OPENING THE FIRST THEORETICAL COURSE OF NGUYEN AI QUOC SCHOOL*

(September 7, 1957)

Today the theoretical Party school opens. On behalf of the Party Central Committee, I wish you to make efforts and wish the school success.

Why do we have to study theory?

Our Party has established the theoretical school for cadres to raise the level of their understanding in order to meet the requirements of its revolutionary tasks and the practical situation so that it can better carry out its work and fulfill its great revolutionary tasks.

Our Party is a Marxist-Leninist Party that has been tested and tempered for a long time in hard struggles. That is why it has a great many strong points, for example: loyalty to Marxism-Leninism and to proletarian internationalism, determination in fighting, great revolutionary ardor, and traditional solidarity and unity. However, our Party has also many weak points, and a great one is the low level of its ideological understanding.

* The first theoretical course of Nguyen Ai Quoc School, Branch 1, opened on September 7, 1957. This was the first long-term theoretical course offered in Viet-Nam by the Central Committee of the Viet-Nam Workers' Party with a view to fostering and raising the level of political and ideological understanding of Party cadres. (*It is patterned on the Lenin School in Moscow.*— ED.)

315

Because of its many strong points, our Party has led the Revolution to great and fundamental successes. But on the other hand, due to the low level of its ideological understanding, when facing new and more complicated revolutionary tasks, perplexity and errors are inevitable in our Party leadership. For example, we have committed errors in the carrying out of land reform and the readjustment of organization and economic management.

At present, what are the revolutionary tasks of our Party? On the national level, we have not yet completed the task of a national people's democratic revolution. As for the North alone, since the restoration of peace it has been liberated completely and has stepped into the transitional period to socialism. In the South, we are carrying on the task of a national people's democratic revolution and are struggling for national unity. Socialism has become a powerful world system; the movement for peace, democracy, and national liberation is on the upgrade; the liberated North is being built up and consolidated; our people in the South have been tempered in the Resistance War and in these three years of struggle by peaceful means. Nevertheless, these tasks also have many difficult and complicated aspects; for example, changes in international and home situations require from us the proper line, principle, and method of action; our enemy is very wicked; our cadres and people have not thoroughly understood that the struggle for national reunification by peaceful means is a long and hard struggle. This demands that our Party raise its ideological understanding; to do so, Marxist-Leninist studies must be conducted in the whole Party, first of all among high-ranking cadres.

The North is in the transitional stage to socialism. The socialist revolution is the most difficult and far-reaching change. We have to build up a completely new society unknown in our history. We have radically to change thousand-year-old customs and habits, ways of thinking, and prejudices. We have to change old relationships in production, abolish the exploiting classes, and establish new relationships without exploitation and oppression. Therefore, we have gradually to turn our country from a backward agricultural country into an industrial one. Step-by-step collectivization of agriculture has to be implemented. Private industry, commerce, and handicrafts must go through socialist transformation. Our ignorant and poverty-ridden country must be turned into one with an advanced culture and a happy and merry life.

These tasks must be undertaken in the particular conditions of our country, that is, on the basis of a very backward country, newly freed from colonialist and feudal rule and divided into two zones.

In such conditions, what must be our method, form, and speed gradually to advance to socialism? These are problems facing our Party at the present time. To solve them with fewer gropings and errors, we must learn from the experiences of the brother countries and apply them in a creative way. We have to intensify our Marxist-Leninist training in order to apply the Marxist-Leninist stand, viewpoint, and method in summing up our Party's experience and correctly analyze the peculiarities of our country. In this way we shall gradually succeed in grasping the laws governing the development of the Vietnamese revolution and in working out the line, guiding principle, and concrete steps of socialist revolution adequate to the situation in our country. Thus, the Party's general level of Marxist-Leninist understanding must be raised, and Marxist-Leninist studies carried on by the Party, primarily by high-ranking cadres.

On the other hand, in the period of socialist revolution, the Party must be stronger than ever. Society cannot be transformed unless the Party members transform and elevate themselves. The socialist revolution demands of the Party members and cadres a firm proletarian stand and high socialist consciousness. It demands of them to sweep clean the influence of the exploiting classes' ideologies and of individualism, and to forge collectivism. It requires them to overcome bureaucracy and narrow-mindedness in order to maintain close contact with the masses, thereby to develop to the full the creativeness of the masses of people in building socialism, because socialism can be built only by the creative labor of millions of fully conscious people. Consequently, the general level of ideological understanding of the Party must be raised, and Marxist-Leninist studies made in the Party, first of all among high-ranking Party cadres.

Thus, we see that Marxist-Leninist studies are an urgent need for our Party.

What is the importance of theory to our Party? Lenin, our great teacher, summarized the importance of theory in the following sentences: "There cannot be a revolutionary movement without revolutionary theory," and "Only a party guided by a vanguard theory can possibly fill the role of vanguard fighter." The Communist Party of the Soviet Union, the first party which blazed the trail of liberation for mankind, has always paid attention to theory because it has realized that theory shows it the correct path to Communism.

The Chinese Communist Party, which is the model of the Communist Party in a semicolonial and semifeudal country, has long paid great attention to theory. Mao Tse-tung said that if among the leading Party cadres there were one or two hundred who succeeded in making a systematic and practical study of Marxism-Leninism, then it could be considered that they were able to defeat the Japanese imperialists. When summing up experiences, the Eighth Party Congress concluded that good or bad Party leadership depended first of all on whether training in Marxism-Leninism of high-ranking cadres was good and that the carrying on of Marxist-Leninist studies for Party cadres and members was the key to better work thenceforward.

Through the experience of brother countries, we all the more see the pressing need and importance of theoretical study for the Party, in the first place in high-ranking cadres.

What is our cadres' attitude to theoretical study? It can be said that our Party has never been confronted with so many complicated, big, and difficult problems as at the present time. In this situation, our cadres, in general, have felt that their weakness lies in lack of theory, and consequently they have understood the need for theoretical study and have asked the Party to organize theoretical study for them. This is a very good sign. We must promote this yearning for study and for progress in order to step up the movement for theoretical study in our Party. However, this does not mean that all our cadres have understood this need. For example, at present, there are many cadres who bury themselves all day long in routine work without being aware of the importance of theory. Hence there are signs of slighting study or lacking determination to find ways and means to combine work with study. After a period of study on the job, there are some cadres— chiefly those with low education who are not used to reading and meditation—who grumble when encountering difficulties inherent in reading documents, in going deeply into and pondering over them. Having fruitlessly applied a number of experiences without creativeness, we also lack conviction of the need to study theory and to learn from the experiences of brother countries. These are manifestations of empiricism to be overcome. These are also expressions of a revisionist character to be watched in order to step up the present movement for theoretical study.

I have dealt with the importance of theoretical study. Now I shall speak of integration of theory with practice. Theory is very necessary, but unmethodical study yields no result. Therefore, in studying theory we have to stress that *theory must be integrated with practice*.

Unity of theory and practice is a fundamental principle of Marxism-Leninism. Practice without the guidance of theory is blind practice. Theory without integration with practice is mere theory. For that reason, while laying stress on the importance of theory, Lenin repeated over and over again that revolutionary theory is not dogma but a guide to revolutionary action; that it is not something rigid but of a rich creative nature; and that it should be constantly improved by new conclusions drawn from living practice. Communists of various countries must put Marxism-Leninism in concrete form proper to circumstances of the given time and of the given place.

The Party school is the school to train outstanding fighters devoted to the proletarian cause. You are all high-ranking cadres of the Party. Your theoretical study does not aim at turning you into mere theoreticians but at enabling you to work well. It means that you must study the spirit of Marxism-Leninism, its stand, viewpoint, and method, and put them into practice in order satisfactorily to solve practical problems in our revolutionary work.

How is theory integrated with practice? We study theory in order to apply it, not for its own sake and not to make capital for ourselves later to bargain with the Party. All bad motives should be extirpated.

We do not carry on studies to learn by heart every sentence and every word and apply the experience of brother countries in a mechanical way. We must learn Marxism-Leninism to analyze and solve the actual issues of the revolution in our country according to its particular conditions. While applying theory, we must improve and enrich it with new conclusions drawn from our revolutionary practice.

Theory is the summing up of the experiences of mankind, the synthesis of knowledge of nature and society in the course of history. Marxist-Leninist theory is the summing up of experiences of workers' movements of all countries down to the present time. Stalin said that theory is the science of laws governing the development of nature and society, the science of revolution of the oppressed and exploited masses, the science of success of socialism in all countries, the science of Communist construction.

Reality is problems to be solved and contradictions lying within things. We are revolutionary cadres, our reality is problems to be solved that the revolution puts to us. Real life is immense. It covers the experience drawn from the work and thought of an individual, the Party's policies and line, its historical experiences, and issues at home and in the world. In the course of our study, these are realities to be kept in contact with. However, in this school we must primarily compare theory with our thought and work, that is, to use the theory we have acquired to make an analysis of the success and failure in our work and to discover the origin of our correct or wrong stand, viewpoint, and method. To do so is to sum up in order to improve our approach to these issues and to work with better results. We carry out the revolution with a view to transforming the world and society. To transform the world and society, we must first and foremost transform ourselves. Therefore we must, in the first place, integrate theory with our actual work and thought in order to transform ourselves, to improve our Marxist-Leninist stand, viewpoint, and method.

In our study, we have also to bring into focus the actual issues in the country and in the world and the revolutionary problems and tasks ahead of our Party, using the acquired understanding to find the correct line and method for the solving of these issues, or to analyze the experiences drawn from work done by the Party and to discover the causes of its successes and failures. This will help us consolidate our stand and enhance our viewpoint and method.

However, it is necessary to refrain from demanding the solving of all actual issues in the course of the study. The practice of the revolution is very extensive and the solving of all the issues put forth by this practice is a long-term work for the whole Party. At school we can only lay the foundation for integration of theory with practice. The experience of brother parties as well as ours has given many lessons in the harm done by dogmatism divorced from real life. The Twentieth Congress of the Communist Party of the Soviet Union, while criticizing the cult of personality, pointed out the harm done in ideological work. As a result, the Party succeeded in correcting its mistakes and obtained big achievements. Since the Twentieth Congress, the brother parties have actively overcome the bad consequences of dogmatism, which were manifested in the fact that in many places experiences of brother countries were applied mechanically, disregarding the peculiarities of one's own country. Many times, the Chinese Communist Party also made mistakes in its line and suffered losses from dogmatism. In the fight against it, the Chinese Communist Party, under Mao Tse-tung's leadership, succeeded in combining the universal truth of Marxism-Leninism with the revolutionary practice of China, thereby taking steps proper to the Chinese society, and made a great contribution to the treasure house of Marxist-Leninist ideology and experience.

Thanks to its ability to combine Marxism-Leninism with the actual situation in our country, our Party has scored many successes in its work. However, the combination of Marxist-Leninist truth with the practice of the Vietnamese revolution was not complete and brought about many mistakes, namely those committed in the land reform, readjustment of organization, and economic construction. At present, in building socialism, although we have the rich experiences of brother countries, we cannot apply them mechanically because our country has its own peculiarities. Disregard for the peculiarities of one's nation while learning from the experiences of the brother countries is a serious mistake; it is dogmatism. But undue emphasis on the role of national peculiarities and negation of the universal value of the great, basic experiences of the brother countries will lead to grave revisionist mistakes. For that reason, while laying emphasis on the importance of theoretical study, stress must always be laid on the principle of integrating theory with practice. We have to overcome dogmatism and also to be on guard against revisionism. In short, we must be aware of the importance of theory to study enthusiastically. In the course of your study, only by making use of what you will have learned to analyze and solve the practical questions in your ideological work and in the Party, can you obtain good results.

To put into practice the principle of integration of theory with practice and to reach the aim of your study—that is, highlighting theory, ideological transformation, and strengthening Party spirit—it is necessary to have a correct attitude to study:

1. To be modest and frank. The level of ideological understanding of our Party is rather low; nobody can boast about being good at it. Therefore modesty and frankness are to be emphasized: to go deep into and ponder over Marxist-Leninist works and the lectures given by the professors from friendly countries, modestly to learn from them, recognizing what one knows and what one does not know. Conceit, self-assumption, and self-complacency are the number-one enemies of study.

2. Voluntarily and consciously to consider study as a task to be completed at all costs by a revolutionary cadre, thereby actively and on one's own initiative to fulfill the plan for study, highlighting industriousness and unflinching efforts when confronted with difficulties in study.

3. To stress independent and free thinking. To go deep into and thoroughly understand the documents without having blind faith in every word and phrase of the documents, boldly to put forth for discussion the questions one has not thoroughly understood until one fully grasps them. To ask "Why?" when faced with any question and to consider carefully whether it is in conformity with real life and reason, to refrain absolutely from obeying the book blindly. There must be mature thinking.

4. To defend truth and stick to principle; indiscriminate "yeses" and compromise are not allowed.

5. To help each other in study, to conduct bold criticism and sincere self-criticism from a desire for solidarity, with the aim of building new solidarity on a new basis.

This attitude toward study must become a habit. Only in this way can you realize the principle of integration of theory with practice and enable your study to reach its aim: to train cadres capable of applying the Marxist-Leninist stand, viewpoint, and method in solving concrete revolutionary issues.

These are my views, for you to examine. I again wish the school success.

THE OCTOBER REVOLUTION AND THE LIBERATION OF THE PEOPLES OF THE EAST*

(November 6, 1957)

The October Revolution brightened the history of mankind with a new dawn.

Like the rising sun driving away the shadows, the October Revolution brightened the history of mankind with a new dawn.

Forty years ago, under the leadership of the Leninist Party, the Russian proletariat, firmly united with the working peasants, overthrew the power of the capitalists and landlords. The Soviet state, the state of proletarian dictatorship, bringing a genuine democracy to the people, has given proof of its vitality and invincible strength.

The October Revolution was the victory of the revolutionary forces of the toiling masses; it was an extremely violent upheaval creating conditions which clearly showed the creativeness of the toiling masses. The victory of the October Revolution confirmed the correctness of Marxism-Leninism; it paved the way to new victories of the working class in social life, on the basis of great loyalty to Marxist-Leninist principles. Thanks to the clear-sightedness and heroism of the Leninist Party, the Party of the proletarian class, the October Revolution

* This article was written at the invitation of the National Political Publishing House of the U.S.S.R. for the fortieth anniversary of the October Revolution.

won victory and ushered in a new era in the history of mankind and a new stage on the long and glorious path covered by the revolutionary Party of the Russian proletariat.

Owing to the success of the October Revolution, the Leninist Party was able successfully to fulfill the historical tasks of great significance entrusted to it. Peoples who were once oppressed have become masters of their own destiny. The Czarist empire was suppressed; this empire was formerly the prison of many nations and at the same time was enslaved by a handful of cosmopolitan financiers. The people were no longer the toys, the slaves, the cannon fodder of rival imperialists. The toiling masses wiped out the wretchedness of bourgeois Russia where, as in other countries, they had suffered under the dreadful yoke of the capitalists and landlords. The laboring people were the creators of all wealth but were kept in misery and ignorance—the atrocious and age-old fate of the overwhelming majority of mankind. For the first time in human history, the working people started to build a society without class exploitation and national oppression—a socialist society. With their exemplary enthusiasm in labor, high consciousness, ever-growing labor efficiency, and with boundless faithfulness to their own cause, that of their children, and of their brothers who still suffer in slavery, the Soviet people have transformed their age-old dream of happiness into a dazzling reality over a sixth of the earth.

The October Revolution has nationalized factories, mines, and principal means of communication and liaison. It has brought land to the peasants. On the basis of socialist industrialization and socialist transformation of the countryside along the path drawn by Lenin, the Soviet Union has developed its economy at a prodigious speed, at a pace hitherto unknown. The socialist economy has proved its superiority over the capitalist economy.

The fundamental law of the socialist economy is to satisfy the ever-growing material and cultural needs of the working people. It is completely contrary to the monopolistic capitalist economy, which relies on the ever-increasing exploitation of the working class, on the impoverishment of the laboring masses, and on the plundering of the enslaved peoples. The Soviet workers, peasants, and intellectuals, who have wiped out the regime of exploitation of man by man and of class antagonism on the vast Soviet territory, are constantly consolidating their socialist brotherhood, which is growing more splendid and blooming with every passing day. The glorious achievements of the Soviet people are preparing the way for the future society—a Communist society.

The October Revolution has proved the possibility of overthrowing the dictatorship of the exploiting class and establishing a socialist society that ensures the country's brilliant development at an unprecedented speed and takes the toiling masses to a dignified, glorious, and ever more prosperous life. It brings to the working people a free, happy, and powerful Fatherland and leads them toward a bright horizon, formerly undreamt of. This is an inspiring example for the working people throughout the world, especially for the peoples of the East, who were and are still being enslaved by imperialism. The monopolist imperialists want to keep the Eastern countries in a backward economic state, keeping the masses in misery and always trampling on their nationalism.

The October Revolution has opened up the era of a new foreign policy, the policy of peace and friendship among nations. On October 26, 1917—the day following the establishment of worker-peasant power—the Second Congress of Soviets adopted a decree concerning peace, which was the basis of the Soviet state's foreign policy. Since then, the Soviet Union has constantly been carrying out an active struggle for peace and against the warmongers. This policy was prompted by the very nature of the socialist Soviet state. The truth is that the working people hate all aggressive wars because, first of all, they bring profit to the exploiters and cause ravages and sufferings to the broad masses. That is why the working people's power genuinely defends peace, in which the peoples of all lands display keen interest.

The October Revolution overthrew the capitalists' and landlords' state in a vast country, shattered the imperialists' chains, and thus eliminated all power of the exploiting class for whom war is a source of profit. The Soviet Union consistently stands for peaceful coexistence among nations, whatever their political and social systems.

The Communists are convinced of the superiority of the socialist system. The Soviet Union is cogent proof of this. For this reason it does not fear peaceful competition; on the contrary, it advocates it. Not long before the October Revolution, Lenin quoted the principle expressed by Engels in 1822: *"The victorious proletariat cannot impose any happiness whatever on another people without in this way undermining its own victory.*" He regarded this principle as indubitable and absolutely conforming to the spirit of internationalism.

At the same time, the Soviet Union unceasingly supports other nations in their struggle for international independence, against imperialist enslavement and aggression. The firm peace policy of the Soviet Union constitutes a decisive mainstay for all nations in their struggle against the forces of war. This policy is of particular importance for the peoples of the East, considered by the imperialists as ready prey and as sources of manpower and material wealth for the stepping up of their predatory wars.

A bulwark of peace, the Soviet Union is at the same time an invincible force ready to repel any aggression. From 1918 to 1920, Soviet power, actively supported by the international proletariat, crushed the internal counterrevolutionary forces and wiped out the armies of fourteen interventionist imperialist powers. During World War II, the Soviet Union annihilated the huge armed forces of the fascist aggressors, which had been carefully prepared with the assistance of all imperialist countries. Thus, it saved the world from the barbarous Hitlerite enslavement and dealt a decisive blow to the main forces of Japanese militarism. All the peoples, especially the peoples of the East, felt gratitude for the Soviet Union. Full of enthusiasm, the peoples of the East were aware that the imperialists who enslaved other peoples were not invincible. The fascist aggressors were crushed, despite their modern weapons and their long preparation before World War II for their criminal aggression.

The October Revolution and the building of socialism in the Soviet Union have considerably increased the revolutionary forces of the working class in the capitalist countries. The laboring peoples of many European and Asian countries have followed the example set by the Russian revolutionary proletariat.

In a short space of history, socialism has become a world system, now embracing twelve countries with more than 900 million people.

The October Revolution has shattered the fetters of imperialism, destroyed its foundation, and inflicted on it a deadly blow. Like a thunderbolt, it has stirred up the Asian peoples from their centuries-old slumbers. It has opened up for them the revolutionary anti-imperialist era, the era of national liberation.

The Soviet Union is the strongest and most powerful bulwark of progress, democracy, and peace. Its invincible and constantly developing strength and its consistent peace policy constitute the firmest guarantee for the independence of all nations, big and small. The Soviet Union has always made worthy efforts and has tabled practical proposals for arms reduction. It has persistently struggled for the suppression of nuclear and thermonuclear weapons which are threatening all nations. It has many a time asked other states to adopt collective security systems aimed at safeguarding peace in Europe and Asia. It has always upheld the five principles of peaceful coexistence and has endeavored to make these five principles the basis of international relations between countries throughout the world.

Contrary to the peace policy of the socialist states, the aggressive warmongering imperialists, first of all the U.S. imperialists, are aggravating international tensions. They refuse arms reduction and prohibition of nuclear and thermonuclear weapons, which are a terrible threat to mankind. They cherish the senseless hope of keeping the whole world under the threat of their military bases. They form aggressive blocs like fetters, in an attempt to reshackle and re-enslave the free and independent nations. They resort to every maneuver to threaten the peoples of the East and to re-establish colonial rule in the countries which have recovered their independence. This is the true nature of the war unleased against Egypt by the aggressors in London and Paris, with the practical assistance of the U.S. imperialists. While fostering the aggressive schemes of the others, the U.S. imperialists make an attempt to impose their yoke on the peoples in the Near East, Southeast Asia, and the Pacific, to turn those countries into new bases of aggression and to oust from these countries their allies and rivals—the English, French, Dutch, etc.

The imperialists seek to sow discord and division in the great family of socialist countries. This is the very nature of their aggression against the Hungarian People's Republic, against the heroic achievements of the Hungarian people, who, thanks to the heroism of the Soviet people during World War II, were liberated from the fascist yoke. But events have confirmed the assessment made by the Twentieth Congress of the Communist Party of the Soviet Union: "Thanks to the powerful socialist camp which loves peace, the forces of peace have not only moral means but also material means to check aggression." Owing to this fact and the existence of a "vast zone of peace," to the peace movement of the broad masses, and to the development of the workers' movement in the capitalist countries, today "powerful social and political forces have sufficient means to prevent the imperialists from unleashing war, and will deal them deadly blows and frustrate their adventurist plans if they venture to launch war."

In Egypt, the aggressors met with ignominious defeat. The plot of subversion against the Hungarian People's Republic was foiled. Everyone sees that the powerful strength, vigilance, and determination of the Soviet Union have crushed the plot of the warmongers and aggressors. At the same time, this is also the victory of the cause of peace and independence of all nations. The Soviet Union does not step back when facing the imperialist maniacs who want to sow trouble among the peoples so as to carry out easily their wicked schemes. The Soviet Union is determined to defend freedom and the peaceful labor of all peoples and the security of all nations, big and small. The Soviet Union constantly shows loyalty to international solidarity, sympathizes with and supports the struggle for liberation of all oppressed nations. All countries of the East, whatever their state or social regime, are deeply grateful to the Soviet Union for its peace policy and its proletarian internationalism. These policies inspire the peoples of the East with an ever-growing confidence in the great socialist ideology.

The power brought into being by the October Revolution set an example of genuine freedom and friendship between nations. Comrade Mao Tse-tung said: "The gunshots of the October Revolution have brought us Marxism-Leninism. It has helped the whole world and the progressive elements in China to examine the destiny of the country in the world outlook of the working class and revise their own problems. The conclusion was to follow the path of the Russians."

As early as 1913, Lenin said: "Everywhere in Asia a strong democratic movement is growing, spreading, and being consolidated. There the bourgeoisie is still siding with the people to fight the reactionaries. Hundreds of millions of people are rising up in life, light, and liberty. . . . All young Asia, that is, hundreds of millions of toiling masses in Asia have a staunch ally—the proletariat of all civilized countries. No force on earth can prevent its victory, which will liberate all the peoples of Europe as well as of Asia."

In 1919, at the Eastern Communists Congress, Lenin said: "A task is laid before you here, which has previously not been laid before the Communists of the whole world: basing yourselves on the general theory and practice of Communism, you must, in adapting yourselves to specific conditions which do not exist in the European countries, learn how to apply this theory and this practice to the conditions, when the peasantry forms the basic masses, when it is necessary to settle the task of struggle not against capitalism but against medieval vestiges."

Dealing a telling blow to the common enemy—imperialism—the October Revolution has brought to the Eastern peoples assistance of a decisive character; it has given them the example of the liberation struggles of the countries once oppressed by Czarism.

The October Revolution has brought to the people of all nations the right to decide their own fate and the practical means to implement this right. It is well known that Lenin attached particular importance to the recognition of the right of all nations to secession and to build up independent states. Opposing Bukharin's theories, Lenin resolutely demanded that this right should be inserted into the Party's Political program expounded at the Eighth Congress in March, 1919. The Soviet Union of the October Revolution recognized the independence of Mongolia and Finland, which seceded to build up independent states. Of course, for the formerly oppressed nations, the right to secession does not signify the obligation to secede from a state where the people have overthrown the oppressors. On the contrary, it creates conditions for a voluntary alliance between free nations on the basis of complete equality of interests. It was on this basis that in December, 1922, the Union of the Soviet Socialist Republics was founded—a great example of a multinational socialist state built on friendship, mutual confidence, and cooperation between nationalities.

Today, in the Soviet Union, thanks to the friendly assistance of the Russian people, the nationalities formerly oppressed by the Czarist regime have reached an unprecedented level of development. They are able to establish their own institutions and to restore and develop their own culture in their own language. All Soviet citizens, regardless of nationality and race, enjoy complete equality and the same freedoms, not only written on paper but actually ensured. This is a situation unknown to the workers of even the most democratic bourgeois countries, where acknowledged freedoms guaranteed by law are canceled out by actual social conditions. That is why the freedoms enjoyed by the Soviet peoples have fired the hearts of millions of people who are living under colonialist oppression. The ruling circles in the imperialist countries are stifling the most elementary freedoms of the colonial and dependent peoples while inscribing the ironic legend "Liberty, Equality, Fraternity" in jails and places where tortures are carried out.

The Soviet Union establishes the equality of peoples by basing itself on special concern for the interests and requirements of the once oppressed nationalities. It helped them build up a modern economy and sweep away the centuries-old backwardness bequeathed them by their exploiters. The national republics of the Soviet Union have developed even more rapidly than the Russian Republic in industry as well as in other fields. The recent measures taken in the light of the decision of the Twentieth Congress of the Communist Party of the Soviet Union to improve the organization of industrial and construction management bring a new contribution to the bold and ingenious policy steadily carried out by the Soviet power since the October Revolution. They will further accelerate the economic and cultural development of all the republics in the Soviet Union. The peoples of these republics are setting for the peoples of the whole world an example of socialist peoples united into a monolithic bloc in political, social, and moral fields, a solidarity unknown in the conditions of the capitalist regime.

All the Soviet nationalities are animated by an ardent and genuine patriotism—a patriotism inseparable from proletarian internationalism.

For the first time in history, the national question has been solved by the victorious working class in a satisfactory way, on the basis of Marxist-Leninist principles.

Marxism-Leninism has elaborated a just and complete theory of anti-imperialist national revolution. The era of monopolist capitalism is also one when a few great powers, swayed by a handful of financiers, exercise their domination over dependent and semidependent countries; therefore, the liberation of the oppressed countries and peoples has become an integral part of the proletarian revolution.

Hence, there arise in the first place the possibility of and the need for a close fighting alliance between the colonial peoples and the proletariat of the imperialist countries to triumph over the common enemy. The revolutionary struggle of the workers of the capitalist countries directly helps the oppressed peoples free themselves, by striking direct blows at the heart of the oppressors. This was vividly demonstrated by the October Revolution, which has overthrown the power of the exploiters in Russia and resolutely abolished the oppressive colonial policy of the Czarist regime and the Russian bourgeois class. In its turn, the revolutionary struggle of colonial and semicolonial peoples directly helps the proletariat of the capitalist countries in their fight against the ruling classes to free themselves from the yoke of capitalism. The unity of the anti-imperialist struggle carries the certainty for victory for all colonial and semicolonial peoples and for the proletariat in the capitalist countries.

Therefore, the national question can no longer be viewed from an abstract and isolated point of view. Marxism-Leninism has shown that national movements effectively directed against imperialism unfailingly contribute to the general revolutionary struggle and that national claims and national movements must not be estimated according to their strictly local political and social character in a narrow-minded way, but according to the part they play against the imperialist forces in the world. Marxism-Leninism has unmasked bourgeois democracy, which dissimulated behind sermons on the abstract "equality" between nations to conceal the oppression and exploitation of the great number of nations in the world by a handful of imperialist countries. Marxism-Leninism makes a clear distinction between "oppressed, dependent, and subject nations, and the oppressing, exploiting, and sovereign nations."

To handle in a scientific way those problems on the basis of Marxism-Leninism and of the inexhaustible theoretical and practical experiences of the Soviet Union and at the same time to pay heed to the peculiarities of all dependent countries, it is of great importance for the study of political lines to continue the development of the national liberation movement and the organization of social forces in the revolutions for liberation in the Eastern countries. In 1923, Lenin wrote on the dependent countries as follows: "Our European philistines never even dream that the subsequent revolutions—in Oriental countries, which possess much vaster populations and a much vaster diversity of social conditions—will undoubtedly display even greater peculiarities than the Russian Revolution."

During the course of the emancipation struggles of the Eastern peoples, the Marxist-Leninist principles in the question of colonial liberation have been triumphantly confirmed. The October Revolution provided strong impetus for this struggle, and the existence of the Soviet Union constituted an important historic factor which helped that struggle develop rapidly.

The revolution in the colonial and semicolonial countries is a national democratic revolution. To make it successful, it is possible and necessary to form a very wide national front, uniting all social strata and classes longing for liberation from the colonialist yoke. In particular, one should bear in mind that the role played by the bourgeoisie in colonial and dependent countries in general is not similar to that played by the bourgeoisie in capitalist countries. The national bourgeoisie can be won to participate actively in the national democratic revolution.

The revolution in the colonial and semicolonial countries is first and foremost a peasant revolution. It is inseparable from the antifeudal revolution. The alliance of the broad peasant masses with the working class is the fundamental base on which a wide and firm national front can be formed. Consequently, agrarian reform is a fundamental task of the national democratic revolution.

To lead the national revolution to victory and to cover the successive stages of the development of the national democratic state, the working class and its Party must take up their role of leading the revolution.

The revolution for liberation of the oppressed countries and the revolution of the proletariat of the oppressing countries must support each other. In the oppressing countries, the central task in the education of internationalism is to help the toiling people clearly understand the right of oppressed nationalities to secession and to found independent states. In the oppressed countries, this task consists in allying the various nationalities on a voluntary basis. Lenin said: "The situation which presents itself provides no other path leading to internationalism and the concord between peoples, no other path leading to this goal."

The October Revolution gave an impetus to the movement of national liberation, which has become a surging wave in all Eastern countries: China, India, Indonesia, Viet-Nam, etc. After World War II, many colonial and semicolonial countries have shattered imperialist chains. Several of them have broken away from the capitalist system.

The victory of the Chinese revolution was a historical event of great significance. It struck a new blow at the imperialist system, the severest since the October Revolution.

Today, more than 1,200 million inhabitants of Asia and Africa have already freed themselves from colonial and semicolonial enslavement.

The colonial system of imperialism is collapsing beyond remedy; the question of total liquidation of the colonial system is the foremost one. The peoples of the East are rising up against their aggressors and are determined not to let anyone oppress them.

As Lenin had foreseen, the time has now come when, heads held high, these peoples enter the international arena.

The Vietnamese people advance toward socialism under the glorious Marxist-Leninist banner.

Thanks to the French Communist Party and the Chinese Communist Party, the Vietnamese revolutionaries have received the invigorating influence of the October Revolution and of Marxism-Leninism. That is like a thirsty and hungry traveler who, after a long journey, receives water and rice.

The Indochinese Communist Party was founded on February 3, 1930, thirteen years after the October Revolution. It became the undisputed leader of the whole people in the struggle against imperialism.

In September, 1930, in Nghe An province, under the leadership of the young Indochinese Communist Party, the peasants seized power and established the Soviets, marking a step in their heroic struggle. The Soviets adopted a resolution on agrarian reform which was put into effect by the peasants. But going mad before the development of the movement of national liberation and activities of the Soviets, the French imperialists savagely repressed and terrorized the Vietnamese people. They succeeded in crushing the Soviets only by mobilizing all their available forces, bombing the liberated zones, razing whole villages to the ground, and setting up a regime of bestial terror everywhere. However, the Indochinese Communist Party throughout the country kept on struggling persistently and heroically to lead the movement of national liberation of the Vietnamese people.

Twenty-eight years after the October Revolution, the victory of the Soviet army over the Japanese imperialists created favorable conditions for the August Revolution which brought independence to Viet-Nam.

But the French imperialists were not content with their defeat and wanted to re-enslave Viet-Nam. For nine years, the Vietnamese people had to wage a hard and heroic Resistance War against the colonialists. United in a broad patriotic front and standing around the Viet-Nam Workers' Party, which inherited the experiences and traditions of the Indochinese Communist Party, the Vietnamese people have defeated the forces of French and world imperialism.

In 1954, the Geneva Agreement was signed, thanks to the help of the Soviet Union and China and to the support of peace-loving peoples all over the world. It put an end to the aggressive war of the colonialists. The independence, unity, and territorial integrity of Viet-Nam were officially recognized.

Since then, the Vietnamese people have perseveringly carried on the struggle for the implementation of the Geneva Agreement to reunify the country, because South Viet-Nam is still ruled by the U.S. imperialists and their henchmen. In completely liberated North Viet-Nam, power is in the hands of the people; this is a firm basis for the peaceful reunification of Viet-Nam, a task which receives ever-growing and generous help from the Soviet Union, China, and other brother countries. Thanks to this assistance, the consolidation of the North has scored good results.

The victory of the August Revolution in Viet-Nam has proved once again the soundness of Marxism-Leninism on the national and colonial question, the correctness of the line mapped out by the Socialist Revolution of October, 1917. It confirms that to be successful, the national revolution must: rely upon a broad national front against imperialism; solve the peasant question; organize a people's army; have the brotherly support of the people and proletariat of other countries; and be led by the Party of the working class.

The October Revolution teaches us to unite closely the efforts of the world proletariat, of the oppressed peoples, and of other peace forces in the whole world to struggle against imperialism and war.

"Unless the proletariat and, following it, all the toiling masses of all countries and nations all over the world voluntarily strive for alliance and unity, victory over capitalism cannot be successfully accomplished," said Lenin. And he added: "In the last analysis, the outcome of the struggle will be determined by the fact that Russia, India, China, etc., account for the overwhelming majority of the population of the globe. And it is precisely this majority that, during the past few years, has been drawn into the struggle for emancipation with extraordinary rapidity, so that in this respect there cannot be the slightest shadow of doubt as to what the final outcome of the world struggle will be. In this sense, the complete victory of socialism is fully and absolutely assured."

The forty years that have elapsed since the October Revolution are years of uninterrupted marching forward of socialism.

In the face of the imperialists who seek to prolong their tottering regime, detested by every people, we, revolutionaries of all countries, must at all times strengthen our unity around the U.S.S.R. and the Communist Party of the U.S.S.R. The Leninist theories of the Twentieth Congress strengthen this union still further and tighten the bonds of friendship and mutual trust between the socialist countries. The declaration by the Government of the Soviet Union on October 30, 1956, defined anew the relationship between socialist countries, established on principles of equality, mutual respect, confidence, and friendly cooperation.

The celebration of the fortieth anniversary of the great October Revolution is an opportunity to mobilize the great mass of workers of the whole world, to appeal to them to unite and struggle to achieve new and yet greater victories.

Under the glorious banner of Marxism-Leninism and following the path marked out by the October Revolution, with complete faith in the masses and absolute confidence in victory, we march forward with courage and resolution toward a future radiant with happiness, friendship, and lasting peace, toward a socialist society.

EXCERPT FROM A TALK AT A CADRES' MEETING DEBATING THE DRAFT LAW ON MARRIAGE AND THE FAMILY*
(October, 1959)

There are people who think that as a bachelor I may not have a perfect knowledge of this question. Though I have no family of my own, yet I have a very big family—the working class throughout the world and the Vietnamese people. From that broad family I can judge and imagine the small one.

At present, our entire people want socialist construction. What is to be done to build socialism?

Production must certainly be increased as much as possible. To increase production there must be much labor power, which can be obtained satisfactorily only by emancipating the women's labor power.

Women make up half of society. If they are not liberated, half of society is not freed. If women are not emancipated only half of socialism is built.

---

* On December 28, 1959, at its Eleventh Session, the National Assembly adopted the law on marriage and the family. This law is based on four fundamental principles: freedom of marriage, monogamy, equality between men and women, and defense of children's rights and interests.

It is correct to take a keen interest in the family; many families constitute the society. A good society makes a good family and vice versa. The core of the society is the family. It is precisely to build up socialism that due attention must be paid to this core.

"Living in concord, husband and wife may empty the East Sea," the proverb runs. To enjoy concord in matrimonial life, marriage must be based on genuine love.

The law on marriage to be presented to the National Assembly is a revolution, an integral part of the socialist revolution. Therefore, we should adopt the proletarian stand to understand it. It is not correct if our understanding is based on the feudal, bourgeois, or petit-bourgeois stand.

The law on marriage aims at emancipating women, that is, at freeing half of society. The emancipation of the women must be carried out simultaneously with the extirpation of feudal and bourgeois thinking in men. As for themselves, women should not wait until the directives of the Government and the Party free them but they must rely upon themselves and struggle.

The Party must give this law leadership from its preparation to its presentation and execution, because this is a revolution. The leadership by the Party means that all cadres and Party members must apply this law strictly and lead all youth and women's organizations resolutely and correctly put it into effect.

The execution of this law is, on the one hand, favorable, because our people have received the Party education and have made much progress; and on the other, difficult, because of the long-standing and deeply rooted old habits and traditions among the people. That is why everything is not over with the promulgation of this law, but long-term propaganda and education needs to be carried on to obtain good results.

I hope that all of you will do your best, be patient, have a thorough knowledge of this law, and carry it out satisfactorily. In particular, you must be very careful, because this law exerts great influence on the future of the family, the society, and the nation.

SPEECH OPENING THE CEREMONY COMMEMORATING THE THIRTIETH ANNIVERSARY OF THE FOUNDATION OF THE PARTY

(January 5, 1960)

On behalf of the Party Central Committee and the Fatherland Front, I welcome the comrades present at this celebration of the thirtieth birthday of the Party.

In recent times, throughout the North of our country, in town and countryside, in the factories, farms, cooperatives, army, offices, schools, etc., everyone enthusiastically emulates to make achievements in honor of the Party. On behalf of the Party, I convey praise and thanks to all the compatriots.

The Southern compatriots, who took a heroic part in the Revolution and the Resistance War, are now closely united and are perseveringly struggling against the cruel U.S.-Diem regime for improved living conditions, democratic freedoms, and peaceful national reunification and have constantly turned their mind toward the North. On behalf of the Party, I send most affectionate greetings to them and tell them that our just struggle, though protracted and hard, will certainly win.

Dear comrades, with all the modesty of a revolutionary, we still have the right to say: *Our Party is truly great!*

Our Party is a thoroughbred, born of the toiling class. In the great international proletarian family under the Marxist-Leninist banner, our Party has such great elder brothers as the Communist Party of the Soviet Union, the Chinese Communist Party, the French Communist Party, and other brother parties embracing 35 million vanguard fighters of the working class.

Our Party is truly great. From the day our country was invaded by French imperialism and turned into its colony, our people were reduced to slavery and our Fatherland was trampled under the iron heel of a cruel enemy. For tens of years before the birth of our Party, the situation was gloomy and seemed hopeless.

Since its inception, our Party has raised aloft the banner of Revolution and Solidarity and led our entire people to march forward, struggling for national and class liberation. As bright as the rising sun, the Party's red flag tore down the black curtain of darkness and blazed the way, leading our people's steady advance to victory in the anti-imperialist and antifeudal revolution.

"When eating fruit one must think of the fruit grower." In today's merry celebration, we must turn our mind toward the heroes and martyrs of our Party and people.

During the fifteen years of struggle preceding the August Revolution and during the nine years of Resistance War, many outstanding Party members and many men and women among the revolutionary masses have made extremely heroic sacrifices for the people and the Party. Speaking merely of the comrades in the Party Central Committee, fourteen have been shot, guillotined, or beaten to death in prison by the French imperialists. The crimson blood of these martyrs has made the revolutionary red banner brighter. Their heroic sacrifices were to bring to our country the flower of independence and the fruit of freedom. Our people will forever remember these martyrs' deeds, and we must constantly take inspiration from their courageous spirit in order to overcome all difficulties and hardships and achieve the revolutionary task they have handed down to us.

On this occasion, I wish to remind you that thirty-one of the comrades who are now in the Central Committee were given altogether 222 years of imprisonment and deportation by the French imperialists before the Revolution, not to mention the sentences to death *in absentia* and the years of imprisonment evaded by those who escaped from prison. Turning what was a bad thing into a good thing, our comrades made up for the years in prison in discussing and studying political theory. Once more, this not only proves that the enemy's extremely savage policy of repression could not check the progress of the revolution but, on the contrary, it became a touchstone, it has further steeled the revolutionaries. And the result was that the Revolution has triumphed, the imperialists have been defeated.

Our Party is truly great. Here is an example of it: It is recorded in our history that a national hero, Thanh Giong, drove the invaders out with bamboo trunks. In the first days of the Resistance War, our Party led thousands, tens of thousands, of heroes to follow Thanh Giong's example of fighting the French colonialists with bamboo spears.

But victory over imperialism and feudalism is relatively easy; it is much harder to defeat poverty and backwardness. At present, the North is completely liberated. The Party unites and leads our people to vie with one another in socialist construction and to build a happy and comfortable life with admirable customs and fine habits. As long as a Vietnamese is still exploited and reduced to misery, the Party still suffers, considering it has not yet completed its task. For that reason, while attending to big affairs, such as turning our backward economy and culture into advanced ones, the Party constantly takes care of small things such as fish sauce, salt, etc., indispensable to the people's everyday life. Our Party is great because it covers the whole country and is at the same time close to the heart of every compatriot.

Our Party is great because it has no other interests besides those of the class, the people, and the nation.

Our Party's immediate task is to lead the people to intensify the emulation to increase production and practice economy to build socialism in the North in order to serve as a firm base for the struggle for national reunification.

The brother countries in the socialist camp have all advanced by leaps and bounds, e.g., the Soviet Union will fulfill, in the main, its Seven-Year Plan of building Communism from one to three years ahead of schedule. In only two years, China has basically fulfilled its Second Five-Year Plan. Korea has fulfilled, in the main, its Five-Year Plan in two-and-a-half years, etc.

Our people are traditionally industrious and enjoy wholehearted assistance from the brother countries. We must resolve to study and catch up with them.

The good results of the emulation drive to make achievements in celebration of the Party's birthday show that our people are rich in creativeness and great in strength. Once one has a thorough understanding in doing something, however great it may be, one can overcome all difficulties and bring it to a success.

The Party Central Committee appeals to all members of the Party and the Labor Youth Union, of every position and occupation, to improve revolutionary virtues, wipe out individualism, make efforts in political, cultural, scientific, and technical studies, satisfactorily to carry out economic and financial work, to set an example in everything. They must unite with and learn from the non-Party and non-Union friends, to progress together with them.

At the time of the General Insurrection, our Party had less than 5,000 members, yet it led the people throughout the country to bring the August Revolution to success. Now, its ranks have increased nearly 100 times, to approximately half a million members. We have, in addition, over 600,000 members of the Labor Youth Union. Our people's power is steady, the People's Army powerful, and the National Front broad. Our workers, peasants, and intellectuals have been tested and tempered and have made constant progress. In a word, our big force is growing bigger. Under the clear-sighted leadership of the Party, we will certainly be successful in socialist construction and in the struggle for national reunification, contributing a worthy part to the defense of peace in Asia and in the world.

Our Party is as great as the immense sea, the high mountain. It has won so much love in thirty years of struggle and success. Our Party is virtue, civilization, unity, independence, a peaceful and comfortable life.

Its acts of kindness and services are really great. Its thirty-year history is a whole golden book of history.

Long live the great Viet-Nam Workers' Party!

Long live a peaceful, unified, independent, democratic, prosperous, and strong Viet-Nam!

Long live the socialist community headed by the great Soviet Union!

Long live Communism!

Long live world peace!

PART FIVE

At War Again
(1960–66)

SPEECH OPENING THE
THIRD NATIONAL CONGRESS OF
THE VIET-NAM WORKERS' PARTY
(September 5, 1960)

Today, the Third National Congress of our Party opens at a time when our entire people are joyfully celebrating the fifteenth anniversary of the founding of the Democratic Republic of Viet-Nam. This Congress of our Party is attended by over 500 delegates representing more than 500,000 Party members throughout the country and personifying the heroic militant tradition of our Party over these thirty years. On behalf of the Central Committee, I extend cordial greetings to you, to all the cherished members of our Party, to the representatives of the Viet-Nam Socialist Party and the Viet-Nam Democratic Party, and to the representatives of the member organizations of the Fatherland Front.

Our Congress is very happy to extend its warm welcome to the Comrades delegates of: the Communist Party of the Soviet Union; the Communist Party of China; the Albanian Party of Labor; the Bulgarian Communist Party; the Polish United Workers' Party; the Socialist Unity Party of Germany; the Hungarian Socialist Workers' Party; the Mongolian People's Revolutionary Party; the Rumanian Workers' Party; the Korean Workers' Party; the Communist Party of Czechoslovakia; the French Communist Party; the Communist Party of India; the Communist Party of Indonesia; the Communist

Party of Japan; the Communist Party of Canada; and other fraternal Communist Parties.

Prompted by lofty sentiments of international brotherhood, our comrades have come to take part in our Congress and to bring to us the friendship of the fraternal Parties. So,

Though frontiers and mountains stand between us,
Proletarians of the whole world come together as one family.

On behalf of the Congress, I heartily salute all the workers, peasants, intellectuals, armymen, cadres, youth, and children who have been enthusiastically engaged in emulation in recording new achievements in honor of the Party Congress and the Fifteenth National Day.

Over the past thirty years, large numbers of our comrades and compatriots have heroically made the supreme sacrifice for the cause of the Revolution. During the War of Resistance, how many fighters gave their lives for the Fatherland! Over the last six years, how many brave fighters in the South have in their turn given their lives for the Nation! Our Party and our people shall forever treasure the memory of their most splendid sons and daughters who have fallen in the fight for the cause of national liberation and the ideal of Communism.

More than nine years have elapsed since our Party's Second National Congress. Over the past nine years, our Party, implementing the line of the Second Congress, led our people's bitter, difficult, and heroic War of Resistance. The brilliant victory of Dien Bien Phu put an end to the aggressive war unleashed by the French colonialists assisted by the American imperialists. The Geneva Agreement was signed; peace was restored in Indochina on the basis of international recognition of the sovereignty, independence, unity, and territorial integrity of our country. North Viet-Nam was completely liberated. Six years have elapsed, but our country has not yet been reunified as stipulated by the Geneva Agreement. Our Government and people have always correctly implemented the Agreement signed. But the U.S.-Diem clique is deliberately partitioning our country and shamelessly sabotaging the Geneva Agreement, so that the South of our country is still going through hell under its ruthless rule.

That is why our people have been struggling constantly to achieve the peaceful reunification of the country, for the freedom of our compatriots in the South who are being dragged through blood and fire. The widespread, deep-going, and powerful struggle of our compatriots in the South is continuing. The South has proved worthy of its glorious title: "Brass Wall of the Fatherland."

Since the re-establishment of peace, the North, completely liberated, has shifted over to the stage of socialist revolution. This is a change of great significance in the Vietnamese revolution. Under the leadership of the Party, the land reform has been victoriously carried through, liberating the toiling peasants, translating the slogan "Land to the Tillers" into reality.

We have successfully restored our economy and are now victoriously fulfilling the Three-Year Plan for the development of the economy and culture. In the socialist transformation of agriculture, handicrafts, and private capitalist industry and commerce, we have won a victory of a decisive character. We have recorded many achievements on the agricultural and industrial production fronts and in cultural and educational work, and have made the first improvements in the people's living standards. The North is becoming more and more consolidated and transformed into a firm base for the struggle for national reunification. The big victories won over the past nine years have testified to the correctness of our Party's line and the firmness of our Party's leadership. They are victories of Marxism-Leninism in a country which has suffered imperialist oppression and exploitation. Our Party is worthy of the confidence of our people from North to South.

Our Party can be proud to be the heir to our people's glorious traditions, and the guide of our people on the road to a bright future.

All these victories are not the work of our Party alone. They are the common work of our entire people all over the country. The revolution is the work of the masses, not that of a few heroic individuals. The success of our Party lies in the fact that it has organized and developed the boundless revolutionary power of the people and led the people in battle under the invincible banner of Marxism-Leninism.

The victories of the Vietnamese revolution are also due to the wholehearted assistance of the fraternal socialist countries, especially the Soviet Union and China. We avail ourselves of this opportunity to express our warm feelings of gratitude toward the fraternal socialist countries headed by the great Soviet Union. We are also sincerely grateful to other fraternal Parties, first of all, to the French Communist Party, for their active support to our people's just struggle. We sincerely thank all colonial nations and peace-loving people throughout the world who have always given us their sympathy and support.

The history of the thirty-year-long struggle of our Party has taught us this: The best guarantee of victory for the revolution is to steep ourselves in Marxism-Leninism, to remain loyal to the interests of the working class and the people, and to preserve solidarity and unity within the Party, between all Communist Parties, and all countries of the big socialist family.

Our Party has in the past always fulfilled these tasks. In the future, too, our Party will undoubtedly continue to do so.

Our Party has won many big victories, but it is not faultless. We have not, however, concealed our mistakes. On the contrary, we have frankly practiced self-criticism and actively corrected our mistakes. Victories have not made us dizzy with success, or complacent. Today, armed with our own experiences and those of the fraternal Parties, we resolutely strive for further and ever greater progress.

The present task of the Vietnamese revolution is to lead the North forward to socialism and to struggle for national reunification by peaceful means, to complete the national people's democratic revolution throughout the country.

The decisions of this Congress will guide our whole Party and our whole people in the successful construction of socialism in the North, endowing the North with modern industry and agriculture, advanced culture and science, making our people's life more and more abundant and happy.

The Second Party Congress was the Congress of Resistance. This present Party Congress is the Congress of Socialist Construction in the North and of the struggle for Peaceful National Reunification.

Our people, who showed their heroism in the War of Resistance, are now showing heroism in their labor for national construction. We will undoubtedly succeed in building glorious socialism in the North.

A prosperous and strong North is the firm base of the struggle for national reunification. This Congress will shed new light on our people's path of revolutionary struggle leading to peaceful national reunification.

Our nation is one, our country is one. Our people will undoubtedly overcome all difficulties and "achieve national reunification and bring the North and the South together again."

The Vietnamese revolution is a part of the world forces of peace, democracy, and socialism. The Democratic Republic of Viet-Nam is a member of the big socialist family headed by the great Soviet Union.

It is our duty to defend the advance post of socialism in Southeast Asia, to endeavor to contribute to the strengthening of the forces of the socialist camp, and to safeguard peace in Southeast Asia and the world.

Today socialism has become a powerful world system, as firm as a brass wall. Our people are greatly encouraged by the momentous achievements of the Soviet Union in the building of Communism and the big victories of China and the other fraternal socialist countries in the building of socialism. Our people strongly support the foreign policy of peace and the disarmament program advanced by the Soviet Union and other countries in the socialist camp. Our people also rejoice profoundly at the victories won by the peoples of Asia, Africa, and Latin America in their great struggle against the imperialists, especially the American imperialists. It is crystal-clear that the forces of peace, democracy, national independence, and socialism throughout the world have become definitely stronger than the imperialist camp. The peoples of the world, uniting closely with one another and struggling actively, will undoubtedly be able to prevent a world war and establish a lasting peace. The resolute struggle of oppressed peoples will undoubtedly defeat the imperialists and colonialists. Socialism will ultimately triumph throughout the world.

In this great struggle, solidarity between the forces of the socialist countries and the complete unity of the Communist and Workers' Parties of all countries is of the utmost importance. We are confident that "the Communist and Workers' Parties will continue to strengthen the cohesion of the countries of the world socialist system and will preserve, like the apple of the eye, unity in the struggle for peace and the security of all peoples for the triumph of the great cause of Marxism-Leninism (Bucharest communiqué)."

In our time, the imperialists can no longer rule the roost in the world as before. But so long as imperialism exists there remains the danger of war. The Declaration of the meeting of Representatives of the Communist and Workers' Parties of the socialist countries held in Moscow in 1957 reminds us that the Communist and Workers' Parties "regard the struggle for peace as their foremost task. . . . All the nations must display the utmost vigilance in regard to the war danger created by imperialism." We must also bear in mind that "the greater and stronger the unity of the various patriotic and democratic forces, the greater the guarantee of victory in the common struggle."

The imperialists have in the past caused our people much suffering; the U.S.-Diem clique is now partitioning our country and trampling on the South of our country. So long as we have not driven the American imperialists out of the South, liberating it from the barbarous rule of the U.S.-Diem clique, our people can know no peace of mind. That is why the struggle for the defense of peace and for national reunification cannot be separated from the struggle against American imperialism.

In the common struggle to safeguard peace and national independence in Indochina, the Vietnamese people resolutely support the Laotian people's present heroic struggle against American imperialism. The Laotians' struggle has the aim of leading Laos along the road to national concord, independence, unity, peace, and neutrality. We sincerely hope that friendly relations between our country and neighbor countries, especially Cambodia and Laos, will be established and promoted in a satisfactory manner.

The cause of socialist revolution in the North and the struggle for national reunification, which are contributions to the safeguarding of peace in Southeast Asia and the world, set heavy but glorious tasks for our Party. To ensure the victory of the revolution, a question of decisive significance is the further heightening of the capacity for struggle of our whole Party and the promotion of the leading role of our Party in all fields of work.

Our Party has always endeavored to integrate Marxism-Leninism closely with the actual practice of the Vietnamese revolution. In general, our Party cadres and members are of good revolutionary substance. But we still have many shortcomings, such as subjectivism, dogmatism, empiricism, bureaucratic style of work, individualism. . . . These shortcomings are hampering the progress of our comrades. We must endeavor to study Marxism-Leninism, to strengthen ideological education in the Party, and to struggle to overcome these shortcomings. We must further heighten the class character and vanguard character of the Party, constantly strengthening the Party's ties with the masses, uniting with all patriotic and progressive people in order to win victory in the construction of socialism and the struggle for national reunification. We must strive to learn in a creative way from the experiences of the fraternal Parties. We must never fall into arrogance and conceit; we must be modest, as Lenin taught us.

This present Party Congress will elect the new Central Committee of our Party. We are confident that, with the new Central Committee, our Party will be more closely united and will further mobilize the people throughout the country to strive to fulfill the great task now facing us, which is to build socialism in the North and to struggle for national reunification by peaceful means.

Long live great Marxism-Leninism!

Long live the heroic working class and people of Viet-Nam!

Long live the Viet-Nam Workers' Party!

Long live the solidarity and unity of the fraternal Parties and of the big socialist family headed by the great Soviet Union!

Long live a peaceful, unified, independent, democratic, prosperous, and strong Viet-Nam!

Long live world peace!

A TALK WITH HO CHI MINH*

(*Prime Minister Pham Van Dong, wearing a khaki Mao Tse-tung suit, met me in the corridor of the presidential residence and invited me into a sitting room overlooking the formal gardens.*)

PHAM: Please make yourself at home. Take off your jacket. (*He takes off his own jacket.*) I hope you are enjoying your trip throughout North Viet-Nam, and that you find us cooperative.

FALL: Thank you, Mr. Prime Minister, your subordinates indeed have generally been cooperative.

PHAM: I remember, however, that you said in your book *Le Viet-Minh* that we are not a democratic country. Do you still feel the same way about this?

FALL: Well, Mr. Prime Minister, all my color films were impounded upon my arrival at Hanoi airport. I don't think you would call this in accordance with democratic procedures. . . .

PHAM (*laughing*): Oh, those are general rules which apply to everybody.†

---

* The following interview is based on a conversation that took place in the presidential palace in Hanoi in July, 1962. It is a verbatim translation from the original French, omitting only some of the usual banter. Present at the interview, in addition to President Ho Chi Minh and the editor, was Prime Minister Pham Van Dong, probably Ho's closest associate since 1955. This interview is reprinted, by permission, from The New Republic, *October 12, 1963. © 1963 by Harrison-Blaine of New Jersey, Inc.—*ED.

*† While theoretically true, the rule obviously applies to Westerners only. In addition, all black-and-white film has to be exposed prior to departure and the developed film submitted to the Foreign Ministry for censorship. Even so, the airport police again inspected my films prior to departure.—*ED.

FALL: Mr. Prime Minister, North Viet-Nam has had some serious economic difficulties. Do you believe that they have been mastered?

PHAM: As you know, the recent seventh plenary session of the [Vietnamese] Communist Party's Central Committee has decided to give priority to basic heavy industries, although attention will be paid to a proper balance with agriculture and consumer goods production.

We base ourselves upon the Marxist economic viewpoint: Heavy industrial development is essential to socialist construction, but we also understand the importance of the "full belly." In any case, we do not seek to bluff and will not put emphasis on "showpiece" industries but on sound and useful economic development.

Yes, we have made economic mistakes, due mainly to our backwardness and ignorance in the field of economic planning. Not all of those errors have yet been corrected and some of their effects are still felt, but we try to overcome them rapidly, thanks to help from friendly countries.

FALL: Mr. Prime Minister, President Ho Chi Minh made a declaration to the *Daily Express* [London] in March, 1962, referring to the conditions under which North Viet-Nam would negotiate a settlement with the South. Has anything happened in the meantime that would change those conditions?

PHAM: Our position has remained largely unchanged since President Ho Chi Minh's declaration. What has changed, however, is the extent of American intervention in South Viet-Nam, which has continued to increase and to take over increased responsibilities and control over the Diem regime.

The real enemy is American intervention. It is of little importance who the American agent in Viet-Nam might be.

FALL: Mr. Prime Minister, the International Control Commission [composed of Indian, Polish, and Canadian members] has recently accused the North Vietnamese Republic of aiding and abetting the South Vietnamese rebellion. What do you think of that accusation?

PHAM (*deprecating gesture*): We understand under what outside pressures the [Indian and Canadian] members of the ICC labor. After all, India does depend for development upon large-scale American aid.

FALL: But would it not at least be conceivable that some of the almost 100,000 South Vietnamese who went north [of the 17th parallel] in 1954, and whose relatives are now fighting against South Vietnamese forces, would attempt to slip across your border back into

South Viet-Nam in order to help their relatives—even without the permission of the North Vietnamese government? Wouldn't that be at least conceivable?

PHAM: Sir, in our country one does not cross borders without permission.

FALL: Would not a spreading of the guerrilla war entail a real risk of American reaction against North Vietnamese territory? You have been to North Korea last year, Mr. Prime Minister; you saw what American bombers can do. . . .

PHAM (*very seriously*): We fully realize that the American imperialists wish to provoke a situation in the course of which they could use the heroic struggle of the South Vietnamese people as a pretext for the destruction of our economic and cultural achievements.

We shall offer them no pretext that could give rise to an American military intervention against North Viet-Nam.

(*Ho Chi Minh suddenly enters, unannounced. He is also wearing a Mao Tse-tung suit, in suntan cotton. Spry and tanned looking, he has a springy step, firm handshake.*)

FALL: I thought you were in Moscow on vacation!

HO: You see, people say a lot of things that aren't true. (*He looks at my jacket, tape recorder, book, next to me on the sofa.*) My, you have brought a lot of things with you.

FALL: I am sorry, Mr. President. (*I push things together. Ho sits down next to me, a humorous gleam on his face, and slaps me on the thigh.*)

HO: So, you are the young man who is so much interested in all the small details about my life.*

FALL: Mr. President, you are, after all, a public figure, and it certainly would not be a violation of a military secret to know whether you had a family or were in Russia at a given date.

HO: Ah, but you know, I'm an old man, a very old man. An old man likes to have a little air of mystery about himself. I like to hold on to my little mysteries. I'm sure you will understand that.

FALL: But. . . .

HO: Wait until I'm dead.†

* *In* Le Viet-Minh, *I had included as complete a biographical sketch of Ho Chi Minh as possible. During my stay in Hanoi, I had also interviewed many of Ho's old friends, and he apparently had been informed of this.*—ED.

† *In spite of this, I received just before I left Hanoi a letter containing six manuscript pages of details about Ho's life, filling in most of the gaps—no doubt on Ho's own orders.*—ED.

PHAM: Dr. Fall brought you a book on the Indochina War that contains a drawing of you by his wife.

Ho (*with an old man's impatience*): Where? Where? Let me see it. Providing she's got my goatee right. Providing the goatee looks all right. (*He unwraps the book and looks.*) Mmm—yes, that is very good. That looks very much like me. (*He looks around, grabs a small flower bouquet from the table, and hands it to me.*) Tell her from me that the drawing is very good and give her the bouquet and kiss her on both cheeks for me.

PHAM: Dr. Fall is interested in the present situation in South Viet-Nam. . . .

FALL: Yes, Mr. President, how do you evaluate the situation in South Viet-Nam?

HO: Ngo Dinh Diem is in a very difficult position right now and it is not likely to improve in the future. He has no popular support.

FALL: But would you negotiate with South Viet-Nam?

PHAM: The situation is not yet ripe for a real negotiation. They [the South Vietnamese] don't really want to negotiate.

HO: That is absolutely true. They are showing no intention to negotiate.

FALL: But are you not afraid that the situation might degenerate into a protracted war?

HO (*earnestly, turning full face*): Sir, you have studied us for ten years, you have written about the Indochina War. It took us eight years of bitter fighting to defeat you French in Indochina. Now the Diem regime is well armed and helped by many Americans. The Americans are stronger than the French. It might perhaps take ten years, but our heroic compatriots in the South will defeat them in the end. We shall marshal world public opinion about this unjust war against the South Vietnamese people.

PHAM: Yes, the heroic South Vietnamese people will have to continue the struggle by their own means, but we watch its efforts with the greatest sympathy.

HO: I think the Americans greatly underestimate the determination of the Vietnamese people. The Vietnamese people have always shown great determination when faced with an invader.

FALL: But are you still willing to come to a negotiated settlement if the occasion presented itself?

HO: Yes, but only with people who are willing to sit down with us at one and the same table and "talk" [*causer*].

FALL: You mean you would negotiate with any South Vietnamese government?

Ho: Yes, with any.

FALL: But what kind of relations would you envisage?

Ho: Of whatever type they [South Vietnamese] wish. After all, the East and West Germans have flourishing trade relations in spite of the Berlin Wall, haven't they? (*After some further amenities, Ho left.*)

FALL: Mr. Prime Minister, what do you think of Ngo Dinh Diem's personal position as of right now?

PHAM: It is quite difficult. He is unpopular, and the more unpopular he is, the more American aid he will need to remain in power. And the more American aid he gets, the more of an American puppet he'll look and the less likely he is to regain popularity.

FALL: That sounds pretty much like a vicious circle, doesn't it?

PHAM (*a humorous gleam in his eye*): No, sir. It is a descending spiral.

FALL: But you must understand, Mr. Prime Minister, that South Viet-Nam is in a different situation from the non-Communist parts of Germany and Korea. In the latter two cases, the non-Communist part is by far the more populated, whereas in the case of Viet-Nam, the non-Communist part has 13.8 million people against your 17 million. You can clearly see that they have good reason to fear North Viet-Nam, which also has the larger army, and one with a fearsome reputation, as we French well know.

PHAM: Certainly, we realize that we are in the stronger position. Thus, we are also willing to give all the guarantees necessary for the South to be able to come out fairly [*pour que le Sud trouve son compte*] in such a negotiation.

You will recall President Ho's declaration with regard to maintaining the South's separate government and economic system. The Fatherland Front embodies those points in its program, and the South Vietnamese Liberation Front likewise.

We do not envisage an immediate reunification and are willing to accept the verdict of the South Vietnamese people with regard to the institutions and policies of its part of the country.

FALL: What, then, would be the minimal conditions under which the Democratic Republic of Viet-Nam would accept a settlement of the conflict which at present exists in South Viet-Nam?

(*Pham makes a statement, as below.*)

FALL: Would you object to my making a tape recording of that answer? It is a reply that I would like to have verbatim, if possible.

(*Pham thinks it over, makes notes, agrees.*)

PHAM: This is a very timely question: The D.R.V.N. Government has made some sufficiently explicit declarations on the subject [but] let me underline what follows: The underlying origin and immediate cause of the extremely dangerous situation in the South of our country is the armed intervention of the United States and the fascist dictatorship of Ngo Dinh Diem, the creation and instrument of that intervention.

It is obvious, then, that in order to normalize the situation in our whole country, those factors of dissension must disappear. We support with determination the patriotic struggle of our Southern compatriots and the objectives of their struggle—I mean, the program of the Southern Liberation Front.

We are certain that the massive help of all classes of South [Viet-Nam's] society and the active support of the peoples of the world shall determine the happy outcome of the dangerous situation that exists in the South of our country.

The people of Viet-Nam and the D.R.V.N. Government remain faithful to the Geneva Agreements [of July, 1954] which establish our basic national rights. We shall continue to cooperate with the International Control Commission on the basis of those agreements, and hope that this cooperation shall be fruitful—providing that all members of the Commission respect the agreements.

FALL: Thank you, Mr. Prime Minister, for that statement.

PHAM: I would like to say something about a remark you made in your book on our Republic about our alleged "isolationism" from neutral and pro-Western countries and from international organizations. No, no, and no, we are not isolationists! On the contrary, we seek "open windows" toward any country or organization that will deal with us on a matter-of-fact basis. We are willing to trade with them and make purchases from them.

FALL: What would be the position of the foreign community in South Viet-Nam, if the war worsens? There are still 15,000 French citizens living there.

PHAM: As you know, the Southern Liberation Front has repeatedly shown that it does not wish to hurt the legitimate interests of the Europeans who live in South Viet-Nam. We make a distinction between France's position and that of the American imperialists.

FALL: What is the attitude of the D.R.V.N. toward Laos and Cambodia?

PHAM: We shall respect the Laos agreements,* and shall at all costs maintain good relations with Cambodia.

* *This was stated soon after the signature of the 1962 Geneva agreements on Laos. It became obvious afterward that North Vietnamese troops were still operating in Laos to some extent, or were traveling through South Viet-Nam.*—ED.

U.S. IMPERIALISTS, GET
OUT OF SOUTH VIET-NAM!*

Our National Assembly is holding the present session in a very urgent situation but full of enthusiasm and confidence. The movement to oppose the United States and save the country is seething everywhere. Many great successes have been recorded in both North and South Viet-Nam.

Over the past ten years, the U.S. imperialists and their henchmen have carried out an extremely ruthless war and have caused much grief to our compatriots in South Viet-Nam. Over the past few months, they have frenziedly expanded the war to North Viet-Nam. In defiance of the 1954 Geneva Agreements and international law, they have sent hundreds of aircraft and dozens of warships to bomb and strafe North Viet-Nam repeatedly. Laying bare themselves their piratical face, the U.S. aggressors are blatantly encroaching upon our country. They hope that by resorting to the force of weapons they can compel our 30 million compatriots to become their slaves. But they are grossly mistaken. They will certainly meet with ignominious defeat.

Our Vietnamese people are a heroic people. Over the past ten years or more, our 14 million compatriots in the South have overcome all hardships, made every sacrifice and struggled very valiantly. Starting with their bare hands, they have seized guns from the enemy

* An address to the National Assembly, printed in the *Vietnam Courier* (Hanoi), April 15, 1965.

to fight against the enemy, have recorded victory after victory, and are launching a continual attack inflicting upon the U.S. aggressors and the traitors ever greater defeats and causing them to be bogged down more and more deeply. The greater their defeats, the more frantically they resort to the most cruel means, such as using napalm bombs and toxic gas to massacre our compatriots in the South. It is because they are bogged down in South Viet-Nam that they have furiously attacked North Viet-Nam.

As the thief crying "stop, thief!" is a customary trick of theirs, the U.S. imperialists, who are the aggressors, have impudently slandered North Viet-Nam as committing "aggression" in South Viet-Nam. The U.S. imperialists are precisely the saboteurs of the Geneva Agreements, yet they have brazenly declared that because they wished to "restore peace" and "defend the Geneva Agreements" they brought U.S. troops to our country to carry out massacres and destruction. The U.S. imperialists are precisely those who are devastating our country and killing our people, yet they hypocritically declared that they would give $1 billion to the people in Viet-Nam and the other Southeast Asian countries to "develop their countries and improve their life."

U.S. President Johnson has also loudly threatened to resort to violence to subdue our people. This is a mere foolish illusion. Our people will definitely never be subjugated.

The Taylor plan has been frustrated. The McNamara plan has also gone bankrupt. The "escalation" plan which the U.S. imperialists are now endeavoring to carry out in North Viet-Nam will certainly fail, too. The U.S. imperialists may send in dozens of thousands more U.S. officers and men and make all-out efforts to drag more troops of their satellite countries into this criminal war, but our army and people are resolved to fight and defeat them.

The statement of the South Viet-Nam National Front for Liberation has upheld that heroic will. The appeal of the Viet-Nam Fatherland Front has clearly underlined that iron-like determination.

We love peace but we are not afraid of war. We are resolved to drive away the U.S. aggressors and to defend the freedom, independence, and territorial integrity of our Fatherland.

The people throughout our country are firmly confident that with their militant solidarity, valiant spirit, and creative wisdom, and with the sympathy and support of the world's peoples, they will certainly lead this great Resistance War to complete victory.

Our people are very grateful to and highly value the fraternal solidarity and devoted assistance of the socialist countries, especially the Soviet Union and China, of the people in all continents who are actively supporting us in our struggle against the U.S. imperialist aggressors, the most cruel enemy of mankind.

With regard to the Laotian and Cambodian peoples who are valiantly struggling against U.S. imperialism and its henchmen, our people constantly strengthen solidarity with them and unreservedly support them.

We warmly welcome the youth of various countries who have expressed willingness to come to Viet-Nam and join us in fighting the U.S. aggressors.

The American people have been duped by the propaganda of their government, which has extorted from them billions of dollars to throw into the crater of war. Thousands of American youths—their sons and brothers—have met a tragic death or have been pitifully wounded on the Vietnamese battlefields thousands of miles from the United States. At present, many mass organizations and individuals in the United States are demanding that their government at once stop this unjust war and withdraw U.S. troops from South Viet-Nam. Our people are resolved to drive away the U.S. imperialists, our sworn enemy. But we always express our friendship with the progressive American people.

The Government of the Democratic Republic of Viet-Nam once again solemnly declares its unswerving stand: to resolutely defend Viet-Nam's independence, sovereignty, unity, and territorial integrity. Viet-Nam is one, the Vietnamese people are one, no one is allowed to infringe upon this sacred right of our people. The U.S. imperialists must respect the Geneva Agreements and withdraw from South Viet-Nam. That is the only way to solve the problem of war in Viet-Nam, to carry out the 1954 Geneva Agreements, to defend the peace in the Indochinese and Southeast Asian countries. There is no other solution. That is the answer of our people and Government to the U.S. imperialists.

Our people are living in an extremely glorious period of history. Our country has the great honor of being an outpost of the socialist camp and of the world's peoples who are struggling against imperialism, colonialism, and neocolonialism.

Our people have fought and made sacrifices not only for the sake of their own freedom and independence, but also for the common freedom and independence of the other peoples and for peace in the world.

On the battlefront against the U.S. aggressors, our people's task is very heavy but also very glorious.

At present, to oppose the United States and save the country is the most sacred task of every Vietnamese patriot. Under the leadership of the South Viet-Nam National Front for Liberation, the genuine and only representative of the South Vietnamese people, the heroic people and fighters in South Viet-Nam are marching forward to record ever greater successes so as to liberate the South and defend the North.

The armed forces and people of the North are eagerly engaged in emulation to build socialism while valiantly struggling to defend the North and wholeheartedly support the South.

I propose that the National Assembly warmly support the statement of the South Viet-Nam National Front for Liberation and the appeal of the Viet-Nam Fatherland Front. Warm welcome to our heroic compatriots and fighters in South Viet-Nam! Warm congratulations to our armed forces and people in North Viet-Nam, now enthusiastically emulating with one another in production and fighting against the enemy to record new exploits!

I call on our compatriots and fighters to constantly heighten their revolutionary heroism, vigilance, and fighting spirit—to promote the "everyone redoubles his efforts" emulation movement, resolutely overcome all difficulties, endeavor to build and defend socialist North Viet-Nam and wholeheartedly support the patriotic struggle of our compatriots in the South!

Let all of us single-mindedly unite as one man and be determined to defeat the U.S. aggressors!

For the future of our Fatherland, for the happiness of our people, let all compatriots and fighters throughout the country valiantly march forward!

OUR PEOPLE HAVE THE DUTY
OF DEFENDING THE FATHERLAND*

Question: What are the causes of the struggle in South Viet-Nam?

Answer: The main cause of the South Vietnamese people's patriotic struggle is the barbarous aggression of the United States imperialists, by which they are trying to turn the southern part of our country into a new-type colony, a military base for the expansion of their war of aggression in realizing their aim of world domination.

Question: What are the basic aims of the National Liberation Front in South Viet-Nam? What is the relation between the policy of the Democratic Republic of Viet-Nam and that of the South Viet-Nam Liberation Front?

Answer: The program of the South Viet-Nam National Front for Liberation clearly specifies its principal aims. These are: to struggle against aggressive U.S. imperialism, to liberate the South, to achieve independence, democracy, peace, and neutrality, and advance step by step toward the reunification of the country. The South Viet-Nam National Front for Liberation is an organization of the patriotic movement, set up by the mass of the people. The Front is the leader, the organizer of the South Vietnamese people's struggle against U.S. imperialism to recover national independence. The Front is the only genuine representative of the South Vietnamese people. It is the sacred duty of the whole people of Viet-Nam to support the South

* Excerpts from an interview in the *Daily Worker,* as reprinted in the *Vietnam Courier,* July 15, 1965.

363

Vietnamese people's liberation struggle, waged under the leadership of the National Front for Liberation. We respect the policies of the Front and hold that the two zones must take their respective characteristics into account, understand each other, restore normal relations between them and gradually achieve national reunification. Viet-Nam is one. The Vietnamese are one people. Our entire people have the duty of opposing foreign aggression and defending the Fatherland.

Question: Do you still think that the Geneva Agreement provides the basis for the solution of the war in Viet-Nam?

Answer: Yes. The Geneva Agreements are still the basis for the peaceful solution of the war.

Question: What in your view are the most important provisions of the Geneva Agreement?

Answer: I think that the most important provisions are: the sovereignty, independence, unity, and territorial integrity of Viet-Nam must be respected; no military base under the control of a foreign state may be established in Viet-Nam; Viet-Nam shall not join any military alliance; democratic freedoms must be guaranteed to create favorable conditions for the restoration of normal relations between the North and South of Viet-Nam with a view to the reunification of the country.

Question: What do you consider to be necessary at the present time for the implementation of the Geneva Agreements?

Answer: The 1954 Geneva Agreements on Viet-Nam are an important international agreement. All countries participating in the Geneva Conference, including the United States, must respect these agreements and carry them out correctly. A country which is Co-chairman of the Geneva Conference, like Great Britain, should all the more respect its obligations and carry them out correctly.

Question: What have you to say about the latest proposal of [Prime Minister] Harold Wilson for a Commonwealth mission?

Answer: Mr. Wilson has not correctly carried out his obligations as Co-chairman of the 1954 Geneva Conference on Viet-Nam. He has tried to support U.S. imperialist aggression in Viet-Nam. He cannot engage in peace negotiations since he has himself supported the U.S. policy of aggression and expansion of the war.

LET THE U.S. IMPERIALISTS
WITHDRAW THEIR TROOPS FROM
SOUTH VIET-NAM AND PEACE WILL
BE IMMEDIATELY RESTORED*

Question: Thoughtful people all over the world are greatly concerned about the war that is now taking place in your country. I feel very grateful to you, President Ho Chi Minh, for allowing me to come and ask you some questions—and for allowing these cameras to record our conversation so that it may be shared with many others in all parts of the world.

President Johnson has said over and over again that he is ready to begin unconditional discussions with you at any place and at any time to bring this war in Viet-Nam to an end. It is said you do not accept this offer. May I know the reason?

Answer: In essence, President Johnson's so-called offer of "unconditional discussions" means that the Vietnamese people must accept U.S. conditions. These are: U.S. imperialism will cling to South Viet-Nam, carry on its policy of aggression, and refuse to recognize the South Viet-Nam National Front for Liberation as the sole genuine representative of the people of South Viet-Nam. Those are conditions imposed by the aggressors, which the Vietnamese people will never accept, nor world public opinion tolerate.

* An interview granted to the British journalist Felix Greene, as printed in the *Vietnam Courier*, December 16, 1965.

The Vietnamese people eagerly want peace to build up their country. But genuine independence must be achieved if there is to be real peace. The question is very clear: U.S. imperialism is the aggressor. It must stop its air attacks on the North; put an end to its aggression in the South; withdraw its troops from South Viet-Nam; and let the Vietnamese people settle themselves their own affairs, as provided for in the Geneva Agreements. Peace will then be immediately restored. In short, the U.S. Government must declare and prove by actual deeds its acceptance of the four-point stand of the Government of the Democratic Republic of Viet-Nam, which fully conforms to the main political and military provisions of the 1954 Geneva Agreements on Viet-Nam. This stand is the only basis for a correct settlement of the Viet-Nam question.

The truth is that President Johnson wants neither peace nor peace negotiations. As a matter of fact, at the very moment when he talks a lot about peace discussions, the U.S. imperialists are further expanding the war of aggression in South Viet-Nam, massively sending there tens of thousands of U.S. troops and extending "escalation" in North Viet-Nam. The peoples of the world have clearly seen this. That is precisely the reason why the progressive American people are actively opposing the U.S. war of aggression in Viet-Nam.

Question: The Government of the United States says that the reason why North Viet-Nam is being bombed is to discourage you from helping the revolutionary forces in the South, and that the bombing would stop immediately if you would leave your neighbor alone. What do you have to say about this?

Answer: The U.S. Government has launched savage air attacks on the territory of the Democratic Republic of Viet-Nam, an independent and sovereign state. In so doing, it has grossly trampled underfoot international law, most seriously violated the 1954 Geneva Agreements on Viet-Nam, and flouted humanity and justice.

U.S. imperialism is the aggressor. The U.S. Government must stop its criminal actions against the Democratic Republic of Viet-Nam. It must put an end to the war of aggression in South Viet-Nam.

The contention that the southern part of our fatherland is "a neighbor country" separate from the North is a misleading one. It is just like saying that the southern states of the United States constitute a country separate from the northern states.

Question: The United States says that it has in its possession overwhelming evidence of your support for the National Liberation Front in South Viet-Nam—what we refer to as the "Viet-Cong." They specifically refer to your 325th Division and other units of your regular army that are fighting in South Viet-Nam. What help are you giving to the Viet-Cong? What troops? What weapons? How many volunteers from North Viet-Nam have gone to fight in the South?

Answer: To fabricate false evidence in order to slander North Viet-Nam is a deceitful trick of the U.S. Government to cover up its aggression in South Viet-Nam. The truth is that the United States and its satellites have brought in foreign troops to wage aggression on South Viet-Nam, in contravention of the 1954 Geneva Agreements. The present patriotic struggle against U.S. aggression in South Viet-Nam is being waged by the people and liberation forces of South Viet-Nam under the leadership of the National Front for Liberation.

The U.S. imperialists have sent troops for aggression in South Viet-Nam, and launched continual air attacks on North Viet-Nam, thus committing barbarous crimes against the Vietnamese people in both zones.

Viet-Nam is one, the Vietnamese people are one. As sons and daughters of the same fatherland our people in the North are bound to extend wholehearted support to the patriotic struggle waged by the people of the South against U.S. aggression; likewise, our people in the South are duty-bound to fight with all their forces to contribute to the defense of the northern part of their fatherland.

Question: The United States began to bomb your country on August 5, 1964. According to the French Press Agency, from February 7, 1965, to the first half of November, 1965, there have been 17,400 raids by U.S. aircraft against targets in North Viet-Nam. We have been told that your communications and your productive capacity have been seriously damaged. However strenuously your people are resisting, how long can your country sustain this intensity of bombing without being forced to seek some way of ending the conflict?

Answer: As the saying goes, "seeing is believing." You have visited a number of areas in the North which have been savagely attacked by U.S. aircraft, you have seen the facts for yourself. So you may draw yourself the necessary conclusions.

In a war, there must be, of course, losses and sacrifices. Our people are determined to persevere in the fight, and to undergo sacrifices

for ten or twenty years or a longer time, till final victory, because
there is nothing more valuable than independence and freedom. We
are determined not to flinch before difficulties and temporary losses.
We are determined not to submit to U.S. aggression. We are determined to defend the freedom and independence of our fatherland.
At the same time, we are determined to help prevent the U.S. imperialists from inflicting the calamity of aggression on other nations.

Question: As you well know, President Ho, the people of the
United States look upon Communism as an evil force which should
be resisted wherever possible. One reason why the United States is
involved in Viet-Nam is because it is thought that if they withdraw
their forces from South Viet-Nam the country would inevitably be
unified under a Communist government.

But more than that, they feel that the whole of Viet-Nam would
fall under the influence of China and would then not be able to develop as she herself would wish but only in a way that would further
China's expansionist aims. So my question is this: Are you not already receiving great quantities of military aid from China? Would
you perhaps not be ready to come to the conference table if it were
not for pressure from China? And could you look easily upon the
possibility of the whole of your country being dominated by an
immensely more powerful country?

Answer: The capitalists hate Communism, which is part of their
class nature. As for the working people, they like Communism, which
is to their class interest. No doubt, you know very well that to misrepresent Communism to fool the people is a customary method of
the U.S. imperialists' policy of aggression.

As for the relations between the Vietnamese people and the
Chinese people, they are fraternal relations as close as the relations
between the lips and the teeth. China's sympathy, support, and assistance to Viet-Nam are most valuable and effective.

China, like the Soviet Union and the other socialist countries, fully
agrees with the line of struggle of the Government of the Democratic
Republic of Viet-Nam and the South Viet-Nam National Front for
Liberation, they wholeheartedly support the Vietnamese people's
fight against the U.S. imperialist aggressors. All U.S. attempts to
divide Viet-Nam and China, and to divide the socialist countries, are
doomed to ignominious failure.

The above question shows that there are still many people in the
West who do not understand that the close relations among the

socialist countries are based on the principles of Marxism-Leninism and proletarian internationalism.

Question: President Ho, our time is almost up. You have heard of the protest movement in the United States and, judging by your newspapers here, I think the scope and influence of this movement is being greatly exaggerated here. The great majority of the people of the United States support President Johnson. I am not an American but have lived there for many years. I believe Americans are essentially a well-intentioned and humane people. Have you any special message you might like to send to the people of the United States?

Answer: As you have just said, the American people are essentially well-intentioned. That is why the great majority of the American people cannot support President Johnson's policy of aggression.

I would like to tell the American people that the aggressive war now being waged by the U.S. Government in Viet-Nam not only grossly flouts the national fundamental right of the Vietnamese people, but also runs counter to the aspirations and interests of the American people. This aggressive war has also besmeared the good name of the United States, the country of Washington and Lincoln. I wish to tell the American people about the determination of the entire Vietnamese people to fight the U.S. aggressors till complete victory. But as for the American people, we want to strengthen our relations of friendship with them.

The Vietnamese people are strong because of their just cause, their unity and gallantry, and because they enjoy the support of all peace-loving peoples in the world, including the American people. It is because of their love of justice and humanity that many progressive Americans from all walks of life, hundreds of thousands of youths, students, professors, scientists, lawyers, writers, artists, clergymen, and working people have courageously raised their voices and staged huge demonstrations against the Johnson Administration's policy of aggression in Viet-Nam. For their part, the American youth resolutely refuse to be sent to Viet-Nam as cannon fodder for the U.S. imperialists.

Our people highly value this struggle of the American people. We are deeply moved by the heroic sacrifices of Helga Herz and other peace fighters like Norman Morrison, Roger Laporte, and Celene Jankowski. I wish to convey to the families of these martyrs my feelings of affection and admiration and those of my compatriots.

I take this opportunity to extend our sincere thanks to the Ameri-

can people who are resolutely fighting for the cessation of the U.S.
'Government's war of aggression in Viet-Nam.

U.S. imperialism is the common enemy of our two peoples. With
our united struggle, it will certainly be defeated. Our peoples will be
victorious.

REPLIES TO AN INTERVIEW
WITH JAPANESE NDN TV*

Question: Mr. President, would you please tell us about the characteristic feature of the war in Viet-Nam in the recent period and its prospects?

Answer: This characteristic feature is: The more the U.S. imperialists bring troops into South Viet-Nam and intensify the air raids against towns and villages of the Democratic Republic of Viet-Nam, the heavier are their defeats.

In South Viet-Nam: During the first two months of 1966 alone, the South Viet-Nam army and people wiped out 32,000 enemy troops (including 16,000 Americans), neatly annihilated seven enemy battalions and thirty enemy companies (including four U.S. battalions), shot down or destroyed over 500 planes, and destroyed about 300 military vehicles.

In North Viet-Nam: The U.S. air attacks have also been defeated. Up to March 8, 1966, the North Viet-Nam army and people have downed over 900 U.S. planes.

On the international front, the U.S. so-called peace offensive has also failed. It has not been able to deceive anybody; instead, it has only increased U.S. isolation.

Now, President Johnson is feverishly preparing to dispatch tens of thousands of additional U.S. troops to South Viet-Nam. The army of

* As printed in the *Vietnam Courier,* April 21, 1966.

371

aggression from the United States and its satellites is carrying out the savage and criminal "kill all, burn all, destroy all" policy.

But as the enemy grows more ferocious, the Vietnamese people become more closely united and firmly determined to defeat him. In the end, the U.S. imperialists will inevitably be defeated. Although the Vietnamese people's Resistance War against U.S. aggression for national salvation is to be a protracted and arduous one, its victory is left in no doubt.

Question: Mr. President, could we know your views on the recent Honolulu Conference between the U.S. authorities and the South Viet-Nam Administration?

Answer: That conference discussed the question of stepping up *real* war and *sham* peace in Viet-Nam. It was a most serious challenge to the Vietnamese people, to the American people, and to peace-loving people in the world. It laid bare the deceitfulness of President Johnson's so-called peace offensive.

The Thieu-Ky puppet clique were summoned to Honolulu to receive directly from their U.S. masters instructions to prepare conditions for an intensification and expansion of the aggressive war in Viet-Nam. This exposed further their nature as traitors to their country and faithful lackeys of the U.S. aggressors, to the peoples of all countries.

Question: How do you assess, Mr. President, the threats uttered by a number of people in the U.S. ruling circles to send U.S. troops for expanding the war in central and southern Laos and the repeated provocations staged by Thailand and South Vietnamese troops against the Kingdom of Cambodia?

Answer: The acts of aggression by the U.S. imperialists and their henchmen against Laos and Cambodia are part of the U.S. scheme to extend the war of aggression to the whole of Indochina.

The United States has been carrying out this scheme step by step: In Laos, it has been savagely intensifying its air attacks on the Liberated Zone. It has been using puppet troops to launch repeated attacks against the Lao people's Liberation Forces. It has been stealthily bringing Thailand troops in increasing numbers into Laos. It is now contemplating to dispatch U.S. troops to central and southern Laos for direct aggression.

With regard to the Kingdom of Cambodia, the U.S. aggressors have not only incited their South Vietnamese and Thailand henchmen to stage repeated provocations on the border, but have also arrogantly stated that U.S. troops may violate the Cambodian territory at any time. These are most brazen encroachments on the independence, sovereignty, and neutrality of the Lao and Khmer peoples, and a serious threat to peace in Indochina and Southeast Asia.

Since the U.S. imperialists want to turn the countries of Indochina into a single battlefield, the Indochinese peoples will unite still more closely and struggle resolutely to defeat them.

Question: Recently, the Japanese Government has engaged in certain activities with a view to carrying out its so-called peace work. What is your opinion on this subject?

Answer: President Johnson's "search for peace" is a hoax. The activities of the Japanese Government to carry out its so-called peace work are aimed at giving publicity to this U.S. swindle. They are also designed to lull into inactivity the Japanese people's resolute struggle against the U.S. war of aggression in Viet-Nam. Another purpose is to cover up the fact that the Japanese Government is helping the U.S. imperialists expand the war in Viet-Nam and allowing them to use Japanese territory as an important base for this war.

Should the Japanese Government really want to contribute to the restoration of peace in Viet-Nam, it would not have colluded with the U.S. aggressors. Unfortunately, it has worked hand in glove with the U.S. imperialists.

Question: As far as we know, your January 24, 1966, letter to the Heads of State of a number of countries has had widespread impact throughout the world. Will you kindly tell us about the significance of that letter?

Answer: The U.S. imperialists are waging aggression against Viet-Nam and jeopardizing ever more seriously the peace and security of the peoples of Indochina and Asia. This is an extremely gross violation of the 1954 Geneva Agreements on Viet-Nam and all norms of international law. Our people have to fight in self-defense, for the independence of their Fatherland, and for world peace.

In the letter I sent to the Heads of State of a number of countries on January 24, 1966, I pointed out these facts and voiced the Vietnamese people's determination to fight against the U.S. imperialist aggressors and fulfill their national and international obligations. Though protracted and arduous, this just struggle of ours is sure to end in victory. I also expounded the fair and reasonable stand of our

Government and people regarding a settlement of the Viet-Nam problem.

This stand is a just stand of peace; therefore, it is gaining increasing approval and support from many Heads of State, governments, and the peoples of the world. I take this opportunity to convey our sincere thanks to all our friends throughout the five continents for their valuable support.

Lastly I wish to express our heartfelt thanks to the Japanese people for their warm support of our people's struggle against U.S. aggression, for national salvation.

OUR ENTIRE PEOPLE, UNITED AS ONE MAN, ARE RESOLVED TO DEFEAT THE U.S. AGGRESSORS*

This session of our National Assembly meets at a time when our entire people's resistance against U.S. aggression, for national salvation, is becoming fiercer and fiercer with every passing day and we are winning many glorious victories.

Suffering heavy defeats in the southern part of our country, the U.S. aggressors have recklessly thrown into that battlefield 250,000 expeditionary troops of the U.S. and its satellites to frantically step up, together with the puppet army, their war of aggression. They have been launching large-scale terrorist operations. Wherever they go, they carry out the "burn all, kill all, and destroy all" policy. They have been using napalm bombs, poison gas, and toxic chemicals to massacre our compatriots and ravage our villages. They are mistaken in thinking that the barbarous power of weapons can bring our compatriots in South Viet-Nam to their knees. But the heroic people of South Viet-Nam do not flinch at all and will never flinch! Like pouring more oil on the flames, the extremely savage crimes perpetrated by the U.S. aggressors and their henchmen only exasperate further the hatred of our people throughout the country. With marvelous valor and with the resolve to annihilate the enemy and save the country, the South

* A speech to the National Assembly, printed in the *Vietnam Courier*, April, 28, 1966.

Viet-Nam armed forces and people have been marching onward heroically, launching repeated attacks on the enemy on all battlefields, putting out of action tens of thousands of U.S. troops, and wiping out and disintegrating hundreds of thousands of puppet troops. Our compatriots in South Vietnamese cities are also standing up to struggle with a very powerful mettle. The glorious exploits, the big victories of the South Vietnamese armed forces and people are inspiring our people throughout the country and rejoicing our friends all over the five continents.

I propose that our National Assembly warmly hail the heroic fighters and people of South Viet-Nam.

It is because of their increasing predicament and passivity, and to get out of such an impasse, that the U.S. imperialists have recklessly extended their aerial war of destruction to North Viet-Nam. For over a year now, they have been daily using hundreds of aircraft to continually bomb and strafe the northern part of our country. They are also mistaken in thinking that their bombs and bullets can shake the determination of our people. But our armymen and compatriots in the North have been fighting very heroically. So far, 973 U.S. aircraft have been shot down and a number of U.S. aggressors piloting those aircraft have been captured.

For the beloved Fatherland, for our brothers in South Viet-Nam, and for socialism, our army and people in the North have been showing a very high fighting spirit, and a very powerful fighting strength. Making all-out efforts in production while standing ready to fight, our compatriots and armymen all prove very heroic. The revolutionary mettle is growing and the patriotic emulation movement is becoming more and more stirring with every passing day. From old people to children, particularly the youth, men and women, everybody is enthusiastically engaging in emulation to make his contribution to the resistance against U.S. aggression, for national salvation.

I propose that our National Assembly warmly hail our armed forces and people in the North for their great achievements in both fighting and production.

We have won glorious victories, but these are but initial victories. The U.S. aggressors and the Vietnamese traitors have not yet been completely defeated, they are still hatching many perfidious schemes. The more savage crimes they perpetrate, the more loudly they prattle about "peace" and "negotiations."

Although our fight will be long and hard, our people are resolved to fight till final victory. Our people cherish peace, but genuine peace can only be achieved when there is real independence and freedom. Our people are a heroic people; we are resolved to fight till complete victory to achieve real peace, independence, and freedom.

Our armed forces and people in North Viet-Nam who have already made great efforts should make still greater efforts, march forward resolutely, emulate one another in production, in the fighting against the enemy, step up the anti-U.S. struggle for national salvation, and push forward the anti-air-raid work. We should militarize our life and our work. We should strive to defend and build North Viet-Nam into a stronghold and wholeheartedly assist the liberation of South Viet-Nam, fulfill our duty as the big rear that North Viet-Nam is, toward that big front line, South Viet-Nam.

Under the clear-sighted leadership of the South Viet-Nam National Front for Liberation, our people in South Viet-Nam from the rural areas to the towns and cities, from the mountain areas to the plains, are increasing their solidarity, fighting resolutely, and advancing valiantly to liberate South Viet-Nam, thus contributing to the defense of North Viet-Nam and to eventual peaceful national reunification.

We have the responsibility and great honor to stand in the front line of the world people's struggle against U.S. imperialist aggression. For the independence and reunification of our country, for the security of the socialist camp, for the revolutionary cause and defense of peace of the world peoples, our entire people, united as one man, are resolved to fulfill their heavy but extremely glorious duty—to defeat the U.S. aggressors.

The people of the fraternal socialist countries and the progressive people in the world are daily following our great Resistance War with love and admiration and are giving us increasing support and assistance to help us fight and win. In response to this lofty internationalism, our people should enhance their revolutionary spirit and enthusiastically march forward to win complete victory.

On this occasion, on behalf of our people, the National Assembly, the Government, and the Viet-Nam Workers' Party, I again convey our profound gratitude to the fraternal socialist countries, our thanks to the progressive people in the world for having warmly supported and assisted our struggle against U.S. aggression for national salvation. I express our deep appreciation for the progressive American people's valiant struggle against the criminal war of the U.S. Government in Viet-Nam.

The only correct solution to end this war has been expounded in my message to the Heads of State and Governments of many countries. It has also been pointed out in the five-point statement of the South Viet-Nam National Front for Liberation—the sole genuine representative of the South Vietnamese people.

Again we say to President Johnson: "If the U.S. really wants peace, it must withdraw all U.S. and satellite troops from South Viet-Nam and stop the aggressive war there; and stop at once and unconditionally the war of destruction against North Viet-Nam. The problem of reunification of Viet-Nam must be settled by the Vietnamese people themselves without foreign interference, as stipulated by the Geneva Agreements."

Justice is on the side of our people.

The Vietnamese people will certainly be victorious. The U.S. imperialists will surely be defeated.

Let our people and armed forces throughout the country march forward heroically!

Let us fight resolutely to defeat the U.S. aggressors!

FIGHT UNTIL COMPLETE VICTORY*

Compatriots and fighters throughout the country!

The barbarous U.S. imperialists have unleashed a war of aggression in an attempt to conquer our country, but they are sustaining big defeats.

They have rushed an expeditionary corps of about 300,000 men into the southern part of our country. They have used a puppet administration and a mercenary army fostered by them as instruments of their aggressive policy. They have resorted to extremely savage means of warfare—toxic chemicals, napalm bombs, and so forth. With such crimes they hope to subdue our southern compatriots.

But under the firm and wise leadership of the NFLSV, the South Viet-Nam army and people, closely united and fighting heroically, have scored very glorious victories and are determined to struggle until complete victory with a view to liberating the South, defending the North, and subsequently achieving national reunification.

The U.S. aggressors have brazenly launched air attacks on North Viet-Nam in an attempt to get out of the quagmire in the South and to impose negotiations on us on their terms.

But North Viet-Nam will not falter. Our army and people have shown redoubled eagerness in the emulation to produce and fight heroically. So far we have blasted out of the skies more than 1,200 aircraft. We are determined to defeat the enemy's war of destruction and at the same time to extend all-out support to our dear compatriots in the South.

* A speech over Radio Hanoi, July 17, 1966.

379

Of late the U.S. aggressors hysterically took a very serious step further in the escalation of the war: They launched air attacks on the suburbs of Hanoi and Haiphong. That was an act of desperation comparable to the agony convulsions of a grievously wounded wild beast.

Johnson and his clique should realize this: They may bring in 500,000 troops, 1 million, or even more to step up the war of aggression in South Viet-Nam. They may use thousands of aircraft for intensified attacks against North Viet-Nam. But never will they be able to break the iron will of the heroic Vietnamese people to fight against U.S. aggression, for national salvation. The more truculent they are, the further they will aggravate their crime. The war may still last ten, twenty years, or longer. Hanoi, Haiphong, and other cities and enterprises may be destroyed, but the Vietnamese people will not be intimidated! Nothing is more precious than independence and freedom. When victory day comes, our people will rebuild our country and endow it with bigger and more beautiful construction.

It is common knowledge that each time they are about to step up their criminal war, the U.S. aggressors always resort to their peace talks swindle in an attempt to fool world opinion and blame Viet-Nam for unwillingness to enter into peace talks!

President Johnson! Reply publicly to the American people and the peoples of the world: Who has sabotaged the Geneva Agreements which guarantee the sovereignty, independence, unity, and territorial integrity of Viet-Nam? Have Vietnamese troops invaded the United States and massacred Americans? Is it not the U.S. Government which has sent U.S. troops to invade Viet-Nam and massacre the Vietnamese?

Let the United States end its war of aggression in Viet-Nam, withdraw from this country all U.S. and satellite troops, and peace will return here at once. Viet-Nam's stand is clear: It is the four points of the Government of the D.R.V.N. and the five points of the NFLSV. There is no alternative!

The Vietnamese people cherish peace, genuine peace, peace in independence and freedom, not sham peace, American peace.

For the defense of the independence of the fatherland and for the fulfillment of our obligation to the peoples struggling against U.S. imperialism, our people and army, united as one man, will resolutely fight until complete victory, whatever the sacrifices and hardships may be. In the past we defeated the Japanese fascists and the French colonialists in much more difficult junctures. Today the conditions at home and abroad are more favorable; our people's struggle against U.S. aggression for national salvation is sure to win a total victory.

Dear compatriots and fighters, we are strong with our just cause, the unity of our entire people from north to south, our traditions of undaunted struggle, and the broad sympathy and support of the fraternal socialist countries and progressive people throughout the world. We will win!

At this new juncture, we are as one in our determination to undergo any hardships and sacrifices and to strive for fulfillment of the glorious historic task of our people to defeat the U.S. aggressors!

On behalf of the Vietnamese people, I take this opportunity to express warm thanks to the peoples of the socialist countries and progressive peoples in the world, including the American people, for their devoted support and assistance. In face of the new criminal schemes of the U.S. imperialists, I am firmly confident that the peoples and governments of the fraternal socialist countries and the peace-loving and justice-loving countries in the world will still more vigorously support and help the Vietnamese people until total victory in their struggle against U.S. aggression, for national salvation.

The Vietnamese people will win!

The U.S. aggressors will inevitably be defeated!

Long live a peaceful, reunified, independent, democratic, and prosperous Viet-Nam!

Compatriots and fighters throughout the country, march valiantly forward!

INTERVIEW WITH THE
FRENCH MAGAZINE *L'ÉVÉNEMENT**

Question: Certain people hold that the present war is an ideological conflict, others hold that it is a war for national independence. What is your view?

Answer: Our people are deeply attached to peace, independence, and national unity. The United States has sabotaged the 1954 Geneva Agreements on Viet-Nam which solemnly recognize our national rights. It has waged a war of aggression against South Viet-Nam and over the past two years has launched savage air attacks on North Viet-Nam. In face of these attacks, all Vietnamese people have stood up to defend their fatherland to the end.

Question: Since 1965, the Americans have massively dispatched troops to South Viet-Nam in an attempt to avail themselves of the dry season to regain the initiative on the South Viet-Nam battlefield. Would you let us know the result of this campaign?

Answer: Despite very large reinforcements, the U.S. expeditionary army sustained bitter defeats in the [words indistinct] dry-season campaign. Within [six months the United States] and its agents in Saigon suffered 114,000 casualties without being able to regain the initiative. The so-called Saigon government exerts no power, even in

* An interview granted to Emmanuel d'Astier de la Vigerie, editor in chief of the French review *L'Événement;* the article was translated into English in Hanoi and broadcast by the North Vietnamese radio network.

the cities. Its army has sustained heavy losses as a result of massive desertions and frequent mutinies.

On the contrary, the South Viet-Nam National Liberation Front (NFLSV) has more and more proved itself the only genuine representative of the South Viet-Nam people.

Question: As for North Viet-Nam, what lessons has it drawn from the present war?

Answer: The attacks by the U.S. air forces have met with ever more powerful return blows—1,350 attacking aircraft have been downed. Naturally we have also had some losses. But we have adapted our economy to the present situation.

In 1965, rice production continued to rise. Many agricultural cooperatives, including those in the areas most intensively bombed by the enemy, have reaped 5 tons of paddy per hectare in a year. We have developed the local industries. Communications and transport continue to function and the cost of living has not risen.

Despite daily bombing raids, 3 million pupils continued to go to school. The universities and professional schools have an enrollment of 100,000.

These results show to what extent our people are united in their love for their Fatherland and are determined to defeat the enemy, braving all sacrifices.

To mobilize the whole country, to wage a long people's war against the U.S. aggressors, to educate the masses about patriotism and collective heroism, and push forward the broad patriotic emulation movement under the slogan, "All for Victory," that is our experience in the present struggle for national independence.

Question: Do you need volunteers from your allies and friendly countries, or only up-to-date materials?

Answer: The United States has a big economic and military potential. To defeat such an enemy, we first of all rely on our own strength, and at the same time strive to win the most effective international assistance. The assistance and support given us by the brotherly socialist countries are particularly valuable. Hundreds of thousands of volunteers from the socialist countries and other countries have declared their readiness to fight the U.S. imperialists by our side. We warmly thank them for their militant solidarity with us. When necessary, we will appeal to them.

Question: Can we have any hope in the activities of a minority group called liberal in the United States?

Answer: We hold that the movement in the United States in protest against the dirty war is an active support for our cause. Despite the government's persecution, this movement has not ceased to develop.

Question: What can the Vietnamese expect of the moral and material support of all those in the world who support Viet-Nam's independence, and of their French friends in particular?

Answer: To the French people who are bound to our people by a fraternal friendship which has been tempered in the common struggle against colonialism, we once again express our confidence and our gratitude. To our fighting people, the French people's activities constitute a great encouragement and to the whole world, they are an important contribution to peace, national independence, democracy, and socialism.

Question: Where will the Americans come to?

Answer: The Americans are bogged down neck-deep. Yet they are plotting more adventures against us. Our people are ready to cope with them. They are resolved to continue the fight even if it will last five, ten years, or longer. President Johnson and his friends are deceiving their own peoples and making a show of fake optimism about the situation of the United States in Viet-Nam.

Question: What are the prospects of peace?

Answer: Each time they take another step in war intensification, the Americans make noisy propaganda about the so-called peaceful negotiations. That is only a smoke screen. Yet, some people of good will, deceived by U.S. propaganda, have advised us to negotiate with the aggressors at all costs. They have forgotten that to end this war, it is necessary only that the United States undertakes to withdraw. That is the only honorable solution for them.

Question: Although the Americans do not respect the Geneva Agreements, do you think that the principles of these agreements remain valid and peace can be restored on that basis?

Answer: The stand of Viet-Nam is clear: It is the four points of the Government of the D.R.V.N. and the five points of the NFLSV. Our stand embodies the fundamental provisions of the 1954 Geneva Agreements in the present situation. This is the only correct basis to settle the Viet-Nam problem.

Question: After the war, what will be the future of a unified Viet-Nam?

Answer: After peace is restored, the Vietnamese people will devote their might and main to rebuild their Fatherland, turn it into a unified, peaceful, independent, democratic, and prosperous country having friendly relations with all peaceful peoples in the world.

SPEECH IN HONOR OF
CUBAN PRESIDENT OSVALDO DORTICÓS*

Esteemed Comrade Osvaldo Dorticós, dear Comrade Raúl Castro, and the other comrades of the Cuban party-government, dear comrades and friends:

The Vietnamese people, the Viet-Nam Workers' Party, and the Government of the D.R.V.N. are very happy to welcome the delegation of the Republic of Cuba, our brothers and intimate comrades.

You have covered thousands of miles to visit our country and bring to our people the warm friendship of the brotherly Cuban people. This is a great encouragement to the people in our entire country, who are fighting with determination to defeat the U.S. aggressors, defend socialism and North Viet-Nam, and liberate South Viet-Nam, with a view to reunifying their Fatherland.

The Vietnamese people feel greatly inspired to have such a staunch, valiant comrade in arms as the brotherly Cuban people, who are standing shoulder to shoulder with them on the front line against the U.S. imperialists.

Eight years ago, under the leadership of their national hero, Fidel Castro Ruz, and through a long and arduous armed struggle, the Cuban people overthrew the dictatorial regime of Batista—a lackey of the U.S. imperialists—brought the Cuban revolution to victory, and built the first socialist country in Latin America. The victory of

* A speech given at a banquet in honor of the visiting Cuban delegation, November 2, 1966.

the Cuban revolution has raised aloft the ever-victorious banner of Marxism-Leninism in the Western Hemisphere, and constituted a powerful stimulus to the struggle waged by the Latin American peoples for independence and freedom.

Under the leadership of the Communist Party of Cuba and the Cuban Revolutionary Government, the Cuban people have struggled fearlessly and recorded many successes: routing the U.S. aggressors at Giron Beach, defeating the economic embargo, and crushing all other schemes of provocation and sabotage by the U.S. imperialists.

The brotherly Cuban people have also recorded many successes in defending and rebuilding their country in all fields, national defense, economy, and culture, thus making an active contribution to the consolidation of the socialist camp and the safeguarding of world peace.

The Vietnamese people are highly elated at these successes of the brotherly Cuban people and regard them as their own. We sincerely wish the brotherly Cuban people many more and greater successes.

Dear comrades and friends, the cruel U.S. imperialists have waged an aggressive war in an attempt to enslave our country. Yet, they are suffering heavy defeats.

Their special war in South Viet-Nam has failed. They have also sustained heavy defeats in the first round of their local war. The people in both parts of our country have fought very well and continuously won big victories: over 1,500 U.S. aircraft have been shot down over North Viet-Nam. In South Viet-Nam, over 200,000 U.S., satellite, and Saigon puppet troops were put out of action in the first nine months of this year alone.

However, the U.S. imperialists are very stubborn. The nearer their final defeat, the more frantic their acts. They are making active preparations for new steps of escalation with the aim of intensifying and expanding their aggressive war in Viet-Nam. But they will be defeated completely. The Vietnamese people, millions united as one and strong with their rocklike determination and the wholehearted support of the socialist countries, other peace-loving countries, and all progressive mankind, are resolved to fight until final victory.

The U.S. imperialists and their satellites recently held a conference in Manila to peddle their sham peace while actually trying to step up war. What wishful thinking and stupidity on their part! They cannot deceive world public opinion with their insolent and absurd allegations. On the contrary, the world's people are spurning and exposing more and more thoroughly the predatory nature of the U.S. imperialists.

The U.S. imperialists must put an end to their aggressive war against Viet-Nam, stop for good and unconditionally the bombing raids and all other acts of war against the D.R.V.N., and withdraw all troops of the United States and its satellites from South Viet-Nam. Then peace will return to Viet-Nam immediately.

The stand of the Vietnamese people is clear. It is the four points of the D.R.V.N. Government and the five points of the NFLSV.

Having gone through twenty successive years of struggle against foreign invasion, the Vietnamese people more than anyone else ardently cherish peace. But genuine peace must be associated with genuine independence. For the independence of their fatherland and their duty to other peoples now struggling against the U.S. aggressors, for the security of the countries in the socialist camp, the people in our whole country, of one heart and one mind and braving all sacrifices and hardships, are determined to fight until complete victory.

Dear comrades and friends, we are very glad to see that the militant solidarity between our two fraternal countries is consolidating and developing most fruitfully. We avail ourselves of this opportunity to express our deep thanks to all the fraternal socialist countries for their devoted assistance, and other friendly countries in the world for their warm support.

The party, government, and fraternal people of Cuba have devotedly assisted us morally and materially and have firmly supported the four-point stand of the D.R.V.N. Government and the five points of the NFLSV. Comrade Fidel Castro and other leaders of the Cuban party and government have declared on many occasions that to Viet-Nam, the Cuban people are ready to give even their blood. Allow us to express the deep gratitude of the Vietnamese people, the Viet-Nam Workers' Party, and the D.R.V.N. Government for this active support and valuable assistance of the people, Communist Party, and Revolutionary Government of Cuba.

The Vietnamese people have always given unreserved support to the five-point stand of the fraternal Cuban Government in the struggle against the U.S. imperialists to defend the national independence and socialism of Cuba and, at the same time, to contribute to the national liberation struggle in Latin America and the safeguarding of world peace.

Dear comrades and friends, we believe that your present visit to Viet-Nam will help further strengthen the unshakable militant solidarity between the peoples of our two countries and will bring us many new successes, just as is said in a slogan of the brotherly Cuban people: Viet-Nam and Cuba united, we shall win!